Marxism and Education

Series Editor

Anthony Green
Institute of Education
University of London
London, United Kingdom

This series assumes the ongoing relevance of Marx's contributions to critical social analysis and aims to encourage continuation of the development of the legacy of Marxist traditions in and for education. The remit for the substantive focus of scholarship and analysis appearing in the series extends from the global to the local in relation to dynamics of capitalism and encompasses historical and contemporary developments in political economy of education as well as forms of critique and resistances to capitalist social relations. The series announces a new beginning and proceeds in a spirit of openness and dialogue within and between Marxism and education, and between Marxism and its various critics. The essential feature of the work of the series is that Marxism and Marxist frameworks are to be taken seriously, not as formulaic knowledge and unassailable methodology but critically as inspirational resources for renewal of research and understanding, and as support for action in and upon structures and processes of education and their relations to society. The series is dedicated to the realization of positive human potentialities as education and thus, with Marx, to our education as educators.

More information about this series at
http://www.springer.com/series/14811

Mike Cole

New Developments in Critical Race Theory and Education

Revisiting Racialized Capitalism and Socialism in Austerity

Mike Cole
University of East London
London, United Kingdom

Marxism and Education
ISBN 978-1-137-53539-9   ISBN 978-1-137-53540-5   (eBook)
DOI 10.1057/978-1-137-53540-5

Library of Congress Control Number: 2016958123

Cover illustration: jvphoto / Alamy Stock Photo

Printed on acid-free paper

This Palgrave Macmillan imprint is published by Springer Nature
The registered company is Nature America Inc.
The registered company address is: 1 New York Plaza, New York, NY 10004, U.S.A.

Series Editor Foreword

It is a pleasure to welcome Mike Cole's latest contribution to the *Marxism and Education Series*. Mike has been the most prolific of any of our Series' authors so far. His work is testimony to both his own continuing critical energy and his expertise in depth and breadth, as well as to the relevance and impact of the broad approach of *open, dialogical* Marxism that the Series represents. With respect to impact, doubly significant is that this book comes hot on the heels of the **second edition** of his influential *Critical Race Theory and Education: A Marxist Response,* first published in 2009. The new book is devoted to updating with further developments on the earlier work in the fast-moving and contentious arena of debate and struggle. It reflects and articulates with shifting alignments of political action and critique around 'race' and *racialization* in relation to and between Critical Race Theory (CRT) and Marxism.

As bodies of ideas in action, CRT and Marxism are not simply alternatives to one another as Mike clearly indicates. Thus, despite differences and tendencies, Mike makes positive links with CRT and his observations and elaboration, along with impassioned comradely engagement to demonstrate these. He does so along with arguing for the continued indispensability of the Marxist case and its contribution to realigning political awareness in these emergently 'interesting' times. As Series Editor, on that note, I have observed, for instance, on either side of the Atlantic, that the Obama presidency, despite all its many disappointments for social and political progressives, and the Corbyn and Sanders phenomena, no matter what their immediate political outcomes, can be read as constituting encouraging signs as new younger generations embark on the struggles across many fronts and as older activists re-engage with renewed vigour in the face of half a century of ever-deepening neo-liberal inequities and the ever-more evident failures of its currently dominating political economy. Concurrently, there are numerous emergent popular forms of critical *educative* engagement with both *capitalism* and *neo-liberalism* across a variety of media, not least cinema, theatre, TV and no end of social media and the emergent renewal of organized labour. And, of course the academic research and debates are as intense as ever. Concurrently, too, the disenchantment with the dominant political, economic and cultural elites' competence and capacity to deliver security and all manner of aspirational respect finds other modes of negativity in ultra-liberal as well as populist authoritarian and/or nationalist movements, and worse. In turn, the flow of the recent Latin American Red Tide as well as South American developments are no longer apparently as strong as they have recently been.

These are all, in each case, materials to be addressed within the spirit and practices of ongoing openly dialogical *educational* dynamics of what Marx referred to in 1845 as 'educating the educators' in his *Thesis III on Feuerbach;* part of our recognizing ourselves in historically constituted struggle in which the educators, ourselves, require education, in, for and as those struggles. That's to say in recognition that 'The coincidence of the changing of circumstances and of human activity or self-changing can be conceived and rationally understood only as *revolutionary practice*'. The horizon is ever shifting. Read on, think on, act on, reflect, debate and reformulate on, organize for social movement...on and on at each and every level. There are endless emergent individual and collective modes of empowerment for democratic socialism available as renewal of Marxist legacies for building a better future! Then some more!

Anthony Green
April 2016

Preface

This book is a sequel to my 2009 book *Critical Race Theory and Education: A Marxist Response*, also published by Palgrave Macmillan. Prior to the publication of this book, that book, to my knowledge, was the only book-length Marxist critique and appraisal of Critical Race Theory (CRT) and education. The rationale for this new book is fourfold: first, to assess what has happened theoretically on both sides of the Atlantic in the realm of CRT and Marxism since 2009; second, to evaluate these *theoretical* developments; third, to relate them to *political and economic* developments in racialized neo-liberal capitalism and imperialism—specifically in the new era of austerity—in order to assess to what extent CRT and Marxism can inform such developments; and, fourth, to examine CRT's and Marxism's respective visions of the future.

Given the major response and reaction to *Critical Race Theory and Education: A Marxist Response*, a **second edition** of it is being published simultaneously with this volume.

Mike Cole
April 2016

ACKNOWLEDGEMENTS

I would like to thank Noel Ignatiev for his generous support and help in the writing of chapter 3 of this volume and for his permission to reproduce his published response to Garvey, J. (2015) 'No More Missouri Compromises' *Insurgent Notes* 11 (Ignatiev, 2015); Dave Hill for his comments on chapter 4; and Alpesh Maisuria for his comments on chapter 5. Special thanks to Charlotte Chadderton, Richard Delgado and John Preston for their quick responses to my queries about Critical Race Theory and to Tony (Anthony) Green for his detailed comments on the penultimate draft of the book, which considerably sharpened up the arguments.

CONTENTS

.

CHAPTER 1

Introduction

SOME FURTHER PERSONAL EXPERIENCES OF RACIST BRITAIN

In order to understand racism's multifarious nature it can be instructive to reflect on one's earliest experiences of racism, even though they may not have been perceived as racist at the time, and to relate such experiences to theoretical developments in understanding racism (e.g. Cole 2016a). In the book to which this book is a sequel, *Critical Race Theory and Education: A Marxist Response* (Cole 2009, **2nd edition**, 2017),[1] I begin with a recollection of some early personal experiences of racist Britain, starting with some childhood recollections in Bristol, UK, in the 1950s, and end with some brief comments on the lives of the African Caribbean children at a primary school in west London, where I taught in the 1970s. Here I will recall further racist experiences from the 1970s up to the present.

The advent of Thatcherism represents a decisive turning point in racialization (falsely categorizing people into the scientifically defunct notion of distinct 'races') in the UK in the last quarter of the twentieth century. In 1978, Margaret Thatcher, then leader of the opposition in the UK parliament, told a television news programme that 'people are really rather afraid that this country might be swamped by people with a different culture' (cited in Trilling 2013).

© The Author(s) 2017
M. Cole, *New Developments in Critical Race Theory and Education,*
DOI 10.1057/978-1-137-53540-5_1

As Daniel Trilling argues, Thatcher's 'swamping' comments reintroduced to mainstream politics racist discourse that had been confined to the Far-Right fringe for a decade. As he explains, the promise to drastically restrict the numbers of Commonwealth immigrants entering Britain was 'no dispassionate economic calculation', but rather founded on the premise that 'people' were 'threatened by the incursion of an unwanted— and, by the use of the pejorative "swamped", harmful—foreign culture' (Trilling 2013).[2]

Most enduringly, Trilling concludes, Thatcher bequeathed us the idea that when confronted with a surge in support for overtly racist parties, all a mainstream politician needs to do is take to the airwaves and adopt some of their rhetoric (Trilling 2013). From the late 1960s, racism had begun to find a growing political expression, in the form of the National Front (NF), a fascist political party that also commanded the support of a section of disgruntled Tories and 'empire loyalists' who could not come to terms with Britain's post-war loss of power. In the 1970s, as economic crisis began to break up the post-war compact between capital and labour, the NF also attracted a layer of working class support, receiving an unprecedented share of the vote (though no seats) in the Greater London Council elections of 1977 (Trilling 2013).

Thatcher's 1978 intervention had an immediate short-term effect on public opinion. After her 'swamping' interpellation,[3] there was a dramatic surge in support for the Conservative Party, who jumped to an 11-point lead over the Labour Party, who they had previously been trailing by two points. On May 3, 1979, Thatcher won the general election, while the NF, which had stood a record number of candidates, failed to win a single seat and collapsed amid bitter recriminations (Trilling 2013).[4]

Then a young adviser to Thatcher, Oliver Letwin (a chief policy adviser to Prime Minister David Cameron's 2015 Tory Government) helped ward off cabinet pleas for assistance for young unemployed black people following the 1985 inner-city riots on the grounds that any help would end up in the 'disco and drug trade' (Travis 2015). In a paper written by Letwin and Thatcher's inner-cities adviser, Hartley Booth, they told Thatcher that 'lower-class unemployed white people had lived for years in appalling slums without a breakdown of public order on anything like the present scale', also warning that setting up a £10 million communities programme to tackle inner-city problems would do little more than 'subsidise Rastafarian arts and crafts workshops', and insisting that what was need were measures to tackle absent fathers, moral education and an end to state funding of left-wing activists (Travis 2015). Trevor Phillips, former chair of the Equality and Human Rights Commission, commented, 'I don't think these remarks would have raised a single eyebrow at the time' (cited in Travis 2015).

It was during the Thatcher years that a number of Left academics were under sustained and prolonged attack by leading figures of the radical Right, being accused of 'Marxist bias' and vilified for promoting anti-racism and other forms of social equality. These offensives incorporated demands for the abolition of teacher education. The deliberate use of the term teacher *training* by those with power rather than *education* served to undermine teacher educators who were viewed (totally ridiculously) as all being socialist revolutionaries.

Condemnation of my own work included official complaints, the publication of my course materials by radical Right ideologues, an article about my teaching in the right-wing *Spectator,* a year-long libel writ from a Tory Peer, verbal criticism from one of Her Majesty's Inspectorate during a seminar and in front of my students, and culminated in denunciation from the prime minister herself. In the section on 'teacher training' in Thatcher's memoirs (Thatcher 1993). Thatcher writes that she could 'barely believe the contents' of my B.Ed. courses. In addition to concerns that I was assessing the extent to which schools were reinforcing gender stereotypes, what she also found worrying was my consideration of anti-racist education (Thatcher 1993, p. 598). She concluded that the 'effective monopoly exercised by the existing teacher-training routes had to be broken' (Thatcher 1993, p. 598). Subsequently two schemes were devised as alternatives to higher-education-based teacher education. Conservative politicians' distrust of and attempts to undermine teacher education based in higher education continue to this day.

It felt as if I were under surveillance at Brighton Polytechnic and subsequently the University of Brighton, and probably was, long after the demise of Margaret Thatcher. However, it was not until 2005 that I was able to leave, when I was appointed Research Professor at what is now Bishop Grosseteste University. This brought an end to the trials and tribulations I had experienced at Brighton and was witness to a long-overdue recognition of my work. It meant that I was now able to work in a pleasant environment where my work was respected.

On the down side, however, it also meant that I had to experience the overt and hostile racism that is the mainstay of Lincoln society. In my professorial lecture in 2006 (Cole 2008), I provide a snapshot of this racism in the form of three conversations overheard in pubs:

> I had gallstones, but they got rid of the c****s. Have to go back. Problem is the NHS is full of fucking ni**ers these days.
>   I'll drop the bomb [someone's 'joke' about the contents of a bag] in the nearest mosque. Anyone object to that? C'mon anyone object to that? C'mon let's hear it [sounds of approval]...Nobody. Right?
>   [Referring to a fatal accident in Lincoln] They're all f***ing asylum-seekers. They don't know our traffic rules. (Cole 2008, p. 13)

The headline of the *Lincolnshire Echo* on November 14, 2006, was 'BNP TO FIGHT FOR 11 CITY SEATS'. In the article, 'local BNP officials' claimed that the white supremacist[5] and fascist party's policies were 'so popular' that it had to reorganize itself to cope with demand in Lincoln. They claimed 150 members in the county of Lincolnshire (Cole 2008, p. 13). One night in Lincoln I took a taxi home, and, after the driver had made a number of comments I assumed he was at least a BNP supporter. I asked him and he replied that he was actually a member of the BNP. Playing the 'devil's advocate', I further enquired whether it was true that they secretly admired Adolph Hitler, to which his reply was enthusiastically in the affirmative, and on the lines of 'oh yes, of course we do!'[6]

Some years later, I was told by a black teacher I know of that when she first started teaching in Lincolnshire, she was told by a year 11 (final year of compulsory school) student: 'Blacks are not wanted here.' She also had students ask her if she smoked weed and listened to Bob Marley.

In 2011, I left Bishop Grosseteste University and in 2013 took up a part-time professorship at the University of East London. To my great relief, this means that I no longer have to travel regularly to the city of Lincoln (although I retain an Emeritus Professorship at the University) and can now spend my time living in Kemp Town Brighton and commuting to the multicultural environment that is East London.

In the same year I left Bishop Grosseteste, I met the woman who is now my wife. This has enhanced my awareness of some of the issues discussed in this volume, such as 'racial' microaggressions (my wife is from South East Asia) that include name-calling and harassment in the street, assumptions about what work she does, being openly under surveillance in a store while looking for clothes to buy and rudeness from some taxi drivers ('racial' microaggressions are discussed in chapter 4 of this volume). It has to be said that despite this, and although there is a sizeable UK Independence Party (Ukip) presence in Brighton and Hove,[7] the city is by and large a tolerant one.

CONTINUING (NEO-)MARXIST ANALYSES OF RACISM

In the Introduction to Cole (2017), I described how I first read Marx in the 1970s, how I was influenced by the neo-Marxist analyses of racism emanating from the Centre for Contemporary Cultural Studies at Birmingham University in the 1970s and 1980s, and by the work of Antonia Darder and Rodolfo Torres with respect to their Marxist critique of Critical Race Theory (CRT). As discussed in chapter 2 of this present book, I have written a number of Marxist critiques of CRT since the first edition of *Critical Race Theory and Education: A Marxist Response*. I have also since then published a number of other more general (neo-)Marxist analyses of racism, including an examination of fascism (Cole 2012); a feminist antiracism analysis of qualitative research on women from a Gypsy community in the UK (Bell and Cole 2013); several dictionary entries (Cole 2013, 2014, 2016b) and a monograph exploring racism in three countries Anglophone continents—the UK, the USA and Australia (Cole 2016c).

All this work has convinced me of the need to consistently and interrogate ongoing developments in CRT, both for their insights and for their limitations in understanding the plethora of forms of racism in the twenty-first century.

CONTINUING INTEREST IN CRT AND OUTLINE OF THE BOOK

I continue to gain awareness from CRT whose perceptions cannot always be generated by (neo-)Marxism, but also continue to witness CRT's shortcomings which, as is argued throughout this volume, need to be supplemented by (neo-)Marxist analysis,[8] hence the raison d'être for a second book on CRT. The main purpose of chapter 2 of this volume is to revisit the central arguments in Cole (2017), which are spelt out in detail in that chapter. However, the chapter is more than a mere précis of the analyses in that book in that I make some critical comments on some of the book's content and also provide a retrospective viewpoint, seven years after the first edition, as well as some additional explanations.

In the first half of chapter 3, I focus on an analysis of an article in a special issue on CRT in England in the flagship international peer-reviewed journal, *Race, Ethnicity and Education,* a publication edited by founding and leading UK Critical Race Theorist David Gillborn. I analyse this paper in depth because, of all the articles in that special edition, it is the one that most promisingly attempts to theoretically develop CRT in the British context, or to use Kevin Hylton's expression to build 'BritCrit'.[9] The article also has most purchase in the furtherance and understanding of the ongoing theoretical debate between CRT and Marxism, in that in it its authors John Preston and Charlotte Chadderton, who are both sympathetic to (neo-)Marxism and CRT, claim that the influential 1990s 'Race Traitor' (RT) movement has resonance for Marxists in the twenty-first century (Chadderton's later work is also discussed in chapter 4 of this volume). My critique of their position entails an extensive consideration of the RT movement and contemporary Marxism, and includes a critical appraisal of *Race Traitor,* the book edited by RT's co-founders, Noel Ignatiev and John Garvey. In the second half of the chapter, I update and assess the (changing?) politics of Ignatiev and Garvey, in relation to their conceptual and theoretical frameworks, and the political implications thereof.

In chapter 4, I begin by looking at recent developments in CRT in the UK. In the Editorial of the special issue of the journal, *Race, Ethnicity and Education (REE* 15 (1)) on 'Critical Race Theory in England' in January 2012, three pioneers of CRT in the UK, Namita Chakrabarty, Lorna Roberts and the aforementioned John Preston, wrote that it is important that CRT develops in the English context in terms of establishing an academic identity. Given this declared aim, in addition to the six articles in that edition I also look at all of the CRT analyses of the UK published in *REE* since the special issue up to the present. My intention in the chapter is to assess the extent to which a quintessentially British CRT, or 'BritCrit', is being established that is able to address the multifarious nature of racism in the UK in four years or so since the special edition. In chapter 5, I turn my attention to the USA, where of course CRT is much more firmly rooted, critically analysing those articles in *REE* since that special issue up to the present.

Critical Race Theory and Education: A Marxist Response (Cole 2009, **2nd edition,** 2017) was written before the effects of the global financial crisis of 2007/2008 had become evident. In the UK, the USA and most other capitalist countries, the crisis was seized upon by the ruling class as an opportunity to bail out the bankers and the ruling class in general, and to make the working class pay for the crisis. In chapter 6, I address the way in which neoliberal capitalism in its austerity/immiseration mode has wreaked havoc on the working class in general, and on the racialized working class in particular. Given the way in which neoliberal capitalism is instrumental in the demolition of the ecosystem and given the fact that the very existence of the planet is at stake (a truism that must consistently be addressed by twenty-first century socialists), I begin the chapter with an assessment of the present state of global environmental destruction, focusing on global warming, in the light of the United Nations Climate Change Conference in late 2015.

In chapter 7 of this volume, I turn to a consideration of the future, and specifically to what Critical Race Theorists and Marxists respectively have to offer. I begin by contrasting the CRT concept of 'race consciousness' with the Marxist concept of 'class consciousness'. I go on to examine CRT and Marxism with respect to their political and economic visions of the future. I consider the implications of some CRT theorizing drawn from the articles discussed throughout this volume, comparing and contrasting these with Marxist visions for twenty-first-century socialism—both actually existing and potential. In chapter 7 of Cole (2009, **2nd edition**, 2017), I defend Marxism against some 15 common objections, ending with the standard, 'ok, show me where it works in practice'. I give as an example the Bolivarian Republic of Venezuela. In this volume, I update recent post-Chávez developments there with respect to antiracism, concentrating on Indigenous Peoples, Afro-Venezuelans and Afro-Descendants Peoples, and Undocumented Workers. Venezuela suffered a major setback in the 2015 legislative elections, and the future is uncertain. In chapter 7 of this volume, I also speculate, therefore, on what the future might hold for that country. I conclude chapter 7 with an assessment of the totally unexpected election in the UK of socialist Jeremy Corbyn, himself a member of the Venezuela Solidarity Campaign, as leader of the British Labour Party, along with the rise of Bernie Sanders in the USA and the potential that these developments hold for future debate around and developments in socialist thinking. Specifically, I pose the question, 'has socialism moved from the margins to the mainstream?'

NOTES

1. The **second edition** is published simultaneously with this volume. From now on, when referring to *Critical Race Theory and Education: A Marxist Response*, I refer to the **second edition** (Cole 2017) unless I am making a historical point, in which case, I sometimes refer to the first edition (Cole 2009).

2. A decade earlier, Thatcher's colleague, the arch racist Enoch Powell had used the same arguments in a series of speeches prophesying 'rivers of blood' and how white people would soon become a minority in the UK, with 'the whip hand' held by the immigrant. In 1968, Powell was condemned by the Conservative leader Edward Heath and dismissed from the Shadow Cabinet (Trilling 2013).

3. The concept of interpellation, as developed by the French neo-Marxist Louis Althusser (1918–1990), a professor of philosophy at the École Normale Supérieure in Paris, and a long-time member of the French Communist Party. Interpellation is the *process* via which the politicians and the media and so on claim to be speaking on behalf of the people: 'what the British have had enough of'; 'what the American people want'. Althusser stressed that it is individuals rather than classes or groups that are interpellated or hailed. For Althusser, the interpellation of subjects—the hailing of concrete individuals as concrete subjects—'Hey, you there!' provides the absolute guarantee that everything really is so, and that on condition that the subjects recognize what they are and behave accordingly, everything will be all right: Amen—'So be it'.

4. A more recent example of mainstream establishment parties adopting the rhetoric and *indeed* policies of a racist fringe party is the reaction of the Conservative/Liberal Democrat (ConDem) Coalition to the xeno-racism (anti-East European migrant worker) of the anti-European union UK Independence Party (Ukip) in the run-up to the 2015 UK general election (see Cole 2016c, pp. 67–83).

5. I am using 'white supremacist' in its conventional sense. 'White supremacy' in both its traditional and wider Critical Race Theory (CRT) usage is discussed throughout this volume.

6. It should be pointed out that my experiences were not all negative. The co-manager of my local pub was notable for his antiracist beliefs and practices. He told me that he was once confronted with a customer who told an Eastern European worker to 'fuck off back to

Poland' (he was actually Lithuanian, if I remember correctly) before hitting him over the head with a chair, after which the publican made a citizen's arrest and marched him off to the local police station.

7. Although it gained no seats, Ukip fielded 25 candidates in the Brighton and Hove City Council elections in 2015. Brighton and Hove Ukip has over 5000 'likes' on Facebook, compared to about 1000 for the Labour Party, the party with the most seats.

8. The development of neo-Marxism (the 'neo'—'new'—in neo-Marxism refers to theoretical developments in Marxism, post-Marx) needs to be seen in the light of the fact that inevitability and imminence of a general transition to socialism proved to be over-optimistic, and severely compromised. This fact meant that some aspects of Marxism had to be rethought. Specifically, what needed to be understood was the role of capitalist institutions in maintaining their power base. As Leszek Kolakowski (1978) has argued, the common element in theories designated as 'neo'-Marxist is a concern with the role of capitalist states' welfare institutions in retarding rather than advancing socialism. The defining features of neo-Marxism are a concern with culture (as in the notion of the forging of a hegemonic culture as elaborated by prominent Italian neo-Marxist Antonio Gramsci) and with ideology (ideas that work in the interests of the ruling class, as in the concept of ideological state apparatuses outlined by French neo-Marxist Louis Althusser) (both theorists are discussed in Cole 2016c, pp. 8–12). Neo-Marxist analysis should be seen as a supplement to rather than a replacement of Marxism.

9. The term 'BritCrit' was coined by Hylton in his keynote address to the Higher Education Academy: Sociology, Anthropology, Politics (C-SAP) conference, *Critical Race Theory in the UK: What is to be Learnt? What is to be Done?*, Institute of Education, London, 25–26 June 2009.

REFERENCES

Bell, S., & Cole, M. (2013). Qualitative research for antiracism: A feminist approach informed by Marxism. In T. M. Kress, C. Malott, & B. Porfilio (Eds.), *Challenging status quo retrenchment: New directions in critical research*. Charlotte: Information Age Publishing.

Cole, M. (2008, November 29). *Maintaining "the adequate continuance of the British race and British ideals in the world": Contemporary racism and the challenges for education*. Bishop Grosseteste University College Lincoln: Inaugural Professorial Lecture.

Cole, M. (2009). *Critical race theory and education: A Marxist response* (1st ed.). New York/London: Palgrave Macmillan.

Cole, M. (2012). Capitalist crisis and fascism: Issues for educational practice. In D. R. Cole (Ed.), *Surviving economic crises through education*. New York: Peter Lang.

Cole, M. (2013). Marxism. In P. L. Mason (Ed.), *Encyclopedia of race and racism* (2nd ed., Vol. 3, pp. 117–124). Detroit: Macmillan.

Cole, M. (2014). Racism and antiracist education. In D. C. Phillips (Ed.), *Encyclopedia of educational theory and philosophy*. London: Sage.

Cole, M. (2016a). *When I became aware of racism—Professor Mike Cole*. https://www.youtube.com/watch?v=3tKyRku12t8

Cole, M. (2016b). Critical race theory: A Marxist critique. In M. A. Peters (Ed.), *Encyclopedia of educational philosophy and theory*. Singapore: Springer.

Cole, M. (2016c). *Racism: A critical analysis*. London/Chicago: Pluto Press/University of Chicago Press.

Cole, M. (2017). *Critical race theory and education: A Marxist response* (2nd ed.). New York/London: Palgrave Macmillan.

Thatcher, M. (1993). *The downing street years*. London: HarperCollinsPublishers.

Travis, A. (2015, December 30). Oliver Letwin blocked help for black youth after 1985 riots. *The Guardian*. http://www.theguardian.com/politics/2015/dec/30/oliver-letwin-blocked-help-for-black-youth-after-1985-riots?utm_source=esp&utm_medium=Email&utm_campaign=GU+Today+main+NEW+H&utm_term=146715&subid=14322859&CMP=EMCNEWEML6619I2

Trilling, D. (2013, April 10). Thatcher: The PM who brought racism in from the cold. *Verso blog*. http://www.versobooks.com/blogs/1282-thatcher-the-pm-who-brought-racism-in-from-the-cold

Critical Race Theory and Education: A Marxist Response—Summary, Critique and Retrospective

INTRODUCTION

As noted in the Introduction to this volume, the main purpose of this chapter is to look again at the central arguments in my book *Critical Race Theory and Education: A Marxist Response* (Cole 2009a, **2nd edition, 2017**). However, the chapter is more than a précis of the analyses in that book in that I critique some of the book's content and also provide some additional explanations, as well as look back seven years since its first edition to highlight specific moments of change and theoretical development, or lack of such development. So while it is of course my hope that this chapter is of sufficient interest for people to seek out a copy of Cole (2017), the chapter is free-standing, and can be read without cross-reference to it. In Cole (2017), I deal with Critical Race Theory (CRT) per se as well as CRT and education. With respect to the former, issues covered include the origins of CRT, CRT's relationship to other theories that prioritize the *Voice* of the Other, some movements and currents of thought within CRT (chapter 2 of Cole 2017), a critique of two of its central tenets—CRT's use of the concept of 'white supremacy' and the prioritizing of 'race' over class; I suggest their replacement with a wide-ranging definition of racism and the deployment of the neo-Marxist concept of racialization (chapter 3 of Cole 2017). (The neo-Marxist concept of racialization is defined in chapter 4 of this volume.) Also addressed in

© The Author(s) 2017
M. Cole, *New Developments in Critical Race Theory and Education*,
DOI 10.1057/978-1-137-53540-5_2

Cole (2017) are what I perceive to be some of the strengths and limitations of CRT (Cole 2017, chapter 4).

As far as CRT and its specific relationship to education is concerned, processes of multiculturalism in both the USA and the UK and the respective antiracist responses based on Marxism in each country are analysed (chapter 5 of Cole 2017). In addition, I engage in a detailed critical assessment of a key monograph in the theorization of CRT and education in the UK: David Gillborn's *Racism and Education: Coincidence or Conspiracy?* (Gillborn 2008) (Cole 2017, chapter 6). The economic backdrop to the first edition is *pre-austerity* neoliberal global capitalism and imperialism (chapter 6 of Cole 2009a, **2nd edition**, 2017), and this is contrasted with the alternative of twenty-first-century socialism (chapter 7 of that book). In chapter 8, I also raise some common objections to Marxism, and attempt a Marxist response. The last chapter (chapter 9) consists of a consideration of classroom practice from both CRT and Marxist perspectives. In the Conclusion to Cole (2017), I discuss CRT and human liberation; the legacy of Martin Luther King; the relationship between classism, Marxism and democratic socialism and the possibility of a realignment between Critical Legal Studies (CLS) and CRT. There is also a Postscript on Barack Obama, written at the time of the election on November 5, 2008, of the US' first black president, a highly significant political event, one, however, which I argued does not spell the end of racism in the USA (in the event, this proved to be an understatement).

CRT AND EDUCATION: A MARXIST RESPONSE—REACTION

The initial publication of *Critical Race Theory in Education: A Marxist Response* (Cole 2009a) caused quite a furore, generating an extensive, protracted and ongoing theoretical debate between Marxists and Critical Race Theorists. Approval from the former was at least matched by disapproval from some of the latter. There have been exceptions to the disapprobation, most notably from one of the founders of the CRT movement, Richard Delgado, who not only commented extensively and instantaneously on various drafts of the original manuscript, but was also kind enough to endorse the book on the back cover. In 2009, the year of the first edition's publication, I delivered over a dozen critiques of CRT in six countries. In addition, from 2009 on, there were interchanges between myself and a number of Critical Race Theorists: David Gillborn (e.g. Cole

2009b, c; Gillborn 2009); John Preston and Charlotte Chadderton (e.g. Preston 2010, 2013; Cole 2012a, b; Preston and Chadderton 2012) and Charles Mills (e.g. Cole 2009d, e; Mills 2009). There have also been altercations between Gillborn and Marxist writer Dave Hill (e.g. Hill 2009a, b; Gillborn 2010). That is not to say, of course, that there are no fundamental agreements between the two camps. Both are united in their determination to challenge racism in all its manifestations, and both believe in a world where there is more justice. As we shall see in chapter 7 of this volume, however, whereas Critical Race Theorists are vague as to the nature of a more just world, Marxists have more concrete visions of a world without exploitation and oppression.

POSTMODERNISM, TRANSMODERNISM AND CRT

What then are the specific arguments that I put forward in *Critical Race Theory and Education: A Marxist Response*? I decided that before dealing with issues specific to CRT, I needed at the beginning of the book to set the scene with respect to other theories which shared with CRT a stress on the importance of the *Voice* of the Other, namely, postmodernism, voguish at the time, and transmodernism, seemingly up-and-coming when I was writing the book, and viewed by some as set to eclipse postmodernism. I begin chapter 2 of Cole (2017) then by briefly tracing the relationship between CRT, postmodernism and transmodernism. Whereas postmodernism stresses multivocality, celebrating 'multiple sites from which the word is spoken' (Lather 1991, p. 112), transmodernism actively sought out not just Others, 'but...suffering Others' (Smith 2003, p. 499). In this respect, transmodernism had similarities with CRT which focuses on 'race' and the oppression of people of colour, and insists that we listen to their *voice*, which is framed by racism and is at variance with mainstream culture.

In retrospect, I realize that I over-emphasize the significance and endurance of transmodernism. I was swayed at the time by the intellectual stature of its founder, Enrique Dussel, in particular in light of his classic texts on Marx and Marxism (e.g. Dussel 1985, 1988, 1990, 1994, 2001, 2003). Moreover, although not discussed in *Critical Race Theory and Education: A Marxist Response*, influential cultural theorist Paul Gilroy (2004, p. 48; see also p. 10 and p. 58) had enthusiastically endorsed transmodernism as 'a geopolitical project with a longer reach and more profound consequences than is customarily appreciated'. He had further stated (Gilroy

2004, pp. 80–81) that 'transmodern dissidence is increasingly connected to the emergence of an anticapitalist culture that aims to make resistance to neoliberalism as global as capital has become'. Some 12 years later, there are no signs that transmodernism has fulfilled any such promise. Whereas postmodernism, like CRT, is ultimately lacking in a specific direction for moving humankind forward progressively, and is thereby not amenable to critiques about the nature of its 'solutions', transmodernist Dussel posited an 'ex nihilo utopia' (a utopians' society from nothing)—a concept increasingly obscure as neoliberal capitalism becomes more and more entrenched. Having a longer history and a more high-profile and multidisciplinary presence, postmodernism is still significant, exemplified by its continuing presence in some academic journals, but its heyday (the 1990s and the earlier years of the first decade of the twentieth century) is now passed.

Critical Legal Studies and CRT

Next in chapter 2 of Cole (2017), I address CRT's historical origins in CLS in the USA. CLS, I note, was a response to the law's role in protecting hierarchy and class. It was in essence a socialist movement, although many commentators on the movement, as is demonstrated in the chapter, tend to use the adjective 'Left' to describe it, perhaps to distinguish 'socialism' from Stalinism, the authoritarian distortion of socialism that many people in the USA are led to believe, incorrectly I would insist, is socialism's only viable form.[1] Mark Tushnet, secretary of the Conference on Critical Legal Studies from 1976 to 1985, is unambiguous about his take on the revolutionary nature of CLS, when he writes that if he were to be asked to decide actual cases as a judge, he would 'make an explicitly political judgement: which result is, in the circumstances now existing, likely to advance the cause of socialism?' (Tushnet 1981, p. 424). His reasoning is that the courts, like the government, are unequivocally on the side of capitalism, and that therefore it is absolutely necessary to take sides.

With respect to socialist practices in the workplace, Duncan Kennedy (1982, p. 615) notes how both Marxist and non-Marxist law teachers were attempting at the time to challenge the dominant mode of production and radicalize their work lives by equalizing all salaries, including secretaries and janitors, and everyone spending one month per year performing a job in a different part of the hierarchy.

CRT was in part a response to the perception that the analyses of CLS were too class-based and underestimated the centrality of 'race', for them the major form of oppression in society. As Kimberlé Crenshaw and her co-writers (1995, p. xix) put it, Critical Race Theorists sought 'a left intervention into race discourse and a race intervention into left discourse'. CRT is derived from a number of sources, in particular from W.E.B. Du Bois, for whom 'the problem of the Twentieth Century [was] the problem of the color-line' (Du Bois 1903).

While there is no definitive birth date for the CRT movement, the key formative event, according to Crenshaw and her co-writers (1995, p. xxvii), was the founding of a workshop in 1989, when the term 'Critical Race Theory' was coined.

Having addressed CLS and the origins of CRT, in other words the usurping of class by 'race', next in chapter 2 of Cole (2017), I look at the variety of identity-specific movements within CRT, including *Asian-American Jurisprudence*, whose first annual conference took place in 1994 to counter stereotypes and differential experiences within that community; *LatCrit*, founded in 1997 to represent Latina/o Americans, and to challenge 'black exceptionalism', the position that the experiences of African Americans must place them at the center of any analysis or movement based on racism in the USA; and *Native Jurisprudence*, formed in the early twenty-first century to campaign for the specific needs of Native Americans centered around land and culture.

I conclude chapter 2 of Cole (2017) with a discussion of Delgado's (2001) distinction between the 'idealistic' and 'materialist' wings of CRT, the former very much related to discourse analysis and poststructuralism,[2] the latter based in material factors 'such as profits and the labor market' (Delgado 2003, p. 124). Materialist CRT, I suggest, 'has an affinity with both sociologist Max Weber and with Marxism. There is an inherent conflict between Weber and Marx.' Although Albert Salomon's famous observation that Weber was involved in a debate 'with the ghost of Marx' (Salomon 1935) may be somewhat overstated, ever since Weber (c. 1915) made a number of criticisms of Marx and Marxism the intellectual struggle against Marxist ideas has been at the forefront of academic writing. Weber suggested that social class might not be solely related to the mode of production, that political power does not necessarily derive from economic power and that status as well as class might form the basis of the formation of social groups.

CRT: Key Themes and Central Tenets

David Gillborn (2008, p. 40) has defined the key themes of CRT as follows:

- racism is endemic, extensive, 'normal', not aberrant;
- it is socially constructed and constantly changing;
- liberalism[3] is not neutral, objective, colour-blind or meritocratic; formal equal opportunity laws are too limited in scope;
- Civil Rights Laws are limited in their progress and apparent advances have been clawed back;
- CRT challenges ahistoricism and emphasizes the importance of experiential knowledge.

There is not much here that Marxists would take issue with. However, as I argue in the third chapter of Cole (2017), from a Marxist perspective two of CRT's central tenets, namely, the favouring of the concept of 'white supremacy' (viewed by Critical Race Theorists as descriptive of everyday racism rather than just the views of convinced racists and fascists in organisations such as the BNP in the UK and the Ku Klux Klan and other Hate Groups in the USA) over racism and the prioritizing of 'race' over class as the primary form of oppression in society, are both extremely problematical. With respect to the former, while I overstate the case in Cole (2017) by suggesting that Critical Race Theorists want to *replace* the concept of racism with 'white supremacy', 'white supremacy' is much too lacking in breadth of application to examine the multifarious forms of racism in the modern world, as argued in chapter 3 of Cole (2017), and in chapter 4 of this volume.

With respect to 'race' over class, in chapter 3 of Cole (2017), I argue that capitalism, albeit massively racialized (and gendered), relies on social class exploitation and reproduction for its very existence. It is possible, I suggest, though extremely difficult because of the multiple benefits accruing to capital of racializing workers (not least forcing down labour power costs), and the unpaid and underpaid labour of women as a whole, to imagine a capitalist world of 'racial' (and gender) equality. It is not logically possible for capitalism to exhibit social class equality. Without the extraction of surplus value from the labour of workers, capitalism cannot exist (Cole 2017, p. 50; Marx's labour theory of value is discussed in the Appendix to chapter 9 of that book).

In addition, in chapter 3 of Cole (2017) (see also chapter 5 of this volume), I offer my own wide-ranging definitions of racism and xeno-racism (racism directed at Eastern European migrant workers) and of the neo-Marxist concepts of racialization (falsely categorizing people into distinct 'races') and xeno-racialization (the way in which Eastern European migrant workers become racialized), arguing that these formulations are better suited in general to understanding and combating racism than is 'race' over class or the CRT concept of 'white supremacy'. These formulations, as I maintain in the second half of chapter 3 of Cole (2017), can in addition facilitate an understanding of how racism can be theorized in a class-based analysis of contemporary neoliberal capitalism. Whereas in chapter 7 of Cole (2017), I briefly described the nature of neoliberalism, in chapter 6 of this volume, I examine its historical origins, before addressing its role along with imperialism in consolidating racialized world capitalism. In the wake of the 2007/2008 financial crisis, and the accompanying onset of austerity/immiseration capitalism, I point out, it is overwhelmingly the racialized working classes of the UK and the USA that bear the brunt.

CRT: Strengths and Limitations

In chapter 4 of Cole (2017), I examine what I perceive to be the strengths of CRT. These include the previously acknowledged insistence on the all-pervasive existence of racism in the world, the importance of *Voice* so that people of colour can be heard (e.g. Delgado 1995) and CRT and the law in the USA, where CRT has performed and continues to perform a useful reformist intervention in the US legal system. Other fortes include the use of the concept of property to explain segregation historically in the USA (DeCuir-Gunby 2006, pp. 101–105); and the concept of chronicle (e.g. Ladson-Billings 2006, pp. viii–xi), a constructed narrative in which evidence and other forms of data are embedded, so that points can be made about the racist nature of given societies or communities or institutions (see chapters 4 and 5 of this volume). Other progressive conceptual tools include contradiction-closing cases (Bell 1985, p. 32), where inequity becomes so visible that the present situation becomes unsustainable. Gillborn (2008, p. 33) gives the example of *Brown v. Board of Education*. In 1954, the ruling stated that segregation based on colour violated the Equal Protection Clause of the Fourteenth Amendment of the US Constitution. Derrick Bell hypothesized that why this happened was that, given the fact that the Second World War had not long ended and the Korean War had ended in 1953, the possibility of mass domestic unrest loomed if African American service personnel, who had featured prominently in both wars, were subject to violent racism in the USA. Moreover, this period was the height of the Cold War, with much of the 'developing world' (much of it black, brown or Asian) uncommitted and up for grabs (Delgado and Stefancic 2001, p. 19, following Bell 1980). As Delgado and Stefancic (ibid.) explain, the 'interests of whites and blacks, for a brief moment, converged' (interest convergence is discussed later in this chapter). Gillborn (2008, p. 33) points out, however, that over 50 years on, de facto many schools remain segregated.

CRT's strengths, however, are not without limitations, and in chapter 4 of Cole (2017), I suggest ways in which some of these strengths could be enhanced by Marxist analysis. The underlying point is that Marxist theory is needed to in order to investigate and *understand* the material and ideological workings of racialized capitalism that underpin the oppression and exploitation of people of colour, and in chapters 4 and 5 of this volume I demonstrate this by evaluating transatlantic theoretical developments in CRT between 2012 and 2016.

MULTICULTURAL EDUCATION AND ANTIRACIST EDUCATION IN THE USA AND THE UK

Having set the theoretical context in some detail in chapters 2 to 4, in chapter 5 of Cole (2017) I look at multicultural education in the USA and the UK, and at the respective antiracist responses (based on Marxism) in each country. I begin by discussing three forms of reactionary multicultural education in the USA identified by one of the world's leading critical educationists, Peter McLaren. I go on to analyse McLaren's advocacy, *in his postmodern phase,* of 'critical and resistant multiculturalism', a form of multiculturalism favoured by Critical Race Theorist Gloria Ladson-Billings. This entailed, in McLaren's (1995, p. 126) words, not seeing 'diversity itself as a goal but rather [affirming] diversity...within a politics of cultural criticism and a commitment to social justice'. Given that McLaren's theoretical orientation in 1995 was poststructuralist 'located within the larger context of postmodern theory' (McLaren 1995, p. 126), like postmodernists in general, he was restrained by postmodernism's internal constraints from making any concrete suggestions as to just what that social justice consisted of (for a Marxist critique of postmodernism and poststructuralism, see Cole 2008, chapter 5).

Soon after his mid-1990s phase, McLaren rejected postmodernism in favour of Marxism, and by 2008, McLaren's vision of a socially just world was no longer open-ended, but was informed by his re-acquired Marxism.[4] For revolutionary multiculturalists, he wrote, 'the pedagogical is the political'; and they need to create pedagogical spaces for self and social transformation in order to come to the understanding 'that both are co-constitutive of building socialism for the twenty-first century' (McLaren 2008, p. 480). In their 2010 article, McLaren and Valerie Scatamburlo-D'Annibale made use of the neo-Marxist concept of racialization to understand 'race' and racism, arguing that 'race' alone was too blunt an analytical tool to effectively elucidate complex social phenomena, even when, as in the case of Hurricane Katrina, social inequalities were expressed in such blatantly 'racial' disparities. As they put it: 'racism in capitalist society results from the racialization of the social relations of capitalist exploitation' (Scanamburlo-D'Annibale and McLaren 2010).

It is worth dwelling briefly on Scanamburlo-D'Annibale and McLaren's comments about Katrina because they underline a key moment of racialization in the USA in the first decade of the twentieth century. Around the time of Katrina in 2005, William Bennet, a key player in Republican politics and a leading neoconservative ideologue, made the statement that if you wanted to reduce crime in the USA, you could abort every black baby (cited in Van Auken 2005). Bennet added: 'That would be an impossibly ridiculous and morally reprehensible thing to do, but your crime rate would go down' (cited in ibid.).

Effectively underling media interpellation at the time, Bennet told ABC News, '[t]here was a lot of discussion about race and crime in New Orleans'. Bennett also told ABC News: 'There was discussion—a lot of it wrong—but nevertheless, media jumping on stories about looting and shooting, and roving gangs and so on' (cited in ibid.). Just a day after Bennett's radio comments, Charles Murray, co-author of the infamous pseudo-scientific and racist tract *The Bell Curve*,[5] declared that the hurricane merely demonstrated that 'the underclass has been growing during all the years that people were ignoring it' (cited in Van Auken 2005). Cementing the racialization inherent in the representations of New Orleans, Murray declared, 'show us the face of the hard problem: those of the looters and thugs, and those of inert women doing nothing to help themselves or their children. They are the underclass' (cited in ibid.).

Murray also delved into a favourite topic of right-wing ideologues and pseudo-moralists like himself and Bennett—the 'illegitimacy rate' among blacks and 'low-income groups' generally (cited in ibid.). Katrina thus portrayed is caused not by decaying infrastructures, not the result of capitalist exploitation and oppression whereby the US government prioritizes the protection and pursuit of profits and global hegemony and war as opposed to addressing economic deprivation and racism, but by a large black underclass, of whom the men are all criminals and the women not fit to look after their children, and of which they have too many. The cause of crime, according to this right-wing racist perspective, is not grinding poverty, mass unemployment and living conditions resembling the developing world—the direct result of neoliberal capitalism—but too many black people.

In the second half of Cole (2017, chapter 5), I turn to the UK and discuss what was in the 1970s and 1980s, and into the 1990s, an ongoing debate over the relative merits of multicultural and antiracist education. I suggest that both are under threat from the imposition of the adherence to 'British values'. The threat was exacerbated in 2011, when the then Prime Minister David Cameron, leader of the ConDem (Conservative/Liberal Democrat) coalition government, made a key speech in which he advocated what he described as a 'muscular liberalism' to replace any semblance of multiculturalism.[6] Cameron declared:

> Under the doctrine of state multiculturalism, we have encouraged different cultures to live separate lives, apart from each other and the mainstream… Frankly, we need a lot less of the passive tolerance of recent years and much more active, muscular liberalism. (David Cameron 2011, cited in GOV.UK)

By 'muscular liberalism', Cameron meant a tough defence of British values. As he explained:

> A passively tolerant society says to its citizens, as long as you obey the law we will just leave you alone. It stands neutral between different values. But I believe a genuinely liberal country does much more; it believes in certain values and actively promotes them. Freedom of speech, freedom of worship, democracy, the rule of law, equal rights regardless of race, sex or sexuality. It says to its citizens, this is what defines us as a society: to belong here is to believe in these things. Now, each of us in our own countries, I believe, must be unambiguous and hard-nosed about this defence of our liberty. (GOV.UK 2011)

While advocates of twenty-first-century socialism (discussed later in this chapter and in chapter 7 of this volume) would certainly advocate 'freedom of worship' and 'equal rights regardless of race, sex or sexuality', we would also want to add other 'protected' grounds recognized, for example, by the UK Equality and Human Rights Commission, such as equal rights irrespective of age and disability, as well as equal rights as far as pregnancy and maternity, marriage and civil partnership and gender reassignment are concerned. Indeed, it is incumbent on twenty-first-century socialists to address all forms of social inequality. This represents a key distinction with respect to its twentieth-century incarnation.

The other values that Cameron exalts are, from a Marxist perspective, more problematic. I will take each in turn. The kind of 'democracy' that he is referring to is capitalist representative democracy, which, in the UK, means in effect once in every five years voting into parliament a choice of neoliberal capitalist parties (but see the Postscript to this volume for a brief discussion of the election of Jeremy Corbyn to the leadership of the British Labour Party, and the significance of the rise of Bernie Sanders in the USA).

With respect to 'freedom of speech', my own view on this is that, while freedom of speech is important, there need to be limitations as far as 'hate' speech is concerned. Indeed, this is enshrined in UK law and includes 'racial' hatred (although, I would say, the law is applied far too cautiously). In addition, I believe that there should be no platform for fascists (see Cole 2012c for a discussion).

When Cameron referred to the 'rule of law', he was signifying, from *his* perspective, an impartial legal system. From a Marxist point of view, however, the 'rule of law' is interpreted very differently. Following Marx, Louis Althusser (1971) described 'law' as an instance of the superstructural layer of society. In addition to the economic base, societies have a superstructure which itself 'contains two "levels" or "instances": the politico-legal (law and the State) and ideology (the different ideologies, religious, ethical, legal, political, etc.)' (Althusser 1971). Althusser identified two types of state apparatus, the repressive (repressive state apparatuses—RSAs) and the ideological (ideological state apparatuses—ISAs), which function primarily by repression and ideology, respectively, although each functions both by violence and by ideology. As he put it, with respect to the legal state apparatus:

> This term means: not only the specialized apparatus (in the narrow sense) whose existence and necessity I have recognized in relation to the require-

ments of legal practice, i.e. the police, the courts, the prisons; but also the army, which (the proletariat has paid for this experience with its blood) intervenes directly as a supplementary repressive force in the last instance, when the police and its specialized auxiliary corps are 'outrun by events'; and above this ensemble, the head of State, the government and the administration. (Althusser 1971)

The crucial point is that, whereas David Cameron believes that the 'rule of law' is neutral, from a Marxist perspective the legal apparatuses of the state uphold the values, and protect the wealth and privileges of the ruling class. As we have seen, this was also the interpretation of bourgeois law articulated by the CLS movement. For Critical Race Theorists, the 'rule of law' upholds the 'the white supremacist state'. For Marxists, the capitalist state exploits the working class as a whole, and oppresses and racializes various groups historically and contemporaneously. In the context of neo-liberal capitalism, and even more especially austerity capitalism, the legal ideological and repressive apparatuses of the state work hard, and with considerable success, to maintain ruling class hegemony and wealth, and to increase working class poverty and immiseration. They also work, via the ideological and repressive apparatuses of the state (ISAs and RSAs), to restrict immigration and to racialize and demonize immigrants and other racialized groups (Cole 2016).

DAVID GILLBORN AND 'BRITCRIT'

With respect to a specifically *British* form of CRT or 'BritCrit', which is the subject of chapter 4 of this volume, it has to be said that Gillborn has done much to develop it. In chapter 5 of *Critical Race Theory and Education: A Marxist Response* (Cole 2009a, 2017), I address what was when writing the book in 2008, and at the time of the publication of the first edition in 2009, the relatively recent arrival of CRT in the UK. I focus on a seminal work by David Gillborn, *Racism and Education: Coincidence or Conspiracy?* (Gillborn 2008).

I begin by referring to Gillborn's hostility to and misrepresentation of Marxists and Marx (Cole 2009a, **2nd edition**, 2017, pp. 125–131). I go on to critique Gillborn for his ahistorical stance and his lack of engagement with economic, political and ideological factors (Cole 2009a, **2nd edition**, 2017, pp. 130–134). I then consider Gillborn's discussion of racist inequalities in the UK education system, and commend his meticulous and painstaking analysis, and make the point that his insights are of use and interest to all of us involved in the antiracist struggle, but state that, rather than inclining me more to CRT, the trends were indicative of the continuing racialization of Asian and black students that had its origins in the British Empire, briefly referred to towards the end of chapter 3 of Cole (2017, pp. 134–135) (see also Cole 2016, chapter 1). I then turn to Gillborn's treatment of education policy under 'New Labour', and once again, I find the analysis useful and important (Cole 2009a, **2nd edition**, 2017, pp. 135–140). However, whereas, for Gillborn, the major problem is 'white powerholders', 'whites', 'white supremacy' or 'white racial violence', from a Marxist perspective, the problem is the violent racist neoliberal capitalist state.

During the course of chapter of Cole (2009a, **2nd edition**, 2017, pp. 125–145), I illustrate how Gillborn has developed 'BritCrit'. Thus, he applies founding Critical Race Theorist Derrick Bell's *Chronicle of the Space Traders* (Bell 1992) (the ultimate sacrifice of black rights or lives is ever present)[7] to events in the UK. The ever-present threat to people of colour, Gillborn argues, has become more explicit with the ongoing 'war on terror'. Extending Bell's chronicle beyond African Americans, he cites a radio phone-in listener, following a high-profile police in London targeted at Muslims, where one was shot (not fatally) by the police: 'It's *good* that these Muslims, Arabs and Asians are having it rough here. I'd rather the odd one got shot than a relative of mine got blown up' (cited in Gillborn 2008, p. 43).

Gillborn (2008, pp. 41–43) also uses the US CRT concept of 'model minorities', a stereotype that generalizes Asian Americans by depicting them as the perfect example of an if-they-can-do-it-so-can-you success story (see Kuo 2015), to try to understand positive perceptions of Indian and Chinese students in the UK, the flip side of which involves the demonization of black students (Gillborn 2008, chapter 7) and the CRT device of chronicle (a constructed narrative which is used to make important theoretical points, as discussed earlier in this chapter) to trace conversations between an older white professor—not him but sharing some of his thoughts, fears and experiences (Gillborn 2008, p. 5)—and a young black male student to introduce and review the main arguments in his book (Gillborn 2008, pp. 5–19; 184–196).[8]

Transposition (adapted from Gregg Beratan 2008, and developed by Gillborn 2008, p. 82) describes 'situations where one form of injustice is legitimized by reference to a different, more readily acceptable form of argument' and is employed by Gillborn to highlight the hypocrisy of Tony Blair (then Prime Minister) deploying gender equity issues (making statements against forced marriage among Muslim communities) as 'an acceptable trope for otherwise aggressively racist attacks on Muslim communities' (Gillborn 2008, pp. 82–86). As Gillborn puts it, while such statements are, of course, just with respect to women's rights, Blair could put forward a concern for equity for women, while at the same time supporting immigration rules which would make it harder for women to get in the country to be with their husbands.

Finally, Gillborn (2008, p. 32) utilizes Bell's concept of 'the contradiction-closing case'. Gillborn (2008, p. 120) describes the Stephen Lawrence case, from the black teenager's racist murder in 1993 to the lengthy public campaign for justice, the Inquiry by Sir William Macpherson published in 1999, the reform of 'race' equality law and the piecemeal changes that followed as:

> the supreme example of a contradiction-closing case in the UK: a case that, after years of the most painful campaigning and mistreatment, was supposed to have changed Britain for ever but which now seems to have left little imprint on the system in general, and education in particular.

As Gillborn points out, related to the 'contradiction-closing case' is 'interest convergence'. The idea of 'interest convergence', also a concept pioneered by Derrick Bell (2004, p. 69), is that where 'the interest of blacks [by extension all people of color] in achieving racial equality will be accommodated only when that interest converges with the interests of whites in policy-making decisions' 'even when the interest convergence results in an effective racial remedy, that remedy will be abrogated at the point that policy makers fear the remedial policy is threatening the superior status of whites'. Gillborn (2008, p. 33) argues that it is dangerous to rely on interest convergence alone without the deployment of 'contradiction-closing case'. As he explains, while landmark cases may appear to advance social justice, in reality, there is foot-dragging at every stage and conservatives redouble their efforts to oppose the change, while using the landmark case as a rhetorical weapon. He cites Delgado:

> Contradiction-closing cases...allow business as usual to go on even more smoothly than before, because now we can point to the exceptional case and

say, 'See, our system is really fair and just. See what we just did for minorities or the poor. (Delgado 1998, p. 445, cited in Gillborn 2008, p. 33)

More recently, Gillborn (2013, p. 1; 2014, p. 33) has deployed the concept of 'interest-divergence'. As he argues, the politics of interest-divergence are clearly evident in England. He is referring to his belief that:

> White power-holders imagine that a direct advantage will accrue from the further exclusion and oppression of Black groups in society. Behind rhetoric that proclaims the need to improve educational standards for all and celebrates a commitment to closing the existing achievement gaps; in reality education reforms are being enacted that systematically disadvantage Black students and demonstrably widen educational inequalities. (Gillborn 2013, p. 477)

As he puts it elsewhere, since the global economic crisis that began in 2008 interest-divergence has meant that 'white people imagine that some benefit will accrue from the further marginalization and oppression of racially minoritized groups' (Gillborn 2014, p. 30). He goes on to argue that a succession of announcements has sought to present the true 'racial victims in education as white working class children, especially boys' (Gillborn 2014, p. 33). As a result, Gillborn states that multicultural programmes have been cut and special programmes targeted at supporting poor white students have multiplied (Gillborn 2014, p. 33). He concludes that the government's new measure of academic success, the English baccalaureate, will particularly adversely affect certain students. This is because teacher expectations tend to be systematically lower of some students than warranted by their actual performance, meaning that they do not get access to high-status courses. He provides a hierarchy of disadvantage, with children with special needs special education needs (SEN) and students in receipt of Free School Meals (indicative of parental or carer poverty) most disadvantaged. In terms of ethnic origin, the highest penalties are experienced by black Caribbean students, followed by Bangladeshi students, dual heritage students (with white and black Caribbean parents and black African students [Gillborn 2014, p. 34]).

Referring to interest *convergence* in the same article, Gillborn, following a discernible trend in BritCrit analysis towards intersectionality (see Chapter 4 of this volume), states that this 'is crucially about an intersectional analysis of race and class interests', viewing non-elite whites as a kind of buffer that secures the interests of elite whites (Gillborn 2014, p. 29).

NEOLIBERAL GLOBAL CAPITALISM AND IMPERIALISM IN THE TWENTY-FIRST CENTURY

In chapter 7 of Cole (2017), I direct my attention to neoliberal global capitalism and imperialism. I begin by defining capitalism—a system in which a minority (the capitalist class) exploits the majority (the working class) by extracting surplus value from their labour power. I go on to argue that globalization has always been a central feature in the maintenance and parasitic growth of capitalism, but would now stress that globalization increases dramatically with advances in capitalist technology or technocapitalism (Suarez-Villa 2012). I then define, following Martinez and García (2000), five identifying features of the global phenomenon of neoliberalism: the rule of the market; cutting public expenditure; deregulation or reducing government regulation of everything that could diminish profits; privatization; elimination of the concept of 'the public good' or 'community'. I note how the signing of the General Agreement on Trade in Services (GATS) in 1994 gave global neoliberalism a major boost by removing any restrictions and internal government regulations in the area of service delivery that are considered 'barriers to trade'. I go on to discuss global environmental destruction, which in the last 30 years or so has accelerated as capitalism's penetration of nature for profit has dramatically deepened. In the chapter I also assess both transmodern and postmodern perspectives on globalization and US imperialism, finding some strengths in the former, but viewing the latter as fantasy. At the time of writing the first edition of the book (Cole 2009a, **2nd edition,** 2017), Iraq had been occupied for over five years, and 1 million plus Iraqis had been killed and a further 4 million had become refugees (World Socialist Website 2008). To exemplify the horrors of war, I provide, as an Appendix to the chapter, the log of a detainee at Guantanamo Bay.

MARXISM AND TWENTY-FIRST-CENTURY SOCIALISM IN VENEZUELA

In the penultimate chapter of Cole (2017, chapter 8), I examine an alternative to neoliberal capitalism, imperialism and war, namely, twenty-first-century socialism in the making in the Bolivarian Republic of Venezuela. The point is that Marxism, like CRT, is a 'living philosophy' continually being adapted and adapting itself 'by means of thousands of new efforts' (Sartre 1960) and not 'simply a discourse nor a body of (academic) knowledge' (Bartolovich 2002, p. 20). However, unlike CRT, which has no definitive vision of a future beyond capitalism, Marxism can envisage a world based on an entirely different economic system, based on production for need rather than profit.

I begin chapter 8 of Cole (2017) with some common objections to Marxism and provide a Marxist response. Turning my attention to Venezuela, I begin by discussing the *misiones*, a series of social justice, social welfare, anti-poverty and educational programmes implemented under the governments of the late Hugo Chávez, and continuing under the incumbent president Nicolás Maduro. Clifford Young and Julio Franco (2013) document the immense scope and reach of the *misiones*, pointing out that, just before the presidential election in April 2013, 88 % of Venezuelans 'reported that they personally, someone in their family or someone else they know has benefited from at least one of these programs'.

While these programmes are essentially social democratic, they are part of twenty-first-century socialism *in the making*. Elsewhere (Cole and Motta 2011), we have made a distinction between twentieth-century 'socialism' and twenty-first-century socialism.

Twentieth-century 'socialism' tended to have the following features:

- (White male) organized working class
- Top-down control as Stalinism became entrenched
- Atheism (except some varieties of Christian social democratic 'socialism')
- Lack of ecological awareness
- A general belief that the end justifies the means

Twenty-first-century socialism, on the other hand, entails:

- Women of colour playing a central role
- The involvement of the informal economy, not just organized labour
- Genuine attempts at participatory democracy
- A central focus on the spiritual
- Ecological awareness
- Central processes viewed as ends as well as means

To this list, I would also add the fact that twenty-first-century socialists also genuinely promote all equality issues, including the nine 'protected' grounds recognized, for example, by the UK Equality and Human Rights Commission—age, disability, gender, 'race', religion and belief, pregnancy and maternity, marriage and civil partnership, sexual orientation and gender reassignment.

What makes the Bolivarian Revolution unique is that under the late Hugo Chávez, and following Chávez's tragic death under President Maduro, the state is furthering and processing the revolution. In classical Marxist theory, the capitalist state must be overthrown rather than reformed. As Althusser (1971: 142) put it:

> The proletariat must seize State power in order to destroy the existing bourgeois State apparatus and, in a first phase, replace it with a quite different proletarian, State apparatus, then in a later phases set in motion...the end of State power, the end of every State apparatus.

However, Althusser's analysis did not extend to the possible existence of states which advocate their own destruction. As Chávez proclaimed at the World Social Forum in 2005, stressing the need to replace capitalism with socialism, and distancing twenty-first-century socialism from Stalinism:

> It is impossible, within the framework of the capitalist system to solve the grave problems of poverty of the majority of the world's population. We must transcend capitalism. But we cannot resort to state capitalism, which would be the same perversion of the Soviet Union. We must reclaim socialism as a thesis, a project and a path, but a new type of socialism, a humanist one, which puts humans, and not machines or the state ahead of everything. That's the debate we must promote around the world. (cited in Curran 2007)

When writing chapter 8 of Cole (2017), I underestimated the role of the Venezuelan people in the revolution. For example, through the eyes and voices of the revolutionaries in the decades that preceded the election of Chávez, and through his own incisive analysis, George Ciccariello-Maher (2013) demonstrates with great skill and clarity the fact that the origins of the revolution predated Chávez, that there is a dialectical relationship between *el pueblo* (the people) and Chávez and that the key to understanding the apparent synthesis of revolution from above and below can be best explained by the formula 'the people created Chávez' (the title of his book). However, in so doing, while he talks of 'a complex and dynamic interplay and mutual determination between the two: movements and state: "the people" and Chávez' (2013, p. 6), and while he notes 'the undeniable importance of Chávez to the *contemporary* moment and his relationship with the revolutionary social movements that created him' (2013, p. 21), for me, the whole thrust of his analysis has the effect of underemphasizing the supreme historical importance of the insertion of Chávez into the history of Bolivarian socialism (see Cole 2014 for a discussion). While participatory democracy—direct rule by the people—predated Chávez by decades (Ciccariello-Maher 2013) and indeed post-dates him, he must be credited with its inclusion in the Bolivarian Constitution of 1999 of which Article 118 enshrines:

> The right of workers and the community to develop associations of social and participative nature such as cooperatives, savings funds, mutual funds and other forms of association is recognized. These associations may develop any kind of economic activities in accordance with the law. The law shall recognize the specificity of these organizations, especially those relating the cooperative, the associated work and the generation of collective benefits. The state shall promote and protect these associations destined to improve the popular economic alternative.

Participatory democracy is in direct contrast to the aforementioned capitalist representative democracy favoured by capitalists and their promoters, including Cameron, as discussed above, which excludes workers from any power except the notional one of the right to vote in elections.

I conclude chapter 8 of Cole (2017) with a discussion of antiracism in practice in Venezuela, pointing to Chávez's pride in his indigenous and African ancestry, and refer to the various advances made by Indigenous Peoples and Afro-Venezuelans since the 1999 Constitution (for an up-to-date analysis of the achievements, but also of the racism of the opposition, see Eisen 2014; see also Cole 2014). As noted earlier in this chapter, given the recent election results, the future of Venezuela remains uncertain. I return to a discussion of Venezuela in chapter 7 of this volume.

CLASSROOM PRACTICE

In the final chapter (chapter 9) of *Critical Race Theory and Education: A Marxist Response* (Cole 2017) I discuss suggestions for classroom practice from Critical Race Theorists and Marxists. I begin with some areas of agreement such as that 'race' and racism should be discussed in the classroom, that racism intersects with other forms of oppression, that there is a need to look analytically at the failure of the education system to properly educate the majority of culturally and 'racially' subordinated groups. I go on to critique John Preston's (2007) arguments for the 'abolition of whiteness' being part of classroom pedagogy. His reasoning is as follows:

1. 'whiteness is a false form of identity and…there is no such thing as white culture';
2. 'whiteness, in terms of a structural system of white supremacy, is oppressive…[and] whiteness is *only* false and oppressive and…there is no possibility of "redemption" or reformation of whiteness';
3. 'whiteness divides humanity against itself and therefore is not in the genuine interests even of white people';
4. 'class, gender and sexuality are important in understanding oppression but race is central to understanding why other forms of political activity are not possible, particularly in the US' (Preston 2007, p. 10).

In Cole (2017, p. 221), I point out that I do not know what Preston means by proposition 4. I now understand that what he means is that the 'racial' divisions that exist in US society and the way in which these are replicated and enforced by the apparatuses of the state, such as the police, schools and other institutions, means that it very unlikely that the sorts of class consciousness necessary to produce a genuinely revolutionary movement in the USA will exist. Preston is not ignoring other divisions but he believes that even if movements like *Occupy* manage to mobilize a class faction, racial divisions are important in preventing a mass political mobilization (e.g. poor whites still think in 'racial' terms, even though they are disadvantaged by class) (personal correspondence). My response is that while I agree with his explanation, I would want to amend 'other forms of political activity are not possible' in proposition 4 to 'other forms of political activity are seriously constrained'.

I go on to argue in Cole (2017, p. 221) with respect to proposition 1 that while I agree that there is no 'white culture' per se, there are white *cultures*. It is particularly important, given the scenario of continuing UK white working class racism (exacerbated by sections of the tabloid press), that educators do not deny the existence of white working class cultures. As far as proposition 2 is concerned, I argued that it is *capitalism* not white supremacy that is a structural system of oppression. Moving on to suggestion 3, a belief that a division of 'whiteness' divides humanity is not surprising, given Preston's claims that whiteness is an objective power structure. For Chakrabarty and Preston (2006, p. 1), white supremacy, along with capitalism, is an objective inhuman system of exploitation and oppression. From a Marxist perspective, it is capitalism that is the objective system that divides humanity against itself, and is against the interests of *all* workers.

In the next part of chapter 9 of Cole (2017), I make some suggestions for classroom practice based on Marxism. These include antiracist multicultural education, the reintroduction of the teaching of imperialism and the teaching of democratic socialism. I will say a few words about each. In the chapter I point out that in the past I had argued consistently *against* multicultural education in that it tended to consist of white people teaching about other people's cultures, and *for* antiracist education. In the chapter I state that I now believe that technological advances in allowing people to speak for themselves—for example, via websites, blogs and email—provide a window of opportunity for multiculturalism and thus for antiracists to modify their position to include multicultural education. The way forward, I say in the chapter, is to promote both antiracism and antiracist multiculturalism: to create opportunities for hearing authentic voices, but, as I argue in chapter 3 of Cole (2017), in conjunction with objective analysis. Using the web creatively, I conclude, antiracist multicultural education should be about the importance of antiracism as an underlying principle, about the need to constantly address institutional racism and 'race' equality and about the promotion of respect and non-exploitative difference in a multicultural world.

I would now amend this position, and make a distinction between multiculturalism and multicultural societies. I am at present of the opinion that multiculturalism remains an essentially liberal concept, in the sense of 'middle of the road politics', not, as noted earlier, in the way 'liberal' tends to be used in everyday discourse in the USA, where it takes on a more politically Left of Center connotation. I believe now that twenty-first-century socialists should reject multiculturalism, even in its revolutionary mode as advocated by McLaren (2008, p. 480), and mentioned earlier in this chapter (McLaren now agrees: see McLaren 2015). Twenty-first-century socialists remain, of course, firm advocates of multicultural societies, in the sense of societies with people from many different cultural and linguistic backgrounds living together with totally equal rights. However,

I now prefer to multiculturalism the concepts of interculturalism (pertaining to two or more cultures) and intraculturalism (variations within one culture) which are key in Latin American politics. Unlike the liberal concept of multiculturalism, both are about the forging of decolonization. Decolonization is viewed as an umbrella term, and is defined as:

> putting an end to ethnic borders that influence opportunities in the area of education, work, politics and economic security, where no one is privileged on the basis of race, ethnicity and or language. It also signifies to avoid [sic] favouring conceptualisations of the Western world as if they are universal, yet valuing that knowledges, skills and technologies of the indigenous civilisations. (Congreso Nacional de Educación 2006, cited in Lopes Cardozo 2013, p. 105)

Benjamin Martinez, critical of 'multiculturalism', argues that 'interculturalism' 'is not simply the recognition of others' but 'the respect for knowledge, culture, and religion that is fundamental in building a truly democratic society. It is not enough to know that we are different, we must also acknowledge and change the inequalities that exist' (cited in Fischer-Hoffman 2014).

Interculturalism and intraculturalism are linked to plurilingualism and unity in diversity, to cohesion between people and between humans and the environment and to critical social awareness, and social justice more generally.[9]

I go on in chapter 9 of Cole (2017) to make the case that for Marxists an understanding of the metanarrative of imperialism, past and present, encompasses but goes beyond the centrality of 'racial' liberation in CRT theory. It takes us to the crux of the trajectory of capitalism from its inception right up to the twenty-first century; and this is why Marxists should endorse the teaching of imperialism, both old and new. Of course, the role of education in general, and teaching about imperialism in schools in particular, has its limitations, and young people are deeply affected by other influences and socialized by the media, by parents/carers and by peer culture (hence also the need for media awareness). Unlike Marxism, CRT does not centralize the fact that Islamophobia, the 'war on terror' and other forms of racism are necessary to keep the populace on task for 'permanent war' and the accumulation of global profits.

Finally, in the last chapter of Cole (2017), I argue that capitalist inroads into UK schools, colleges and universities had been given a boost by the Gordon Brown Labour government of the time, and that since the first election of Tony Blair in 1997 capitalist values in the education system had intensified to such an extent that the stance of Thatcher and the radical Right in the 1980s seemed tame by comparison. All this accelerated even more under the ConDem administration. If we are to have 'corporate values' in the education system, if we are to have 'business-facing' universities, I conclude, then it seems quite reasonable to press for the introduction in education of alternatives to neoliberal global capitalism and imperialism, such as (world) democratic socialism. Following McLaren and Houston (2005, p. 167), I argue, this should incorporate a thorough consideration of ecosocialism.

In the Conclusion to Cole (2017), I begin with a consideration of CRT and human liberation, and exemplify that CRT, unlike Marxism, is vague about the future. According to Crenshaw et al. (1995, p. xiii), Critical Race Theorists also share 'an ethical commitment to human liberation' but 'often disagree among [themselves], over its specific direction' (ibid.). Thus, often in CRT the solution is vague. To take an example, introducing their edited collection, *Critical Race Theory in Education*, Adrienne Dixson and Celia Rousseau (2006) talk about 'the struggle' (pp. 2–3), 'a vision of hope for the future' (p. 3), 'social action toward liberation and the end of oppression' (p. 3), 'the broader goal of ending all forms of oppression' (p. 4) and 'the ultimate goal of CRT—social transformation' (p. 7). To take another example, Dixson and Rousseau (2006, pp. 2–3) argue that 'CRT scholars acknowledge the permanence of racism' but that this should lead to 'greater resolve in the struggle'. They also refer to a CRT focus on 'praxis', which incorporates 'a commitment not only to scholarship but also to social action toward liberation and the end of oppression' (p. 3). They talk of 'eliminating racial oppression as part of the broader goal of ending all forms of oppression' (p. 4), and state that the 'ultimate goal of CRT [is] social transformation'. However, no indication is given of what they are struggling towards, what liberation means to them or what is envisioned by social transformation and the end of all forms of oppression.

I then turn to the legacy of Martin Luther King Jr., influential in the genesis of CRT (Delgado and Stefancic 2001, p. 4), pointing out that while he is quite accurately known for his gradualism and his reformism, in his later life King had moved on to focus on poor people in general, regardless of their colour. In one speech he is not ambiguous about his socialist beliefs:

You can't talk about solving the economic problem of the Negro without talking about billions of dollars. You can't talk about ending the slums without first saying profit must be taken out of slums. You're really tampering and getting on dangerous ground because you are messing with folk then. You are messing with captains of industry...Now this means that we are treading in difficult water, because it really means that we are saying that something is wrong...with capitalism...There must be a better distribution of wealth and maybe America must move toward a democratic socialism. (cited in The Democratic Socialists of Central Ohio 2008)

Penultimately in the Conclusion to Cole (2017), referring to David Gillborn's (2008, p. 13) remark that 'the best critical race theorists are passionate about...classism', I comment that while challenging the *oppression* of people that is based on their social class (classism) is extremely important, and is championed by Marxists, the fundamental point is to also confront the *exploitation* of workers at the point of production, thereby challenging capitalism itself, for therein lies the economic relationship that sustains and nurtures the capitalist system.

My last point is to very briefly suggest a realignment of CLS and CRT, informed by Marxism. While one leading Critical Race Theorist was enthusiastic about this, and, indeed, put out some feelers, nothing has yet come of this. In retrospect, my view is that this proposal was over-ambitious.

After I had written the Conclusion to the first edition of *Critical Race Theory and Education: A Marxist Response*, on November 5, 2008, Barack Obama became the president of the USA. This prompted me to write a Postscript to the book, in which I argue that the first 'election of a black president will not end racism' as some were suggesting (racism under Obama is discussed in Part Three of the next chapter of this volume; see also Cole 2016, chapter 2).

NOTES

1. Stalinism refers to political systems that have the characteristics of the Soviet Union under Joseph Stalin (he was leader from 1928 to 1953). The term refers to a repressive and oppressive from of government by dictatorship, which includes the purging by exile or death of opponents, mass use of propaganda and the creation of a personality cult around the leader.

2. Poststructuralism has two interrelated forms. One is primarily associated with the work of Michel Foucault, and examines the relationship between discourse and power, in particular the notion that power is everywhere and not just located locally. The other form of poststructuralism is to do with the role of language in forming individual subjectivity. Thus whereas *structuralists* aimed to discover uniform linguistic patterns that gave order and coherence to human existence, *post*structuralists highlight what they see as the unstable patterns of linguistic and therefore subjective and social order. Whereas structuralism was a *constructive* project, intent on identifying linguistic and social order, poststructuralism is concerned with *deconstruction* (Seidman 1998, p. 221; see also Cole 2008, pp. 40–45).

3. The term 'liberalism' tends, in popular (and academic) parlance, to be used differently in the UK and the USA. Traditionally, in the UK, it has been used (in popular discourse by Marxists and other Left radicals) to describe 'middle of the road' politics. Gillborn is using it in this sense. In the USA it has often been used in everyday parlance to describe those who are viewed to be on the Left. The 'Marxism-aware' CLS writers discussed in this chapter, including Tushnet, tend to use 'liberalism' to describe 'middle of the road' politics, as do similarly Marxism-aware Critical Race Theorists.

4. In Cole (2005), I trace McLaren's trajectory back into Marxism, a turning point of which was a conference in 1995 that he and I attended in Halle, in the former DDR (German Democratic Republic or 'East Germany' as it was known before the collapse of the Berlin Wall in 1989).

5. The thrust of Herrnstein and Murray's (1994) arguments in *The Bell Curve* is an unabashed defence of social inequality, attributing wealth and poverty to superior versus inferior genetically determined intellectual abilities. The political conclusion of The Bell Curve is a rejection of all policies aimed at ameliorating social injustice and furthering democratic values.

6. More recently in his speech to the 2015 Conservative Party Conference he clarified that he believed in multi-racialism, describing Britain as the 'proudest multi-racial democracy on earth', then reasserted his faith in 'British Values' by adding, '[t]hat's why we're making sure [children] learn British history at school'.

7. Bell's chronicle, set in the USA in the near future, relates how 70 % of Americans vote to exchange to space traders from another planet all the black people in America for enough gold to settle the country's massive debt and sort out the air that is unfit to breathe.

8. In the Appendix to chapter 4 of Cole (2017), I utilize Gillborn's persona of the Professor to make the point that non-colour-coded racism is highly significant in the UK, and to emphasize the shortcomings of CRT's use of 'white supremacy' in a wider understanding of racism's many forms.

9. See Mieke Lopes Cardozo's interesting discussion of Bolivia, in particular, the 2006 *Bolivian Proyecto de Ley* (Lopes Cardozo 2013, p. 25), for similar developments in that country. One practical educational implication is that coupling interculturalism with intraculturalism and plurilingualism means that students learn in the native language local to their area as well as Spanish (Lopes Cardozo 2013, p. 26).

REFERENCES

Althusser, L. (1971). Ideology and ideological state apparatuses. In *Lenin and philosophy and other essays*. London: New Left Books. http://www.marx2mao.com/Other/LPOE70NB.html

Bartolovich, C. (2002). Introduction. In C. Bartolovich & N. Lazarus (Eds.), *Marxism, modernity and postcolonial studies*. Cambridge: Cambridge University Press.

Bell, D. (1985). Foreword: The civil rights chronicles (the Supreme Court, 1984 term). *Harvard Law Review, 99*, 4–83.

Bell, D. (1992). *Faces at the bottom of the well: The permanence of racism*. New York: Basic Books.

Beratan, G. (2008). The song remains the same: Transposition and the disproportionate representation of minority students in special education. *Race, Ethnicity and Education, 11*(4), 337–354.

Cameron, David. (2011, February 5). Speech on radicalisation and Islamic extremism, Munich. *New Statesman*. http://www.newstatesman.com/blogs/the-staggers/2011/02/terrorism-islam-ideology

Ciccariello-Maher, G. (2013). *We created Cháccvez: A people's history of the Venezuelan revolution*. Durham/London: Duke University.

Cole, M. (2005). The "inevitability of globalized capital" vs. the "ordeal of the undecidable": A Marxist critique. In M. Pruyn & L. M. Heurta-Charles (Eds.), *Teaching Peter McLaren: Paths of dissent*. New York: Peter Lang.

Cole, M. (2008, November 29). Maintaining "the adequate continuance of the British race and British ideals in the world": Contemporary racism and the challenges for education. Bishop Grosseteste University College Lincoln: Inaugural Professorial Lecture.

Cole, M. (2009a). Critical race theory and education: A Marxist response (1st ed.). New York/London: Palgrave Macmillan.

Cole, M. (2009b). The color-line and the class struggle: A Marxist response to critical race theory in education as it arrives in the United Kingdom. Power and Education, 1(1), 111–124.

Cole, M. (2009c, April). On 'white supremacy' and caricaturing Marx and Marxism: A response to David Gillborn's 'who's afraid of critical race theory in education'. Journal for Critical Education Policy Studies, 7(1). http://www.jceps.com/index.php?pageID=article&articleID=143

Cole, M. (2009d). Critical race theory comes to the UK: A Marxist response. Ethnicities, 9(2), 246–269.

Cole, M. (2009e). A response to Charles mills. Ethnicities, 9(2), 281–284.

Cole, M. (2012a). Critical race theory in education, Marxism and abstract racial domination. British Journal of Sociology of Education, 33(2), 167–183.

Cole, M. (2012b). "Abolish the white race" or "transfer economic power to the people"? Some educational implications. Journal for Critical Education Policy Studies, 10(2). http://www.jceps.com/index.php?pageID=article&articleID=265

Cole, M. (2012c). Capitalist crisis and fascism: Issues for educational practice. In D. R. Cole (Ed.), Surviving economic crises through education. New York: Peter Lang.

Cole, M. (2014). The Bolivarian Republic of Venezuela: Education and twenty-first-century socialism. In S. C. Motta & M. Cole (Eds.), Constructing twenty-first-century socialism in Latin America: The role of radical education. New York/London: Palgrave Macmillan.

Cole, M. (2016). Racism: A critical analysis. London/Chicago: Pluto Press/University of Chicago Press.

Cole, M. (2017). Critical race theory and education: A Marxist response (2nd ed.). New York/London: Palgrave Macmillan.

Cole, M., & Motta, S. C. (2011, January 14). Opinion: The giant school's emancipatory lessons. Times Higher Education Online.

Congreso Nacional de Educación. (2006). Especial: Congreso Nacional de Educación de Bolivia, July 3 (15).

Crenshaw, K., Gotanda, N., Peller, G., & Thomas, K. (1995). Introduction. In K. Crenshaw, N. Gotanda, G. Peller, & K. Thomas (Eds.), Critical race theory: The key writings the formed the movement. New York: New Press.

Curran, F. (2007). What happened to the global justice movement? Fighting neoliberalism—The view from Scotland. International Viewpoint. Available http://www.internationalviewpoint.org/spip.php?article1365

DeCuir-Gunby, J. T. (2006). "Proving your skin is white, you can have everything": Race, racial identity, and property rights in whiteness in the Supreme Court case of Josephine DeCuir. In A. D. Dixson & C. K. Rousseau (Eds.), *Critical race theory in education: All god's children got a song*. New York/London: Routledge.

Delgado, R. (1995). *The Rodrigo Chronicles: Conversations about America and race*. New York: New York University Press.

Delgado, R. (1998). Rodrigo's committee assignment: A sceptical look at judicial independence. *Southern California Law Review, 72*, 425.

Delgado, R. (2001). Two ways to think about race: Ref lections on the Id, the ego, and other reformist theories of equal protection. *Georgetown Law Review, 89*. Available http://findarticles.com/p/articles/mi_qa3805/is_200107/ai_n8985367/pg_2. Accessed 26 Mar 2008.

Delgado, R. (2003). Crossroads and blind alleys: A critical examination of recent writing about race. *Texas Law Review, 82*, 121.

Delgado, R., & Stefancic, J. (2001). *Critical race theory: An introduction*. New York: New York University Press.

Dixson, A. D., & Rousseau, C. K. (2006). Introduction. In A. D. Dixson & C. K. Rousseau (Eds.), *Critical race theory in education: All god's children got a song*. New York: Routledge.

Du Bois, W. E. B. (1903). The forethought. In *The souls of black folk*. http://www.bartleby.com/114/100.html

Dussel, E. (1985). *La producción teórica de Marx. Un comentario a los Grundrisse*.

Dussel, E. (1988). *Hacia un Marx desconocido. Un comentario de los Manuscritos del 61–63*.

Dussel, E. (1990). *El último Marx (1863–1882) y la liberación latinoamericana: Un comentario a la tercera y cuarta redacción de "El Capital"*.

Dussel, E. (1994). *Las metáforas teológicas de Marx*.

Dussel, E. (2001). *Towards an unknown Marx: A commentary on the manuscripts of 1861–1863*. London: Routledge.

Dussel, E. (2003). *Beyond philosophy: History, Marxism, and liberation theology*. Maryland: Rowman and Littlefield.

Eisen, A. (2014, March 27). Racism Sin Vergüenza in the Venezuelan Counter-Revolution. *Venezuelanalysis.com*.

Fischer-Hoffman, C. (2014, October 14). Honoring indigenous resistance day in Venezuela, the struggle continues. *venezuelanalysis*. https://venezuelanalysis.com/news/10959

Gillborn, D. (2008). *Racism and education: Coincidence or conspiracy?* London: Routledge.

Gillborn, D. (2009). Who's afraid of critical race theory in education? A reply to Mike Cole's "The color-line and the class struggle". *Power and Education, 1*(1), 125–131.

Gillborn, D. (2010). Full of sound and fury, signifying nothing? A reply to Dave Hill's "Race and class in Britain: A critique of the statistical basis for critical race theory in Britain". *Journal for Critical Education Policy Studies, 8*(1), 78–107. http://www.jceps.com/?pageID=article&articleID=177

Gillborn, D. (2013). Interest-divergence and the colour of cutbacks: race, recession and the undeclared war on black children. *Discourse: Studies in the Cultural Politics of Education, 34*(4), 477–491.

Gillborn, D. (2014). Racism as policy: A critical race analysis of education reforms in the United States and England. *The Educational Forum, 78*(1), 26–41.

Gilroy, P. (2004). *After empire: Multiculture or postcolonial Melancholia.* London: Routledge.

GOV.UK. (2011). PM's speech at Munich Security Conference, delivered on: 5 Feb 2011. https://www.gov.uk/government/speeches/pms-speech-at-munich-security-conference

Hill, D. (2009a, June 25–26). *Statistical skullduggery in the case for critical race theory: How statistical tables comparing "race" and class underachievement have been fiddled to prove CRT's point in England.* Paper delivered to *Critical race theory in the UK: What is to be learnt? What is to be done?* Conference organized by C-SAP, BSA, The Institute of Education, University of London.

Hill, D. (2009b). Race and class in Britain: A critique of the statistical basis for critical race theory in Britain; and some political implications. *Journal for Critical Education Policy Studies, 7*(2). http://www.jceps.com/?pageID=article&articleID=159

Kennedy, D. (1982). Legal education and the reproduction of hierarchy. *Legal Education, 32*, 591–615.

Kuo, R. (2015, April 2). 6 reasons we need to dismantle the model minority myth of those "hard-working' Asians". *Everyday Feminism.* http://everydayfeminism.com/2015/04/dismantle-model-minority-myth/

Ladson-Billings, G. (2006). Foreword they're trying to wash us away: The adolescence of critical race theory in education. In A. D. Dixson & C. K. Rousseau (Eds.), *Critical race theory in education: All god's children got a song.* New York: Routledge.

Lather, P. (1991). *Getting smart; feminist research and pedagogy with/in the postmodern.* New York: Routledge.

Lopes Cardozo, M. (2013). *Future teachers and social change in Bolivia: Between decolonization and demonstration.* Delft: Uitgeverij Eburon.

Martinez, E., & García, A. (2000). What is "Neo-Liberalism" A brief definition. *Economy,* 101. http://www.globalexchange.org/campaigns/econ101/neoliberalDefined.html

McLaren, P. (1995). *Critical pedagogy and predatory culture: Oppositional politics in a postmodern era.* London/New York: Routldege.

McLaren, P. (2008). This fist called my heart. *Antipode, 40*(3), 472–481.

McLaren, P. (2015). *Pedagogy of insurrection: From resurrection to revolution.* New York: Peter Lang.

Mills, C. W. (2009). Critical race theory: A reply to Mike Cole. *Ethnicities, 9*(2), 270–281.

Preston, J. (2007). *Whiteness and class in education.* Dordrecht: Springer.

Preston, J. (2010). Concrete and abstract racial domination. *Power and Education, 2*(2), 115–125.

Preston, J. (2013). *Whiteness in academia: Counter-stories of betrayal and resistance.* Newcastle upon Tyne: Cambridge Scholars Publishing.

Preston, J., & Chadderton, C. (2012). "Race traitor": Towards a critical race theory informed public pedagogy. *Race, Ethnicity and Education, 15*(1), 85.

Sartre, J. P. (1960). *The search for method (1st part). Introduction to critique of dialectical reason.* http://www.marxists.org/reference/archive/sartre/works/critic/sartre1.htm

Scatamburlo-D'Annibale, V., & McLaren, P. (2010). Classifying race: The "compassionate" racism of the right and why class still matters. In Z. Leonardo (Ed.), *Handbook of cultural politics and education.* Boston: Sense Publishers.

Seidman, S. (1998). *Contested knowledge: Social theory in the postmodern era.* Oxford: Basil Blackwell.

Smith, D. G. (2003). On enfraudening the public sphere, the futility of empire and the future of knowledge after "America". *Policy Futures in Education, 1*(2), 488–503. http://www.wwwords.co.uk/pdf/validate.asp?j=pfie&vol=1&issue=3&year=2003&article=4_Smith_PFIE_1_3_web

Suarez-Villa, L. (2012). *Globalization and technocapitalism: The political economy of corporate power.* Farnham: Ashgate. https://books.google.co.uk/books?id=y-ChAgAAQBAJ&pg=PA146&lpg=PA146&dq=richard+d+wolff+on+capitalist++technologies+and+globalisation&source=bl&ots=hvLdjWoc1P&sig=bFLQ94BS8bUSkWeFw7lT9dQgo0k&hl=en&sa=X&ei=wmUeVbuvB8vWU9r3ggg&ved=0CD0Q6AEwBA#v=onepage&q=richard%20d%20wolff%20on%20capitalist%20%20technologies%20and%20globalisation&f=false

Tushnet, M. (1981). The dilemmas of liberal constitutionalism. *Ohio State Law Journal, 42,* 411–426.

World Socialist Web Site (WSWS) Editorial Board. (2008, March 19). *Five years after the invasion of Iraq: A debacle for US Imperialism.* http://www.wsws.org/articles/2008/mar2008/iwar-m19.shtml#

Young, C., & Franco, J. (2013, April 12). No matter who wins in Venezuela, Chavez's legacy is secure. *Reuters.* http://blogs.reuters.com/great-debate/2013/04/12/no-matter-who-wins-in-venezuela-chavezs-legacy-is-secure/

CHAPTER 3

Critical Race Theory, 'Race Traitor' and Marxism

INTRODUCTION

In chapter 2, I revisited Cole (2009a, **2nd edition**, 2017), updating it, and providing additional explanations for those who are not familiar with that volume, in order to set the context for this sequel. In this chapter, I look at the influential 'Race Traitor' (RT) movement, and contextualize it within contemporary debates around CRT and Marxism in the UK, before moving on in chapter 4 to look more generally at 'BritCrit'.

In Part One of this chapter, I take as a starting point an article (Preston and Chadderton 2012) in a special issue on Critical Race Theory (CRT) in England in the flagship international peer-reviewed journal *Race, Ethnicity and Education*, a publication edited by founding and leading UK Critical Race Theorist David Gillborn. Of the articles in that special edition, it is the one that most promisingly attempts to theoretically develop CRT in the British context, or to use Kevin Hylton's expression to build 'BritCrit'. Preston and Chadderton (2012) also has most purchase in the further-ance and understanding of the ongoing theoretical debate between CRT and Marxism. My critique of Preston and Chadderton entails an extensive consideration of the RT movement and contemporary Marxism which includes a critical appraisal of *Race Traitor,* the book edited by RT's co-founders, Noel Ignatiev and John Garvey (Ignatiev and Garvey (eds) 1996). In my assessment of RT, I look at its vulnerability of being misun-derstood (its choice of terminology and its rhetorical style, and Ignatiev

© The Author(s) 2017
M. Cole, *New Developments in Critical Race Theory and Education*,
DOI 10.1057/978-1-137-53540-5_3

and Garvey's views on neo-Nazi militia groups), at its emphasis on the black/white binary and its tactics and visions with respect to twenty-first-century socialism.

In Part Two of the chapter, I update and assess the (changing?) political perspectives of Ignatiev and Garvey, looking at Ignatiev's 2010 'Introduction' to some of the writings of C.L.R. James, his speech to 'Occupy Boston' in 2011 and his comments on 'race', capitalism and class following events in Ferguson, Missouri, 2015, after the death of African American teenager Michael Brown in August.

In Part Three of the chapter, I attempt a final assessment of Ignatiev's and Garvey's politics and discover that they now identify squarely with Marxist politics.

PART ONE: RT AND CONTEMPORARY MARXISM

Of all the papers in *Race, Ethnicity and Education* 15 (1), it is the one by John Preston and Charlotte Chadderton (Preston and Chadderton 2012) which has most relevance to the ongoing transatlantic debate between CRT and Marxism. At the time of a severe crisis in (neoliberal) capitalism, and as more and more people are considering the possibility of an alternative to austerity and some on the Left are looking for an alternative to capitalism itself, it is crucial that the Left presents a credible replacement. In chapter 7 of this volume, I discuss *my* preferred alternative to neoliberal capitalism, namely, intercultural and intracultural twenty-first-century socialism, which I see as the viable and plausible option.

Another alternative is represented by the RT movement. RT's core beliefs are given credence by Preston and Chadderton who aim to politically resituate it.[1] In this chapter I focus on RT's strengths and weaknesses. Preston and Chadderton's intention is to counter the arguments of what they refer to 'a left, Marxist, critique' (p. 88) that considers RT misguided and politically untenable. Contrary to this viewpoint, they suggest that RT is 'a political form with resonance for contemporary Marxists' and Anarchists (p. 85). Given that RT has been 'propagated through more recent work in Critical Race Theory', they argue that CRT and public pedagogy can 'produce new political praxis for Race Traitors in the twenty-first century' (p. 1). My view is that while RT has some strengths, it does not have resonance for contemporary Marxists,[2] and that it has three major problems: its vulnerability to being misunderstood; its almost exclusive focus on the 'black/white' binary and its tactics and the lack of clarity in its vision of a just society.[3]

What then is 'Race Traitor'? RT represents a set of beliefs based around a journal of the same name, founded in 1992, and also a co-edited collection of the same name (Ignatiev and Garvey (eds.) (1996)). Its core beliefs are summarized on its website: RT is dedicated to what it terms the 'abolition of the white race' and the eradication of racism.[4] Ignatiev and Garvey (eds.) (1996) (*Race Traitor* the book) consists of an Introduction, 22 chapters, 7 letters and an interview with Noel Ignatiev. On the first page of the Introduction, Ignatiev and John Garvey argue that by the early 1990s all but a few of the Left had given up on the possibility and even desirability of revolutionary change. They thus turn to 'the most radical of all indigenous American traditions—that of John Brown and the 19th-century abolitionists',[5] seeking 'to move the question of race explicitly to the center of the political stage' and to 'abolish the white race from within' (p. 2), i.e., for white people to abolish the white 'race'. There then follow various (mainly informative) accounts of racism the USA in the 1990s before demonstrating very effectively the abject misery and hatred that it generates. Ignatiev and Garvey (in the first chapter) make it clear at the outset that the white 'race', a historically constructed social formation, cuts across ethnic and class lines, and that it does not imply powers emergent from differential distribution of economic wealth. It 'consists of those who partake of the privileges of the white skin' in the USA (p. 10). This immediately distances RT from Marxism which has social class and class struggle as central, and clearly differentiates the wealth creators (the working class) and the wealth appropriators (the capitalist class): the exploited and the exploiters. While in the CRT tradition, Ignatiev and Garvey favour the concept of 'white supremacy' to describe everyday racism in the USA,[6] they make it clear that they believe 'that the majority of so-called whites...[in the USA] are neither deeply nor consciously committed to white supremacy' (p. 12). Most 'go along with a system that disturbs them, because the consequences of challenging it are terrifying. They close their eyes to what is happening around them because it is easier not to know' (p. 12).

A recurring theme throughout the book is the need for 'white' people to denounce their 'whiteness' and the privilege that goes with it. What RT means by this is explained by Ignatiev when he contrasts 'whiteness' with 'blackness':

Politically, whiteness is the willingness to seek a comfortable place within
the system of race privilege. Blackness means total, implacable, and relent-
less opposition to that system. Their 'whiteness' can be 'washed away' '[t]
o the extent so-called whites oppose the race line, repudiating their own
race privileges and jeopardizing their own standing in the white race'. In so
doing they have 'taken in some blackness' (p. 289)

Ignatiev and Garvey call on 'a minority' of 'white people' 'to undertake
outrageous acts of provocation, aware that they will incur the opposition of many who might agree with them if they adopted a more mod-
erate approach' (p. 36). A number of examples are given in the book.
For example, on the first (unpaginated) page of the book, there is a
description of several female students at a Junior–Senior High School in
Indiana (which had 2 black students out of a total of 850) who called
themselves the 'Free to Be Me' group, and who, in Hip Hop style,
started to braid their hair in dreadlocks, wear baggy jeans and combat
boots. This resulted in accusations from white people in town that they
were 'acting black'. Males students responded by calling them names,
spitting at them, punching them and pushing them into lockers. There
were also death threats, a bomb scare and a Ku Klux Klan rally at the
school. On the day of the rally, many students braided their hair and
wore hand-written 'Free to Be Me' buttons to school. Ignatiev and
Garvey comment: 'This incident reveals, among other things, the tremendous power of crossover culture to undermine both white solidarity
and male authority'.

In a rare reference to the overthrow of capitalism [but see Parts Two
and Three of this chapter]—'[t]he black proletariat forms the historical
antipode to capital']—Ignatiev (pp. 100–101) describes 'I'm black and
I'm proud' as the modern rendition of 'Workers of all countries, unite'.
When the workers of the world learn to say this, he claims, the new world
will be at hand.

There are some interesting conceptual developments, and suggestions of practical ways to combat racism, such as Christine E. Sleeter's
'white racial bonding' (p. 261). By this she means 'interactions that
have the purpose of affirming a common stance on race-related issues'
(p. 261). Sleeter gives as examples 'inserts into conversations, race-
related "asides" in conversations, strategic eye-contact, and jokes'
(p. 261). As she correctly points out, many whites who do not agree

with racist comments being made keep quiet for fear of loss of approval or friendship (p. 263). Sleeter explains how she challenged a neighbour who was trying to make racist connections between welfare, black women and laziness by talking about the need for more childcare options, corporate greed, the huge military budget, lack of jobs and so on (p. 262).

In a very moving account of his personal battles against segregation in a poor white family in the 1950s and 1960s, at a time of 'white supremacy' *in the traditional sense of the word*, Edward H. Peeples describes attempting to buy the newspaper *Richmond Afro-American*. As he puts it, the white cashier 'stared at me for a moment, as if she was searching her cultural grab bag for the rules and words needed to advise a fool who is about to violate a natural law', and finally proclaimed, '[y]ou don't want this newspaper, it's the colored newspaper' (p. 81). Seeing that he had an audience of black customers, Peeples continues, 'I turned back to the cashier, who by now was informing me where to buy the "white newspaper". I let her finish speaking, and then I said in a loud, crisp voice, "You must think I'm white"' (p. 82). She was startled, Peeples concludes, but 'within seconds she came to realize that these simple words represented a profound act of racial sedition' (p. 82).

As far as mass shifts 'to dissolve the white race' (p. 21) are concerned, Ignatiev cites 'the sudden and near unanimous shift by Afro-Americans in the 1960s from the self-designation "Negro" to "black" or "Black"' (p. 22), since from then on black stood in opposition to white. He also notes the countercultural revolution of young people in the 1970s (p. 22), which Ignatiev believes 'contained the elements of a mass break with the conformity that preserves the white race' (p. 23).

Ignatiev also talks rather unconvincingly of an 'approaching American intifada', which he describes as 'the mass strike of today' (p. 99). He then cites what he describes as three hints of this. These are 'black youth' in the early 1990s taking direct action by refusing to work in the fast food industry, thereby obtaining a rise in the minimum wage, which the unions had failed to achieve; the high proportion of children of black mothers born out of wedlock and the 'a decision not to rise out of the working class but with it' (p. 99) and the rise of neo-Nazi groups, members of which Ignatiev hopes will convert to RT (see the section on 'RT and neo-Nazi military groups' below).

The Vulnerability of RT to Being Misunderstood

The Choice of Terminology and the Rhetorical Style of RT

When one taps in 'Race Traitor' on a Google search, what comes up is the RT website. Apart from references to the new (sic) edition of the journal in 2005, what appears in the second paragraph is the following:

> The key to solving the social problems of our age is to abolish the white race, which means no more and no less than abolishing the privileges of the white skin. Until that task is accomplished, even partial reform will prove elusive, because white influence permeates every issue, domestic and foreign, in US society.[7]

Despite its good intentions, which are manifestly evident when one reads Ignatiev and Garvey (eds.) (1996), I question RT's choice of terminology, its use of words. First, it is well known that 'race traitor' is a term of abuse directed by Nazis and other fascists at white people who are not racist. In addition, RT's stated aim of 'abolishing the white race' is seriously open to misinterpretation. For example, anyone googling 'Race Traitor', and finding RT and the quote immediately above could possibly interpret RT's aim as the abolition of white people as a 'race'. Moreover, in Cole (2017, p. 46) I argue that RT's *style* is reminiscent of Nazi propaganda. The placing of 'style' in italics is important. Preston and Chadderton (2012, p. 88) quote my comment about Nazi propaganda (in Cole 2009a, pp. 32–33, **2nd edition**, 2017, p. 47) but they omit the italics. They also ignore what I write immediately after, namely, that Ignatiev and Garvey—the key figures in RT—do not mean the abolition of white people. As I put it, 'it is made clear [by Ignatiev and Garvey] that this is not the case' (Cole 2009a, p. 33, **2nd edition**, 2017, p. 47). I go on to underline the vulnerability of RT to misinterpretation. Preston and Chadderton are trying to back up their claim of 'a left, Marxist, critique of the supposedly fascist nature of ["Race Traitor"]' (p. 88), (I am the only Marxist cited!), and accordingly imply that I levelled the charge of Nazism at RT's political ideology, since in the next paragraph, they state, '[t]he charge of fascism…is often levelled at radical movements against racial oppression' (ibid.). This is a serious distortion of my views of RT. Later, they qualify their assertion somewhat by acknowledging that I was indeed making comments about RT's rhetoric (Preston and Chadderton 2012, p. 91) but the point had already been made. I am also identified by Preston and Chadderton as a Marxist who is 'wilfully unaware' (Preston and Chadderton [2012, p. 88]) of the origins of RT. There is no basis for this assertion. I would like to point out that I was then and am now quite aware of RT's political origins, and political aims. The point I make is about the rhetorical style of RT.

The reason I compare the style of RT to Nazi propaganda is because if, for example, one replaces 'white' with 'Jewish' in the first and third usages of 'white' in the indented quote from the RT website reproduced at the beginning of this section of the chapter, and 'being Jewish' with 'the white skin' in the same quote, it very much recalls the 'final solution'.[8] Let me reiterate and make it totally clear at this point that I am not levelling the charge of Nazism or fascism or racism at RT. Moreover, I have consistently argued (e.g. Cole 2011, pp. 36–37; 2012b) that it is crucial for the Left to be precise in the way it differentiates racism from fascism, of which Nazism is the most infamous example, and not to use 'fascism' or 'fascist' lightly. This is because racism is an everyday occurrence that saturates all societies in the world, a fact that RT and Critical Race Theorists are particularly adept at pointing out. Most, if not all, states worldwide routinely practise racism in their day-to-day policies and practices, whereas fascism represents an exceptional form of the capitalist state (Poulantzas 1978). To reiterate, I am not questioning the sincerity of the protagonists of 'the abolition of whiteness', nor suggesting in any way that they are anti-white people or are fascists or racists—merely questioning 'RT's vulnerability to misunderstanding.

RT and Neo-Nazi Militia Groups[9]

What may also add to possible misunderstanding are Ignatiev's and Garvey's views on neo-Nazi militia groups, whom they believe are a potential base for recruitment to RT's beliefs. As they put it, referring to such groups, in the Introduction to *Race Traitor*:

> We can imagine nothing more likely to offer an alternative to those forces than an assault on whiteness and all its ways, by a force including a detachment of renegades—race traitors—who believe that a new world, and nothing less, is worth fighting for. (Ignatiev and Garvey 1996, pp. 4–5)

Later in the book (p. 93), following the same theme, they state that time was 'when one might have expected opponents of official society to welcome a grassroots movement arming to defend individual liberties against federal encroachment'. They go on to note that 'many who are pleased to locate themselves on the "left" have raised a cry of alarm at the militia movement' (p. 93). Ignatiev and Garvey castigate the Southern Poverty Law Center for 'snooping and snitching' on the militia (p. 95) on the grounds that this could also apply to left-wing militias. The 'militia movement', they argue 'is a rebellion against the massive, faceless, soul-destroying system that is sucking the life out of ordinary people in this country and around the world' (p. 95). After making it clear that these militias' vision of the future is not RT's vision, the militia movement, they claim, 'has done more to shatter the image of government invulnerability than any other development of recent times'. That the 'left' fails 'to see the potentials it reveals and does less than nothing to develop its own challenge to power is an index of its irrelevance' (p. 95).

In a 1997 interview with Danny Postel (Postel 1997), Ignatiev notes that militia groups are intent on creating a 'violent, poor white man's revolution'. He goes on:

> That's fascism. In a certain sense, the fascists are recruiting and gaining influence among the angriest, the most dispossessed, the most alienated, and potentially most radical sections of white America...There's going to be some kind of fundamental, very dramatic change in the United States. It's evident to me from all of the things I see in popular culture and from listening to how people talk. Either the fascists are going to lead people into a poor white man's revolution, which would open the doors to horrors beyond anything that we've seen—from which I do not exclude Germany in the 1930s and 140s [sic]. Or these people are going to say: To hell with this. We do not wish to be white. We wish to recognize that other people, those fighting hardest against the injustices of this society, the most extreme victims of it—the black youth—who are doing their best to resist what American society is doing to them: therein lie our closest potential allies. In other words, we are not going to be white anymore. We're going to take a chance on being free.

While Ignatiev here makes crystal clear his abhorrence of fascism— 'horrors beyond anything that we've seen', as expressed in the Nazi era—what could be interpreted as the RT's general romanticization of those attracted to neo-Nazi militia groups is open to misunderstanding. While the point I am making here is about misunderstanding, mention should also be made of the misplaced optimism inherent in RT's view of neo-Nazi militia groups. History has shown that fascism and fascists have to be directly confronted rather than 'converted' (something clearly recognized by Preston and Chadderton 2012). A fairly recent example of successful confrontation in the UK is the demise of the fascist British National Party (BNP) which was achieved largely (it also split internally) by sustained anti-fascist activity by organizations such as Hope Not Hate and Unite Against Fascism (UAF) (http://uaf.org.uk/), and by minority ethnic groups.[10]

RT and the Black/White Binary

The chapters in Ignatiev and Garvey (1996) overwhelmingly focus on the black/white binary.[11] Indeed, for Ignatiev, 'the United States is an Afro-American country' (p. 18) and 'core black culture is the mainstream' (p. 21). When he is asked by The Blast!,[12] in an interview at the end of the book, if he has 'ever been accused of ignoring the struggles and perspectives of non-Black people of color', he replies in the affirmative, and states: 'I think that the line between black and white determines race in this country, and all groups get defined in relation to that line.' He cautions The Blast!: 'Don't forget, I am using black and white as political, not cultural, categories' (p. 291). Elsewhere, in the Editors' Reply to a letter from Jan Clausen, it is affirmed: 'in our view the US displays not a "spectrum of racial constructions" but a "bipolar, black/white model"' (p. 275). They attempt to justify this by adding, '[m]uch of the controversy over the status of the "new immigrants" from Asia and what is called Latin America consist of efforts to determine who will be "white" in the twenty-first century' (p. 275).

In the interview in the book, Ignatiev states that he does not 'mean to neglect the real and independent histories of people of color who are not of African descent' (p. 291). But this is exactly the effect that RT has. RT and Ignatiev and Garvey are, of course, aware of the situation of Native Americans and Alaska Natives both historically and contemporaneously, of racism experienced historically and currently by Latina/o communities and of the history of and the current realities for Asian Americans. I am sure that they are also concerned about Islamophobia, particularly rampant since 9/11 and the antisemitism of the numerous hate groups (Cole 2016, chapter 2); their insistence on the 'black/white binary' obscures and undermines the racism directed at other racialized groups. CRT itself has also been criticized for its adherence to a black–white binary. As leading US-based Critical Race Theorists Richard Delgado and Jean Stefancic put it some 15 years ago: '[t]he black–white'—or any other—binary paradigm of race...weakens solidarity, reduces opportunities for coalition, deprives the group of the benefits of the others' experiences' (Delgado and Stefancic 2001, p. 70). The black–white binary, they conclude, 'simplifies analysis dangerously' (ibid.). While anti-black racism was and continues to be a prominent and abhorrent reality for African Americans, horrific institutional racism existed before enslaved Africans were brought to the Americas, and continues to oppress a wide constituent of peoples (see Cole 2016 for a comprehensive analysis of racism in the USA; and also the UK and Australia).

From my perspective, the (neo-)Marxist concept of racialization is a more nuanced and analytically useful term than the 'black/white binary'. This concept, which describes how people are falsely attributed the membership of distinct 'races', connects racism to the capitalist mode of production, to imperialisms old and new and to political decisions made about immigration and the 'free market in labour'. Such decisions are themselves closely related to economic dynamics as well as populist attempts by politicians to use migrant workers as scapegoats to win support, especially in times of economic crisis. Appeals to 'common sense' racism among the electorate are fostered by the ideological state apparatuses (ISAs), in particular the communications ISA (press, television, radio, etc.) (Althusser 1971) (I return to a discussion of 'common sense' in chapter 4 of this volume). The (neo-)Marxist concept of racialization is able to relate to the real material contexts of existence in capitalist countries. With respect to the USA, racialization processes relating to the racialized groups referred to above are discussed at length in Cole (2016, chapter 2). To take the case also of the UK, the (neo-)Marxist concept of racialization provides an explanation of the racialization of Asian, black and other racialized peoples in the British Empire, and their continued racialization, as they arrived in the UK in the post-Second World War period. Further, it enables an understanding of 'white' racialized groups such as Jewish people, the Gypsy, Roma and Traveller (GRT) communities historically and contemporaneously and recent migrant workers, for example, from Poland, Bulgaria and Romania, who are subject to processes of xeno-racialization (Cole 2016, chapter 1). The (neo-)Marxist concept of racialization also renders possible an understanding of Islamophobia which needs to be understood in relation to the history of both UK imperialism and the new imperialism and the quest for global hegemony and oil, in the context of the permanent 'war on terror' (Cole 2016).

Crucially, from a (neo-)Marxist perspective, racialization is a process that serves ruling class interests by dividing the working class, promoting conflict among that class—the class with least access to power and wealth—and forcing down labour costs.

TACTICS, VISIONS AND SOCIAL MOVEMENTS: RT AND TWENTY-FIRST-CENTURY SOCIALISM

Preston and Chadderton (2012, p. 85) refer to their 'ongoing search for theories which offer a realistic alternative and consideration of the options for building collective resistance', and cite as examples 'culture jamming', protest and community action (p. 86). Later they also advocate physical violence, such as 'initiating a prison riot or attacking fascists' (p. 87). From a Marxist perspective, as the crisis in austerity/ immiseration capitalism deepens (see chapter 6 of this volume), it is absolutely essential for unity against global racialized and gendered capitalism and imperialism among the working class as a whole. While this may involve culture jamming, protest and community action, though not violence as a strategy (except in certain specific instances such as defensive violence) it must also involve far more, such as making the case for the ownership and control of the means of production by those who create the wealth, that is, the working class; for the setting up in the workplace of workers' control and participatory democracy; self-management; workers' cooperatives; democratic planning and, crucially, posing twenty-first-century socialism as an alternative to capitalism. It must also entail arguing for decentralized decision-making (in the workplace and via communal councils and other local bodies) (Burbach and Piñero 2007). All this needs solidarity among the working class as a whole, which is not RT's focus. Moreover, as Wright (2012) puts it, in its fixation on a single issue, RT is prone to isolate itself from more general issues related to equality.

To reiterate, Marxists *have* had to learn from other social movements that a socialism of the twenty-first century must be fully inclusive—not merely the province of the straight, able-bodied, white working class male. Twenty-first-century socialists must take on board the importance of 'race', gender, disability, sexuality, age and other dimensions of inequality including religion and belief, pregnancy and maternity, marriage and civil partnership, and gender reassignment.

What is needed is a fully unifying approach, not disunity. Advocating 'the abolition of the privileges of the white skin' is useless as a unifier and counterproductive as a political rallying point, as is the 'the abolition of the white race'. As Jan Clausen put it in a letter to the editor published in Ignatiev and Garvey (1996, p. 274):

The slogan 'abolish the white race' has a certain shock value, and expresses a real and valid anger and indignation—emotions I share. As a guide to action, it is worthless insofar as it implies that such 'abolition' can somehow happen on a symbolic or mental level, apart from thoroughgoing social transformation...Of course you are quite right that 'whiteness' is an ideological product, but as such it represents not only distorted mental constructs but the distorted structural relations out of which these constructs arise and which they continually reinvigorate.

Moreover, with its single issue focus, it is difficult to see how RT provides a resolution to Preston and Chadderton's 'ongoing search...[for ways of] building collective resistance'. Of course, the 'white race' is a social construct as is the notion of 'race' per se. One day perhaps, in a socialist world, we can do away with all perceptions of 'race' and 'whiteness', but (tactically) now is not the time. For example, were the promotion of 'the abolition of the white skin', or worse 'the abolition of the white race' to be routinely promoted in educational establishments, it would most likely cause severe confusion and indeed mayhem. Unproductive divisions on grounds of 'race', class and culture would undoubtedly accelerate. Could this be one of the reasons why Preston has abandoned his previous focus (e.g. 2007, 2010) on education in schools and concentrated on public pedagogy?

Via public education for political praxis Preston and Chadderton (2012) wish to unite Anarchists and Marxists in the development of public education, as opposed to critical pedagogy, for the abolition of whiteness in England. As they argue, critical pedagogy can easily be 'captured' by the state or by the intellectual elites (p. 98) (critical pedagogy is discussed in chapter 5 of this volume). While this is, of course, true, it is also important that we recognize the valuable work that grassroots Left critical educators have done and are doing in formal school settings. For some examples at the primary level see Hill and Helavaara Robertson (eds) (2011) and for the secondary level see Cole (ed) (2011). 'Public pedagogy', according to Preston and Chadderton, is 'pedagogy...aimed at pedagogical activities in the public sphere' (2012, p. 94), at 'spaces, sites, and languages of education that exist outside schools' (Sandlin and Burdick 2010, p. 349, cited in Preston and Chadderton 2012, 94). Public pedagogy, they go on, 'not only examines popular cultural forms as sites of learning but also understands direct political action to be a site of pedagogy and politics' (ibid.). Marxists would fully agree with Preston and Chadderton about the importance of public pedagogy. In order to fully understand pedagogies, it is useful to make a distinction between schooling, on the one hand, and education on the other, with the former referring to the processes by which young people are attuned to the requirements of capitalism both in the form and in the content of schooling, and the latter, from a Marxist perspective a liberatory process, from birth to death, a process of human emancipation and socialism (Cole 2011). As noted earlier in this chapter, Preston and Chadderton give the examples of culture jamming, protest, community action and physical violence. They conclude by also stressing that [egalitarian] public education should be informed by both RT and CRT, and should foreground the activism of people of colour, that it should make 'explicit the connections between critical race activism, and activism based on Marxist or Anarchist traditions' (2012, p. 98). CRT, they argue, 'provides a useful corrective to the charge that white people can guide a revolutionary struggle against whiteness', and reminds whites of 'the centrality of struggle by people of colour' (p. 97). Finally, it should aim to 'bring together intellectuals and activists across the lines of class and race' (p. 98). Ignatiev and Garvey (1996, p. 95) insist that 'only the vision of a new world can compete with the fascists for the loyalty of... angry whites' who join militia groups. Marxists could not agree more with this last observation.

PART TWO: SOME UPDATES ON THE (CHANGING?) POLITICAL PERSPECTIVES OF NOEL IGNATIEV AND JOHN GARVEY

Update One: Ignatiev on C.L.R. James (2010)

In his 'Introduction' to some of the work of C.L.R. James, Ignatiev (2010) appraises James from the anti-vanguardist (against a small advanced politically conscious section of the working class leading the revolution) Marxist perspective which James adopted in his later writing.[13] There is no hint in this analysis of James that Ignatiev is anything other than a committed Marxist, in the style of the works of James, who believes in the revolutionary potential of the working class as a whole—the sole force that can create a social revolution to overthrow capitalism. There is no mention of RT nor of 'the abolition of the white race'. Underlining his admiration of James, Ignatiev (2010, p. 6) states: 'If the word "genius" has any meaning, then it must be applied to C.L.R. James'. Ignatiev (p. 7) notes that 'James and his co-thinkers focused their attention on the point of production, the scene of the most intense conflicts between capital and the working class'. Referring to James, Ignatiev (p. 6) writes: 'He led in developing a current within Marxism that was democratic, revolutionary, and internationalist'. Ignatiev makes no allusions to the 'privileges of the white skin' when he writes about the working class. For example, he (p. 7) has the working class as a whole in mind, not any section of it, when he describes, following James:

> ordinary people, organized around work and activities related to it, taking steps in opposition to capital to expand their freedom and their capacities as fully developed individuals. It is a leap of imagination, but it is the key to his method. Of course the new society does not triumph without an uprising; but it exists. It may be stifled temporarily; capital, after all, can shut down the plant, or even a whole industry, and can starve out an entire community. But the new society springs up elsewhere. If you want to know what the new society looks like, said James, study the daily activities of the working class. (Ignatiev 2010, p.8)

'James insisted', Ignatiev (p. 8) goes on, 'that the struggles of the working class are the chief motor in transforming society'. Commenting approvingly of Marx, the working class, Ignatiev (p. 8) explains, 'overthrows capital' 'as Marx said, in the revolutionary reconstitution of society at large, or in the common ruin of the contending classes'. James, Ignatiev (p. 7) argues, brought Marxist theory 'into a modern context and developed it'.

Ignatiev has nothing but admiration for the working class internationally as a class, viewing 'the Hungarian Revolution of 1956, the French General Strike of 1968, and the emergence of the US wildcat strikes of the 1950s and the League of Revolutionary Black Workers in Detroit in 1967 as expressions of a global revolt against the domination of capital' (p. 9). 'When the working class moves', Ignatiev (p. 9) notes approvingly, 'the state is powerless against it': 'united, disciplined, and organized by the very mechanism of capitalist production'. As James put it, the working class had 'a special role to play in carrying the revolution through to the end' (ibid, p. 10). Moreover, the day-to-day lives of workers are central in the formation of a new society: '[James] said the working class is revolutionary and that its daily activities constitute the revolutionary process in modern society' (Ignatiev, p. 7). 'James and his co-thinkers', Ignatiev (p. 7) proclaims, 'documented the emergence on the shop floor of social relations counter to those imposed by management and the union, relations that prefigured the new society'. Summarizing the importance of C.L.R. James's work, Ignatiev states: 'James and his co-thinkers [were able] to look in a new way at the struggles of labor, black people, women, youth, and the colonial peoples, and to produce a body of literature far ahead of its time, works that still constitute indispensable guides for those fighting for a new world' (p. 7). As Ignatiev (2010, pp. 7–8) points out, not every example James discusses makes the point of production central. James also recognized the importance of 'community'. James stresses that for 'negroes' and women, 'the community' can be the centre and the 'bulwark of the people against the bureaucratic state' (pp. 7–8).[14] However, it is the working class as a class that constitutes the agents of change. Thus Ignatiev (p. 17) concludes by referring to James's 'undying faith in the power of ordinary people to build a new world'.

Update Two: Ignatiev at 'Occupy Boston' (2011)

The 'Occupy Movement' is the international umbrella group of the 'Occupy Wall Street Movement', which began in 2011 in New York. It protests against world injustice and inequality, its target being large corporations and the global financial system. In the same year, Ignatiev (Ignatiev 2011a, b) was invited to speak at 'Occupy Boston' (http://www.occupy-boston.org/).[15] Here Ignatiev shows approval for 'interracial' struggle, and argues that whites can learn from black people, and that when the latter believe that the 'Occupy' movement is serious, they will join it. He goes on to advise the occupiers that they should have 'no demands', and, then, reiterating Che Guevara's slogan, later adopted by the insurgents in Europe in May 1968, suggests that they be realistic and 'demand the impossible'. He goes on to suggest they demand 'the abolition of prisons'.[16] Prison, like slavery, he suggests, is immoral, and describes prisons as universities of crime. Once prisons are abolished, people will collectively begin to think of alternatives and transform the whole society. In the meantime, Ignatiev advocates reforms now, such as the unionization of prisoners and support for prison strikes. Ignatiev concludes that collectively we can solve all the problems.

Update Three: Garvey and Ignatiev on Ferguson, Missouri (2015)

In the Editorial of the January 2015 edition of *Insurgent Notes*, of which
John Garvey is co-editor with Loren Goldner, they write about the
events in Ferguson, Missouri, following the murder of unarmed African
American teenager Michael Brown in August 2014. They describe the
ensuing movement as 'without doubt the deepest social movement to
emerge in the United States in more than forty years'. While they argue
that it built upon the experiences of 'Occupy', they argue 'by the large
black participation mainly absent from Occupy, much deeper' (Garvey and
Goldner 2015). They point out that its 'innovations in strategy and street
tactics also went well beyond Occupy' (Garvey and Goldner 2015). As
they put it:

> Instead of holding public spaces and remaining vulnerable to the inevitable
> police crackdown, kettling and mass arrests, this movement kept moving,
> blocking streets and freeways here, bridges and Christmas shopping there,
> and generally refusing to become a stable target.

Unlike Occupy, they conclude, the movement 'focused dead center on the
American "blind spot," race' (Garvey and Goldner 2015). I would want
to avoid the disablism inherent in 'blind spot', but also to insist that while
'post-racial' America, following Obama's victory is, of course, as they put
it, 'ideological pretence', crucially absent from everyday discourse in the
USA are the metanarratives of social class and class struggle. This is recognized by Garvey and Goldner at the end of the Editorial when they state,
'[o]ur work in broadening and deepening the post-Ferguson movement
to the larger working population is cut out for us' (Garvey and Goldner
2015). The first comment at the end of the article by L. May suggests that
perhaps Garvey and Goldner 'have written off the "economic" arena as a
terrain for struggle'. May concludes, correctly I believe, 'Ferguson offers
possibilities, but doesn't include an organic pathway to challenging the
heart of capitalism'.

In an individual contribution to the same issue of the journal, Garvey
makes three major points about Ferguson, Missouri. First, he refers to
the predictable scripts of reaction—the police unions insisting on no pre-
judgement, the initiation of legal proceedings that stretch out as long as
possible, leaks that the victim was not a law-abiding citizen in the past and
efforts to support the accused killer such as support organizations, fund-
raising, buttons and rallies (Garvey 2015, p. 3).

Second, he provides a thorough account of the history of Missouri, focusing on the history of slavery; and segregation between African Americans and white people still stark today. Garvey paints a graphic picture of changes in capitalism, describing 'a new era in American social and economic life' in the last four decades, characterized by factory closures and transfers to lower-waged locations, elimination of jobs through automation and other technical innovations, the growth of finance capital as a major form of profit, even for industrial firms, a rise in part-time and/or temporary jobs as primary employment, the depopulation and physical destruction of cities, gentrification of urban neighbourhoods and the rise in political importance of those groups formed by it, decreases in union membership, lower wages and reduced benefits and the establishment of credit (at normal or usury rates) as an indispensable way of life for the middle and working classes (Garvey 2015, p. 8). It is in this depressing scenario that everyday police all across the USA stop mostly young black men. Most are not recorded for others to see 'other than in the memories of the young people themselves and, in quite different ways, in the memories of the cops involved' (Garvey 2015, p. 10).

In a *slight* nod in the direction of RT, followed by a *modification* of 'white privilege', he then stresses that whiteness is historical, 'not a natural condition' but then goes on to say that 'whiteness is not quite what it used to be', given the existence of a black bourgeoisie and the election of Obama on the one hand; and 'the ineffectiveness of the traditional privileges of whiteness in protecting white workers from being thrown out of their jobs when the factories shut down' (Garvey 2015, p. 11). Arguing that 'the white question has not been settled', he refers to 'white supremacy', but not in the CRT usage of everyday racism, but in the sense of 'white supremacist groups on the far right' (Garvey 2015, p. 11).

The 'new whiteness', he goes on, 'is perhaps the lie that does not have to speak in its own name', in the sense that they speak on behalf of whiteness and its privileges, but speaking as 'racially unmarked homeowners, citizens and taxpayers, whose preferred policies just happen to sustain white privilege and power' (Lipsitz 2011, cited in Garvey 2015, p. 11). The job of the police is 'to protect property and to deal with the all but inevitable consequences of the immiseration that has become pervasive in the last forty years' (Garvey 2015, p. 11). It is necessary to support and defend those who have taken the lead in Ferguson, but also to 'confront' the social bloc who are supported by and support the police (Garvey

2015, p. 11). It is not totally clear to me what Garvey means by 'confront'. Earlier he used the expression 'break up' (Garvey 2015, p. 3). If he means desegregate the housing, then it is not clear how this is to be achieved. In order to challenge immiseration/austerity capitalism, it is, of course, from a Marxist perspective, neoliberal capitalism that needs confronting and breaking up, which is recognized by Garvey in his last sentence when he writes that we should not 'underestimate the need to address the profound shaping of the lives of the people involved by the larger set of circumstances created and sustained by the particular ways in which capital rules St. Louis' (Garvey 2015, p. 16).

PART THREE: SO WHAT ARE IGNATIEV'S AND GARVEY'S POLITICAL POSITIONS?

Ignatiev's Politics

So what are Ignatiev's politics?[17] What then can we make of these apparent anomalies with respect to the 1996 Anarchist (?) Ignatiev of RT, the 2010 Marxist à la C.L.R. James and the 2011 Anarchist (?) Ignatiev at 'Occupy Boston'? Preston and Chadderton (2012, p. 90) point out that for the Sojourner Truth Organization (STO), a Marxist organization formed in the late 1960s, and of which Ignatiev was a founding member, abolishing whiteness 'was a necessary step in bringing the US to the historical position' when socialist revolution was possible. In an email to me about the RT project in 2012, which is self-explanatory, Ignatiev stated: '[w]e thought that since whiteness is an obstacle to making revolution, challenging it, even without explicit reference to capitalism, etc. was part of implementing a revolutionary project'. That Ignatiev's Marxist politics have not changed since his STO days is further revealed in another email from him. In reply to my question, so precisely what is your current political position, he said: 'I consider myself thoroughly Marxist (provided I get to define Marxism). And in response to my request for further clarification of his Marxist orientation, Ignatiev responded: 'Rosa Luxemburg (except on the national question; I thought Lenin was more right than she in their exchange); Gramsci; C.L.R. James'. It is also revealed most clearly in Ignatiev's response to Garvey (2015) (discussed in the last section of this chapter) in the 'Comments' section after the article and in the same edition. His response to Garvey is unequivocal and unambiguous, and I reproduce it in full here:

Capital is 'race'-blind; the capitalist mode of production (cmp) tends to reduce all human beings to abstract, undifferentiated, homogenous labor power. However, the pure cmp exists nowhere; all existing societies, including those in which the cmp prevails, contain elements left over from the past as well as elements that are the product of the political intervention of various groups.

Four places developed historically on the basis of racial oppression: the US, South Africa, Ireland, and Palestine. (By racial oppression I do not mean the ethnic or religious bias that exists widely, but a specific system of oppression that incorporates by definition portions of a subordinate class in the subjection of other members of that class; the hallmark of racial oppression is the reduction of every member of the subject group to a status beneath that of any member of the dominant group: in US terms, it meant that Huck Finn's Pap could push W.E.B. Du Bois off the sidewalk.)

The system of racial oppression did not arise out of a bourgeois plot but out of specific historic circumstances; once it developed it became part of the US social formation. Only value production is essential to capital; 'racial' oppression is contingent, although under some circumstances it may become so vital to bourgeois hegemony that its fall would decisively weaken the entire system. (That was the underlying assumption of STO, which argued the centrality of the fight against white supremacy on strategic grounds.)

The attachment of the capitalist class and of individual capitalists to racial oppression is subject to modification based on various considerations, most of all, what is necessary to maintain political stability. Beginning in the 1950s (and perhaps earlier), decisive sectors of capital came to the conclusion that old-style racial oppression, the kind that prevailed in rural Mississippi, was costing more than it was worth. They were pushed to this view in part by the cold war, in part by changes in production (the mechanization of agriculture) and in part by the struggle of black Americans and their allies. And so they moved to introduce change.

The Supreme Court decision calling for desegregation of public schools[18] (followed by other decisions desegregating public facilities) was not mere talk. The Civil Rights and Voting Right Acts were not mere talk. The striking down of provisions that excluded black people from juries was not mere talk. The effort by the Labour Department to force the construction unions to open their doors to black workers was not mere talk. The passing of regulations outlawing 'steering' by real-estate agents was not mere talk. The introduction of affirmative-action policies in education was not mere talk. The Justice Department's order that police keep records by race of those they stop was not mere talk. The multimillion-dollar fines against

oil company executives caught on tape practicing explicit race discrimination was not mere talk. [African American Attorney General] Eric Holder's
visit to Missouri aimed at dragging Ferguson into the twenty-first century
is not mere talk. (By the way, Holder is a prime example of what I mean: a
vigorous defender of corporate interests (including the right to assassinate
US citizens without due process), he is also an opponent of old-style race
discrimination.)

Of course, none of these measures represent the sort of intervention that
revolutionaries would make. At best they are half-hearted, and limited by
the constraints of 'the system'. They do not address, except marginally, the
effects of the past, either on blacks or poor whites. They are all subject to
reversal, depending on estimates by the governing coalition of what is politically desirable at the moment. Most important, none of them threatens the
capital relation; at most they constitute political, not human emancipation.
(See Marx On the Jewish Question.) But they are not trivial, nor are they
merely demagogy and lies.

The most class-conscious, farsighted sectors of the ruling class, represented by Clinton and Obama, have adopted the policy of neoliberalism, which aims at removing all barriers, including race, to the free flow
of capital. It does not follow that they prevail in every situation (any
more than FDR's policy of benevolent neutrality toward labor unions
prevented Chicago police from massacring Republic Steel strikers in
1937). As Engels pointed out, 'the final result always arises from conflicts
between many individual wills, of which each in turn has been made what
it is by a host of particular conditions of life. Thus there are innumerable
intersecting forces, an infinite series of parallelograms of forces which
give rise to one resultant—the historical event. This may again itself be
viewed as the product of a power which works as a whole unconsciously
and without volition.' The strength of capital, as Trotsky said, is not
that it initiates every policy but that it is able to turn every policy to its
advantage.

In Ferguson, the smart thing—and clearly what the Obama
Administration wants—would be for the grand jury to return some kind
of an indictment that made the protesters feel that justice has been served,
without hurling the defenders of the police into the arms of the fascists.
Holder is up against the opposition of police unions local and national,
an entrenched town bureaucracy, white bigotry, inertia, etc. The midterm
elections may well have emboldened those forces to resist the pressure
from Washington. It is impossible to predict the outcome. In this situation, revolutionaries must prepare themselves to oppose concessions just
as they do repression, understanding that both serve the class enemy.
(Ignatiev 2015a)

Although published in 2015, Ignatiev's 'Comment' was written before the grand jury announced its decision, which was 'no indictment'. After the verdict, Obama defended the decision but said a federal investigation proved the community was justified in its concerns about racism in Ferguson's police department (Nather 2015). Holder told reporters that he found the results of the federal investigation 'appalling' and that the Justice Department is 'prepared to use all the powers that we have, all the power that we have, to ensure that the situation changes there', adding that he did not rule out the possibility of dismantling the Ferguson police department: 'if that's what's necessary, we're prepared to do that'. Obama urged the crowd not to let the Ferguson report make them hostile towards police officers around the country: 'I don't think that what happened in Ferguson was typical.' Most police officers, he went on, 'have a really hard and dangerous job, and they do it well...I strongly believe that' (cited in Nather 2015). However, he concluded that the report suggested that the problems in the Ferguson police department and the widespread mistreatment of African Americans go well beyond Brown's death: '[w]hat happened in Ferguson is not a complete aberration. It turns out they weren't just making it up. It was happening' (cited in Nather 2015). The lesson for police departments around the country, he went on, is that when they get enough complaints about unfair treatment of African Americans or other minority groups, 'you've got to listen, to pay attention' (cited in Nather 2015). The job now, Obama concluded, is for police departments and communities to 'work together to solve the problems, and not get caught up in the cynicism of, "Oh, it's never going to change, everything's racist." It's achievable, but we've got to be constructive going forward.'

More recently, Ignatiev (2015b) has written about 'white privilege' historically, and in the context of the election of Obama and the ensuing years of his presidency. As he puts it:

> There was a time when the task of subjugating black people was carried out by the mass of ordinary whites, in return for which they were socially defined as part of the dominant race. While 'white' laborers did not in general receive a share of the profits extracted from the exploitation of black labor, and were often cruelly exploited, they were the favored slaves of capital, holding a monopoly of the better jobs, standing at the front of the hiring line and the rear of the layoff line, and partaking in what Du Bois called a 'public and psychological wage'—in other words, the privileges of whiteness. (Ignatiev 2015b)

At that time, he goes on, the black 'bourgeoisie' (such as it was) played little role in keeping the masses down, and class divisions within the black community, he argues, were *relatively* unimportant. As a symbol of who enforced control, Ignatiev points out, in 1940 there was not a single black police officer in any state in the deep south, where more than half the black population lived, and few elsewhere.

The triumph of the civil rights movement, Ignatiev continues, gave rise to a layer of black people, north and south, whose job is to administer the misery of the black poor: black mayors, black police chiefs, black city councillors, black prison officials, black superintendents of boards of education and welfare departments and black heads of foundations. These black people now do the job once done by whites, who as a consequence have lost a great deal of their social function and the status that was attached to it.

This is not to say that the privileges of whiteness no longer exist; 'but changes in the economy and the decline of many institutions that used to guarantee them—in the first place, the unions—mean that they are no longer what they were' (Ignatiev 2015b). The changes in the mechanisms of control, Ignatiev points out, are not limited to high-level administrators: 'Many of the police in the black neighborhoods are black, along with social workers, schoolteachers, corrections officers, etc.'

The immiseration of the black poor and the existence of a privileged layer of black professionals in previously white spheres, Ignatiev states, appear to be in conflict. In fact, however, there is a necessary connection between the two phenomena: neither could exist without the other:

> Without black faces behind desks, no force could stop the masses of black poor from tearing the country apart; and on the other hand, without the threat of the black poor there would be no black faces behind desks. *To understand the relationship between black progress and black genocide is the heart of class analysis today.* (Ignatiev 2015b)

The supreme example of the interaction of class and 'race' is President Obama. Indicting him for his neoliberal capitalist and imperialist policies, while acknowledging that Obama and his family are subject to racism like all people of colour, Ignatiev concludes:

> A big failing of US political life today, affecting radicals like Cornel West, Harry Belafonte and many others and including most progressive whites, is the insistence on seeing President Obama, Supreme Court Justice Clarence

Thomas, former Chief-of-Staff Colin Powell et al. as traitors to their race or, more gently, brothers gone astray, instead of as the class enemy, and until people make that breakthrough they will continue to be disappointed. (Ignatiev 2015b)

Garvey's Politics

Like Ignatiev, Garvey read an earlier version of this chapter and also declined an interview for the same reasons as Ignatiev, namely, that he had nothing to add. Helpfully for my purposes in this part of the chapter, which is to ascertain his current political position, Garvey spelt this out in the first issue of *Insurgent Notes*. He and co-editor Loren Goldner stated a minimal programme of agreement as follows:

1. commitment to social revolution for the abolition of the wage-labor system, i.e. the capitalist mode of production, and an orientation to the wage-labor proletariat (i.e. the working class) and its potential allies as the main force for such an abolition;
2. an affirmation of the great experiences in direct democratic management of production and society (soviets, workers' councils) that came to the fore in the failed revolutions of the 20th century (Russia, Germany, Spain, Hungary) or, closer to US experience, the self-managed Seattle general strike of 1919 as important antecedents, but hardly the last word, in our project;
3. a commitment to 'activity as all-sided in its production as in its consumption' (Marx, *Grundrisse*), and the 'development of human powers as its own end' (*Pre-Capitalist Economic Formations*) within the expanded reproduction of humanity as the true content of communism ;
4. a deep-seated skepticism about vanguardist notions of revolution; while we at the same time affirm the need for some of kind of organization that emerges practically and concretely from real social struggle—not 'sprung full-blown from the head of some world reformer' (*Communist Manifesto*)—and which conceives of itself not as 'seizing power' but as a future tendency or current in a future self-managed society;
5. a rejection of nationalism of any kind as an obstacle to such a revolution;
6. a rejection of existing Socialist, Communist or Labour (let alone Democratic) parties in the advanced capitalist sector as alien to our project, and as parties whose (well-proven) role is nothing but the management of capitalism in one or another form, as well as rejection of the 'extreme left' groupings (Trotskyists, Maoists) who see such parties as 'reformist'
7. 'workers' parties';

8. a rejection of the few remaining 'real existing socialist states' (Cuba, Vietnam, China, etc.) and their Stalinist predecessors (the defunct Soviet bloc) as any kind of model, degenerated or not, for the kind of society we wish to help build;

9. a rejection of the renascent 'anti-imperialism' of recent years, associated with the loose alliance of Chavez and his Latin American allies, China, Hezbollah, Hamas, Amadinejad's Iran, etc., as an anti-working class ideology serving emergent elites in different parts of the developing world;

10. a rejection of any strategy of 'capturing the unions' for such a project, as practiced since the 1970s by various 'boring from within' Trotskyists, etc.;

11. a rejection of post-modern 'identity politics' as the ideological articulation of the very real problems of race, gender, and alternative sexuality, but which must be relocated in class politics. (Garvey and Goldner 2010)

Thus Garvey and Goldner identify their politics as 'libertarian Marxist' (they use the terminology 'libertarian communist'). There are no vestiges of RT here. My own position is that I would broadly agree with the points made, but as we saw earlier in this chapter, I have much sympathy with Hugo Chávez and the development of twenty-first-century socialism in the Bolivarian Republic of Venezuela, although, as I have stressed, the future there is uncertain. Moreover, I have learnt much from what Garvey and Goldner describe as 'extreme left' groupings, in particular Trotskyists. Thus, as I note in the next chapter in the section on intersectionality under the heading 'Intersections Between Class, 'Race' and Gender' (see also endnote 8 of that chapter), although I reject their class reductionism, in my writings I make frequent use of articles on the World Socialist Web Site under the auspices of the Socialist Equality Party.

CONCLUSION

In this chapter, I began by suggesting that while RT has strengths in its depiction of the horrors of racism in the USA, and in a few practical suggestions for combating racism at an individual level, as a campaigning movement, it is misguided and politically untenable. I identified three major problems with RT: its vulnerability to being misunderstood; its almost exclusive focus on the 'black/white' binary and its tactics and the lack of clarity in its vision of a just society. I concluded with updates on the (changing?) political perspectives of RT's co-founders, Noel Ignatiev and John Garvey.

It is now 20 years since the publication of *Race Traitor* the book, and nearly 12 years since the last edition of *Race Traitor* the journal; Ignatiev and Garvey have both reasserted their Marxist politics (but the former also reaffirmed his RT beliefs in personal emails to me in 2011 and in 2015[19]). Marxism, as we have seen, was not a feature of the RT movement. Despite Preston and Chadderton's enthusiasm for RT and its propagation in CRT, their claims of resonance for contemporary Marxists and Anarchists, and their arguments that CRT and public pedagogy 'can produce new political praxis for Race Traitors in the twenty-first century' (Preston and Chadderton 2012, p. 1), I must conclude that a future for RT either per se or as an inspiration for Marxists today appears incoherent, confused and thus unfounded. This is not merely because as a movement it seems to have faded, but also because its co-founders and leading lights have returned to an identifiable Marxist politics.

The impetus for this chapter was Chadderton and Preston (2012) in the special edition of *Race, Ethnicity and Education* on CRT in England. In the next two chapters, I look at the other articles published in *REE* since that special edition and up to the present (chapter 4), and at the USA (chapter 5) in a consideration of developments in CRT on both sides of the Atlantic.

NOTES

1. The following analysis of 'Race Traitor' draws on Cole (2012a).
2. It is for others to respond to Preston and Chadderton's claims of resonance with contemporary Anarchism. It is also outside my remit to respond to Preston and Chadderton's discussion (pp. 91–94) of whether RT is 'post-racial'.
3. I think Chris Wright (2012), who writes in the tradition of libertarian Marxism (a broad range of economic and political positions that emphasize Marxism as an anti-authoritarian economic and political theory), is wrong in arguing that the 'Race Traitor' position is liberal and reformist. This is based on rather flimsy 'evidence'—that Ignatiev has hopes for America; and that he doesn't talk about the overthrow of capitalism (he does, but only briefly). RT does have hopes for America, but it is for a new post-capitalist

America. The following quote typically sums up the whole tenor of 'Race Traitor':

> A new fault is building up pressure, a new Harpers Ferry [where abolitionist John Brown started an armed slave revolt in 1859] is being prepared. Its nature and timing cannot be predicted, but of its coming we have no doubt. When it comes, it will set off a series of tremors that will lead to the disintegration of the white race. We want to be ready, walking in Jerusalem just like John. (Ignatiev and Garvey 1996, p. 13)

From my reading of 'Race Traitor', the movement is decidedly a revolutionary, though not a Marxist movement. Preston and Chadderton document at length the autonomist Marxist and Anarchist origins of RT in the USA (2012, 86–91), but as constituted in1996, it comes across to me as more Anarchist than Marxist, more akin to the Anarchist groups that Preston and Chadderton mention: Love and Rage; Anarchist People of Color; and Bring the Ruckus in the US; and in the UK the Anarchist Federation; London Class War; and Antifa. Preston and Chadderton (2012, p. 90) point out, however, that 'the Anarchist movement has been largely ignorant of Black Power and Black resistance'.

4. This is most clearly articulated in Ignatiev and Garvey (1996). The RT journal has now ceased production. The last edition was Issue 16 in January 2005. Extracts from earlier issues can be read at www.racetraitor.org/ by clicking on the left-hand side of the page. Other information about RT can be found by clicking other items on the list.

5. Given that indigenous Americans are, in fact, the First Nations (Native Americans) of what is now the USA, the use of 'indigenous' here is problematic.

6. I have critiqued at length elsewhere (e.g. Cole 2009a, b, c) the use of the concept, 'white supremacy' to describe routine everyday racism. I supplement the critique in chapter 4 of this volume.

7. As a statement, this is clearly historically totally inaccurate. Partial reforms have been accomplished by workers and social movements throughout history and internationally.

8. The chapter by Adam Sabra in Ignatiev and Garvey (eds.) (1996) is particularly problematic. In this he states (p. 210) that '[o]nly the abolition of the Jewish caste can prevent the continuation of

the ongoing race war in Palestine by building a society free of race and caste'. Like the RT position on the 'white race', Sabra is arguing that the Jewish 'race' is a 'historical construction' (p. 195), and uses 'caste' instead of 'race' to distance himself from antisemitism (p. 211), and to avoid 'any form of misunderstanding' (p. 211). However, given the fact that he 'regards the terms "caste" and "race" as synonymous' (p. 211), his use of terminology is self-evidently unfortunate to say the least, and, for me, underlines the extent to which RT as a movement is open to misinterpretation. An adequate Marxist analysis of the complexities of the Palestine/Israel situation would require a major project in its own right.

9. Neo-Nazism is not a rare phenomenon in the USA. There are over 140 active neo-Nazi groups in nearly all of the states in the USA (Southern Poverty Law Centre 2015a). There are also some 892 hate groups (Southern Poverty Law Center 2015b). I would argue that this further underlines the importance of restricting the term 'white supremacy' to the beliefs and actions of such people, rather than using it to refer to everyday racism.

10. The BNP took over half a million votes at the 2010 election, but could not even find the necessary 89 candidates at the 2015 general election to qualify for airtime. In 2010, the party stood in 338 seats; in 2015 just 8. In both elections it failed to win any seats.

11. A notable exception is the chapter by the Chicago Surrealist Group who, discussing the Los Angeles Rebellion of April–May 1992, provide a good honest account of interethnic conflict and solidarity.

12. I have been unable to find any information about The Blast!

13. Ignatiev's anti-vanguardism is emphasized when he notes that the function of organizations built by James 'was not to "lead the working class" but to accomplish this or that specific task' (p. 12), and that 'the idea that any self-perpetuating group of people can set itself up to lead the working class is reactionary and bankrupt' (p. 12). Ignatiev is contemptuous of '"condescending saviors" of the working class' (p. 17).

14. Moreover, as James (1939) put it in his earlier work: 'The American Negroes, for centuries the most oppressed section of American society and the most discriminated against, are potentially the most revolutionary elements of the population'. James stressed the

importance of revolutionary socialists connecting with the African American masses.

15. Ignatiev (personal correspondence, 2011) has suggested that '[p] robably the greatest lasting impact of RT was on young Occupy activists, many of whom owe their consciousness of race directly or indirectly to RT.

16. When questioned by a member of the audience, Ignatiev recognizes the contradiction of recommending 'no demands' and then suggesting a 'demand' for the occupiers to make. He responds by saying he is not sure how to respond, but that 'the abolition of prisons' was not so much a 'demand' as something for them to think about. He also, like Ivan Illich (1973), advocates the abolition of schools which are just prisons for the young, and recognizes the contradiction that he teaches in one! He argues that education should be lifelong.

17. Ignatiev read an earlier version of this chapter in 2015, and declined an interview to be included in this chapter on the grounds that it seemed to him that 'there is little [he could] add that will clarify or advance the argument' and wished me good luck with it.

18. Ignatiev is, of course, using 'public schools' in the US sense. In the UK 'state schools' is the common terminology, since 'public schools' in the UK generally refer to elite private schools.

19. Ignatiev wrote: 'There is nothing in [the 1997 interview with Danny Postel] I would retract, so you can say it still represents my views' (May 22, 2015); see also endnote 15.

References

Althusser, L. (1971). Ideology and ideological state apparatuses. In *Lenin and philosophy and other essays*. London: New Left Books. http://www.marx2mao.com/Other/LPOE70NB.html

Burbach, R., & Piñero, C. (2007). Venezuela's participatory socialism. *Socialism and Democracy*, Online, http://sdonline.org/45/venezuela%e2%80%99s-participatory-socialism/

Cole, M. (2009a). *Critical race theory and education: A Marxist response* (1st ed.). New York/London: Palgrave Macmillan.

Cole, M. (2009b). The color-line and the class struggle: A Marxist response to critical race theory in education as it arrives in the United Kingdom. *Power and Education, 1*(1), 111–124.

Cole, M. (2009c, April). On 'white supremacy' and caricaturing Marx and Marxism: A response to David Gillborn's 'who's afraid of critical race theory in education'. *Journal for Critical Education Policy Studies, 7*(1). http://www.jceps.com/index.php?pageID=article&articleID=143

Cole, M. (2011). *Racism and education in the U.K. and the U.S.: Towards a socialist alternative.* New York/London: Palgrave Macmillan.

Cole, M. (2012a). "Abolish the white race" or "transfer economic power to the people"? Some educational implications. *Journal for Critical Education Policy Studies, 10*(2). http://www.jceps.com/index.php?pageID=article&articleID=265

Cole, M. (2012b). Capitalist crisis and fascism: Issues for educational practice. In D. R. Cole (Ed.), *Surviving economic crises through education.* New York: Peter Lang.

Cole, M. (2016). *Racism: A critical analysis.* London/Chicago: Pluto Press/University of Chicago Press.

Cole, M. (2017). *Critical race theory and education: A Marxist response* (2nd ed.). New York/London: Palgrave Macmillan.

Delgado, R., & Stefancic, J. (2001). *Critical race theory: An introduction.* New York: New York University Press.

Garvey, J. (2015). No more missouri compromises. *Insurgent Notes, 11.* http://insurgentnotes.com/2014/11/no-more-missouri-compromises/

Garvey, J., & Goldner, L. (2015). Ferguson and after: Where is this movement going? Insurgent Notes Jan 24, http://insurgentnotes.com/2015/01/

Hill, D., & Helavaara Robertson, L. (Eds.). (2011). *Equality in the primary school: Promoting good practice across the curriculum.* London: Continuum.

Ignatiev, N. (2010). The world view of C.L.R. James. In N. Ignatiev (Ed.), *C.L.R. James a new notion: Two works by C.L.R. James: Every cook can govern and the invading socialist society.* Oakland: PM Press.

Ignatiev, N. (2011a). Noel Ignatiev at Occupy Boston: Video 1 of 2, November 15. Youtube: http://www.youtube.com/watch?v=BFj63NShxsw

Ignatiev, N. (2011b). Noel Ignatiev at Occupy Boston: Video 2 of 2, November 15. Youtube: http://www.youtube.com/watch?v=DSegN9I9y3Q

Ignatiev, N. (2015a). 'Comment' on 'Garvey, J. (2015). No more Missouri Compromises. *Insurgent Notes, 11.* http://insurgentnotes.com/2014/11/no-more-missouri-compromises/

Ignatiev, N. (2015b). Race or class? *PM Press.* http://www.pmpress.org/content/article.php/20150720120508552

Ignatiev, N., & Garvey, J. (Eds.). (1996). *Race traitor.* London: Routledge.

Illich, I. (1973). *Deschooling society.* Harmondsworth: Penguin.

James, C. L. R. (1939). The SWP and Negro work. SWP New York Convention Resolutions, 11 July, http://www.marxists.org/archive/james-clr/works/1939/07/negro-work.htm

Lipsitz, G. (2011). *How racism takes place.* Philadelphia: Temple University Press.

Nather, D. (2015, March 6). Obama on Ferguson: "They weren't just making it up". *Politico*. http://www.politico.com/story/2015/03/obama-ferguson-reaction-doj-115839.html

Postel, D. (1997, January 1). An interview with Noel Ignatiev. *Z Magazine*. https://zcomm.org/zmagazine/an-interview-with-noel-ignatiev-by-danny-postel/

Poulantzas, N. (1978). *State, power, socialism*. London: NLB.

Preston, J. (2007). *Whiteness and class in education*. Dordrecht: Springer.

Preston, J. (2010). Concrete and abstract racial domination. *Power and Education, 2*(2), 115–125.

Preston, J., & Chadderton, C. (2012). "Race traitor": Towards a critical race theory informed public pedagogy. *Race, Ethnicity and Education, 15*(1), 85.

Sandlin, J., & Burdick, J. (2010). Inquiry as answerability: Toward a methodology of discomfort in researching critical public pedagogies. *Qualitative Inquiry, 16*(5), 349–360.

Southern Poverty Law Center (SPLC). (2015a, March 2). *Active Neo-Nazi Groups*. https://www.splcenter.org/fighting-hate/intelligence-report/2015/active-neo-nazi-groups

Southern Poverty Law Center (SPLC). (2015b). 892. https://www.splcenter.org/hate-map

Wright, C. (2012). Marxism and White Skin Privilege. http://libcom.org/library/marxism-white-skin-privilege-chriswright

CHAPTER 4

Transatlantic Theoretical Developments: The Case of 'BritCrit'

INTRODUCTION

In chapter 3 of this volume I focused on the relationship between Critical Race Theory (CRT), 'Race Traitor' and Marxism, in order to critically engage with one article (Preston and Chadderton 2012) in the special issue of *Race, Ethnicity and Education*, the journal edited by David Gillborn, on 'Critical Race Theory in England' published in January 2012 (*REE* 15 [1]). As I suggested in that chapter, of the articles in that special edition, that paper is the one which I consider most advances 'BritCrit', *and* has most purchase in informing the ongoing theoretical debate between CRT and Marxism. In this chapter, I look first at the remaining six articles in *REE* 15 (1) before addressing further developments in CRT in the UK. In the Editorial of *REE* 15 (1), three pioneers of CRT in the UK, Namita Chakrabarty, Lorna Roberts and John Preston, argued that it is important that CRT develops in the English context in terms of establishing an academic identity (Chakrabarty et al. 2012, p. 1). Given this aspiration, in addition to the seven articles in that edition, I also look at all of the CRT analyses of the UK published in *REE since* the special issue.[1] In total, at the time this volume goes to press, there have been a further 174 papers altogether in the journal. Of these, 4 are CRT analyses of the UK (just over 2 % of the total number of articles) and 41 (just under 25 % of the articles published) are CRT analyses of the USA[2] (correct as of issue 19.4). My intention is not primarily an assessment of the articles per se. Rather, I attempt to consider the extent to which a quintessentially British CRT,

© The Author(s) 2017
M. Cole, *New Developments in Critical Race Theory and Education*,
DOI 10.1057/978-1-137-53540-5_4

or 'BritCrit', is being established that is able to address the multifarious nature of racism in the UK since the special edition, and to further analyse the debate between CRT and Marxism.

REE 15 (1): THE REMAINING SIX ARTICLES

Topics covered in the remaining six articles in *REE* 15 (1) range from *Understanding the Place of Black British Intellectuals in UK Society* through *CRT Methodologies; The Experiences of Racialized Existence; Intersections Between Class, 'Race' and Gender;* to *Multicultural and Antiracist Education, CRT and Islamophobia;* and *The Educational Experiences of the Black Middle Class With Respect to Their Children's Schooling.*

Understanding the Place of Black British Intellectuals in UK Society

The first paper in *REE* 15 (1) by Paul Warmington is exploratory, assessing the role of CRT in understanding the place of black British intellectuals in UK society, and in contrast to the USA, their often marginalized status in public life (Warmington 2012). He states that the 'article might be read as a variant of what CRT refers to as "counter-storytelling"' (p. 6), which is defined by Solórzano and Yosso (2009, p. 138) as:

> a method of telling the stories of those people whose experiences are not often told...a tool for exposing, analyzing, and challenging the majoritarian stories of racial privilege. (cited in Warmington 2012, p. 6)

In Warmington's article, the counter-story told is one that resonates with the voices of black British thinkers that have so often been silenced (Warmington 2012, p. 6). Warmington discusses the intellectual contribution of a wide range of black intellectuals since the 1960s (at that time, 'black' was used as an all-encompassing term to include all people who identified politically with the nomenclature: c.f. the US classification, 'people of colour'). While Warmington is informative, particularly to an audience not familiar with the subject matter, beyond 'counter-storytelling' it is difficult to see what is particularly CRT*ist* in his account. Indeed, in his discussion, he draws on a range of theory used by the 'black intellectuals' including Marxism. As I argue in Cole (2017, p. 80) {pp. 49–50 in first edition}, it is important to listen to the stories and lived experiences of 'racialized' peoples, but, from a Marxist perspective these lived experiences need to be related to economic and political structures so that we can all better understand how and why they are racialized and for what reasons, in different geographical locations, and different historical periods and conjunctures, in order to facilitate moving forward in our mutual understanding of racism, so as to devise strategies to combat it.

Warmington's counter-story of 'black' British intellectuals, of which he is one, needs to be contextualized in terms of the overall dimensions of racism in UK society historically and contemporaneously. The backdrop of Warmington's paper is, of course, a form of colour-coded racism which has its origins in Britain's vast colonial empire, and which manifested itself in the UK in the post-Second World War period when Britain was hungry for labour power, and recruited workers from its colonies and ex-colonies.

Warmington deploys the CRT concept of 'white supremacy' in its CRT usage in his discussion of colour-coded racism. There are a number of problematics with the concept of 'white supremacy' as used by Critical Race Theorists (see Cole 2017 pp. 35–48 for an extended discussion of these problematics; see also the last section of this chapter), both with respect to the current manifestations of the colonial legacy and because of the widespread existence in the UK of the multiple forms of racism that are not colour-coded. While the colonial legacy continues in a number of forms, not least poverty figures (see Cole 2016 for a discussion), and while racism directed at Asian and black people is arguably the most publicly recognized form of racism, and while non-colour-coded racism is not Warmington's focus, it is important also to consider this form of racism.

From the immediate post-war period onwards, both non-colour-coded and colour-coded racism were particularly visible as Irish migrant workers were racialized along with Asian and African Caribbean migrants, prompting the infamous signs in windows: 'No Irish, No Blacks, No Dogs'. As immigrants' children entered school, they too were on the receiving end of processes of racialization (Grosvenor 1987, 1989). Another type of non-colour-coded racism is that directed at Gypsy, Roma and Traveller communities. With the mechanization of farming, many English Gypsies moved from rural areas to cities and towns, encountering hostile reactions from the local population and from the authorities (Greenfields 2006), with similar consequences of racialization as their children entered the education system. Given the presence in England of Irish Travellers, Anti-Gypsy Roma and Traveller racism is compounded with anti-Irish racism.

Islamophobia became a major form of racism in Britain after the first Gulf War (1990–1991) (Poynting and Mason 2007), intensifying after 9/11 and 7/7.[3] This form of racism may be termed hybridist in that Muslims may or may not be subject to colour-coded racism and are often marked out not so much by their colour as by their beards and headscarves (Sivanandan 2009).

These various and multifaceted forms of colour-coded, non-colour-coded and hybridist racism were made even more convoluted when in 1993 the Maastricht Treaty created the European Union. The integration of the UK into Europe and the disintegration of Eastern Europe has witnessed yet another form of racism directed at (predominantly) white Eastern European migrant workers and their families: xeno-racism (Sivanandan 2001).[4] In addition, in the 1990s 'asylum seekers' became racialized as both Centre-Right and Centre-Left parties in Europe began implementing laws that criminalized them (Fekete 2009).

All of these types of racism need to be viewed alongside ongoing and continuing antisemitism, still a significant form of non-colour-coded racism in the second decade of the twenty-first century, with racialization dating back centuries. There can, of course, be permutations among these various forms of racism.

Returning to the historical source of Warmington's article: in much the same way as Asian and African Caribbean workers did in the immediate post-Second World War period, Eastern European workers today provide the labour power needed by capitalists (see Cole 2016, chapter 1 for a discussion). It could be argued that in the run-up to the 2015 general election, xeno-racism directed primarily at Bulgarian and Romanian migrant workers vied with Islamophobia as the most prominent form of racism in the UK, with also a measure of anti-asylum-seeker racism (see Cole 2016, chapter 1, for a detailed analysis). It is difficult to see how 'white supremacy' can usefully inform theorization of either non-colour-coded or hybridist racism.

From a (neo-)Marxist perspective, there continue to be contradictions between capital's desire for (cheap) labour and politicians vying for popular racist support. To take one example, in 2015, the then Home Secretary Theresa May's populist anti-immigration speech at the Conservative Party Conference (May was hoping to replace David Cameron as leader of the party) was described by the director general of the Institute of Directors as 'irresponsible rhetoric'.

CRT Methodologies

Kevin Hylton addresses what constitutes CRT methodologies. They
he argues, 'focused on philosophical and ethical imperatives that explore
confront and change negative racialised relations' (Hylton 2012, p. 37).
Hylton provides a thorough summary of developments in CRT methodology so far, and urges researchers to be involved in social change and
social transformation in addition to antiracism. He gives a list of key considerations for CRT methodologies on p. 36 of his paper. Of these, issues
such as 'social justice'; 'a challenge to oppression and subordination'
(Marxists would preface this with 'exploitation'); 'praxis orientation';
'activist scholarship'; 'a participatory approach'; and 'challenging the passive reproduction of established questions and practices' would, from a
Marxist perspective all need to be linked to the economic and political
realities of austerity/immiseration capitalism, coupled with the need to
transcend it, and move towards twenty-first-century socialism (see chapter
7 of this volume).

The Experiences of Racialized Existence

In her contribution, Namita Chakrabarty combines psychoanalytical theory
with CRT to try to understand the former's construction of *buried alive*[5] in
its different manifestations. As she explains, her focus is 'the psychological
experience of being *buried alive* as raced experience' (Chakrabarty 2012,
p. 45). She provided two counter-narratives, one where a BME (Black and
Minority Ethnic)[6] academic is incorrectly reported absent from work by a
white administrative assistant, and her manager refuses to believe that she
was actually present: the 'white male word of absence of race was stronger
that the live presence of BME race' (Chakrabarty 2012, p. 47); the other
is a true story, where a woman with an Afrikaans accent refuses to share a
taxi with her in London in the aftermath of 7/7, declaring: '[w]ho'd want
to share a cab with an Asian on a day like this?' (Chakrabarty 2012, p. 48).
Both stories, fictional and true, demonstrate the feeling of being *buried
alive*. Again, beyond the use of counter-narratives applied in the UK context, there is no *theoretical* development of 'BritCrit'.

From a (neo-)Marxist perspective, the first counter-narrative, as with
Warmington's counter-story, relates to the continuing legacy of a form
of racism that had its origins in British colonialism, and the same provisos
apply with respect to the plethora of other forms of racism in UK society,

 the Afrikaans accent, throws up the complex rela-
talism, racism and apartheid in South Africa, best
xist analysis (see, for example, Wolpe 1988; Fine
ling legacy there today of white corporate capital-
(2015) explains how white supremacy (in its tradi-
persists in South Africa today, with a staggering 80
.5 trillion mineral wealth still in the hands of South
Western foreigners. It is difficult to see how, when
'white supremacy' encompasses not just the atrocities of apartheid, but
mundane everyday racism, CRT can adequately understand developments
in South Africa. This perhaps explains why, as is apparent throughout this
chapter, Critical Race Theorists tend to draw on (neo-)Marxist analysis
to make connections with economics and politics.[7] 'White supremacy' as
an umbrella term is inadequate for the task of explaining the various and
multiple manifestations of racism. I discuss this at more length later in the
chapter.

Intersections Between Class, 'Race' and Gender

In her article on 'the liminal space of alterity', Nicola Rollock (2012,
p. 65) reflects 'critically on…the intersections between social class, race
and gender', thus adopting intersectionality as an analytical tool, another
discernible trend among Critical Race Theorists, as we will see in this
chapter. Gillborn explains intersectionality's connection to CRT. As he
points out, Critical Race Theorists 'often focus on how racism works with,
against and through additional axes of differentiation including class, gender, sexuality and disability'(Gillborn 2008, p. 36). Hence, there are a
number of identity-specific varieties, as discussed in Cole (2017, chapter 2), such as 'LatCrit', 'Asian-American jurisprudence', 'Native jurisprudence', and 'queer-crit', as well as Critical Race Theorists concerned
with 'disability'. As Gillborn argues, this concern with intersectionality is
especially strong in Critical Race Feminism (Gillborn 2008, p. 36), itself
a variety of CRT. Indeed, the very concept of intersectionality is generally
attributed to the feminist Critical Race Theorist Kimberlé Crenshaw in an
article in 1989, in which she sought to challenge both feminist and antiracist theory and practice that neglected to 'accurately reflect the interaction
of race and gender' (Crenshaw 1989, p. 140). As she argued, 'because
the intersectional experience is greater than the sum of racism and sexism, any analysis that does not take intersectionality into account cannot

sufficiently address the particular manner in which Black women are subordinated' (Crenshaw 1989, p. 140). A key aspect of intersectionality is its premise that multiple oppressions are not each suffered separately, but as a single, synthesized experience (Smith 2013/14, p. 3).

Leading UK-based intersectionality theorist Nira Yuval-Davis states that unlike 'many feminists, especially black feminists, who focus on intersectional analysis as specific to black and ethnic minorities women or, at least, to marginalized people', she sees 'intersectionality as the most valid approach to analyze social stratification as a whole'. Intersectional analysis, she claims, 'does not prioritize one facet or category of social difference'. 'As to the question of how many facets of social difference and axes of power need to be analyzed', she clarifies her view of its fluidity:

> this is different in different historical locations and moments, and the decision on which ones to focus involve both empirical reality as well as political and especially ontological struggles. What is clear, however, is that when we carry out intersectional analysis, we cannot homogenize the ways any political project or claimings affect people who are differentially located within the same boundaries of belonging. (Yuval-Davis 2011, p. 4)

Intersectionality can be merely an *academic* discipline, divorced from class struggle, or it can be a healthy counterbalance to what remains of reductionist Marxism, which views any consideration of oppression and exploitation beyond social class to be diversionary.[8] At its worst, intersectionality simply creates 'a list of naturalized identities, abstracted from their material and historical context' (Mitchell 2013, p. 7), of which the 'practical upshot...is the perpetual articulation of *difference*, resulting in fragmentation and the stagnation of political activity' (Rectenwald 2013, p. 2). Intersectionality viewed thus renders social class as non-axiomatic, not the crucial social relation on which depends the ability or otherwise of capitalism to sustain and reproduce itself.

As Epifanio San Juan Jr. argues, unlike the Marxist concept of class as signifying class conflict, class as an element of identity makes it 'incomplete without taking into account other factors like race, gender, locality, and so on' (San Juan 2003, p. 14). In other words the class struggle which, for Marxists, is inherent in the capitalist mode of production gets lost, and social class is considered *only* as subjective identity.

With respect to Rollock's paper, while it is, of course, the case that classism has important effects on people's lives, and is worthy of analysis in its own right, for Marxists there is a fundamental need for an analysis that connects it to the capitalist economy. At its best intersectionality is 'rooted in real material conditions structured by social class' (Collins 1995, p. 345). As Sharon Smith argues, as 'an *additive* to Marxist theory, intersectionality leads the way toward a much higher level of understanding of the character of oppression than that developed by classical Marxists'. Underlying the Marxist position that no academic political theory is valid if it is divorced from workers' struggles, Smith adds that intersectionality thus defined enables 'the further development of the ways in which *solidarity* can be built between all those who suffer oppression and exploitation under capitalism to forge a unified movement' (Smith 2013/14, p. 13) (emphasis added).

Rollock also makes use of the CRT tool of counter-narrative and tells a true story and a fictional one. In the former, she recalls how when she was a child, she shrieked and laughed after being tickled by a school friend, and the teacher responded: '[w]ell, I don't know where *you* come from but *we* certainly don't do that sort of thing here!' (Rollock 2012, p. 69). The purpose of the story is to show how Rollock 'came to class awareness and the beginnings of…[her] understanding of the power and taken-for-granted privileges embedded in Whiteness' (Rollock 2012, p. 70). Rollock uses her fictional story to introduce 'rules of racial engagement for (possible) survival in WhiteWorld' (Rollock 2012, pp. 78–80). These ten rules reveal, in Rollock's (p. 78) words, 'the multilayered and nuanced analysis required for survival for those in the margins'.

Rollock's invocation of 'WhiteWorld' rather than racialized capitalism further serves to lose the exploitative as well as oppressive nature of this world system, exacerbated by its current austerity/immiseration mode (see chapter 6 of this volume for a discussion).

Multicultural and Antiracist Education, CRT and Islamophobia

Shirin Housee's paper (Housee 2012) has three sections: first, there is a discussion of the historical debates between multicultural and antiracist education in the UK, which leads on to an exploration, in the second section, of the theoretical developments in CRT in order to get to the 'deep root' of racism that exists, as argued by the antiracists; third, Housee looks at Islamophobia in the context of her (university) students' perceptions. Having reflected on two seminar sessions on Islamophobia and the comments from the students, she argues that her goal as an educator is to 'teach in a way that engages students and leads them to reflect on the socio-economic political/religious issues' that surround our lives (Housee 2012, p. 118).

CRT is not really drawn on in the substantive parts of Housee's text, except in the general sense that CRT and Critical Race Theorists promote antiracism and social justice, as do all progressive educators, including those who do not associate with CRT or use it, or even reject it in favour of other critical theory. While Housee (2012, p. 111) states that the 'student voice, indeed, counter voice, is central to [her] work of anti-racism in Higher Education', her analysis of work with her students, given that presumably some (many?) are white, her theoretical stance would seem to fall more in the realms of 'student voice' than the CRT concept of 'counter-narrative'. So once again there is no real development of 'BritCrit'.

From a (neo-)Marxist perspective, the debate between multiculturalism and antiracism would indeed, as Housee points out, need to be informed by 'structural and societal inequalities and institutional racism', for antiracists the key to understanding minority ethnic inequalities. Later in this chapter, I argue that a Marxist (re-)formulation of institutional racism better explains current realities in the UK and the USA than the CRT concept of 'white supremacy'. Reflecting 'on the socio-economic political/religious issues' that surround our lives is imperative for Marxist educators, and, in the context of Islamophobia (which I have described as hybridist, in that it is not necessarily colour-coded) (see Cole 2016), would entail a thorough examination of twentieth- and twenty-first-century imperialisms (unmentioned by Housee) and, concomitant on the latter, the 'war on terror' (which is mentioned by Housee) and their roles in exacerbating anti-Asian racism and Islamophobia.

The Educational Experiences of the Black Middle Class with Respect to Their Children's Schooling

In the final article in the special edition, David Gillborn, Nicola Rollock, Carol Vincent and Stephen Ball discuss the findings of an Economic and Social Research Council (ESRC)-funded project that used in-depth interviews to explore the educational experiences of the black middle class with respect to their children's schooling. They argue that although the parents have material and cultural capital, high expectations and support for education, this is thwarted by racist stereotyping and exclusion.

On p. 125, Gillborn et al. (2012) state:

> Drawing on the insights of Critical Race Theory...we reject the automatic focus on White people as the normative centre for analysis and, instead, foreground the experiences and voices of people of colour. In particular, we build on the CRT tenet that scholarship should accord a central place to the experiential knowledge of people of colour as a means of better understanding and combating race inequity in education.

However, beyond this statement of the principle that informed the research there is no use of CRT concepts in this paper, and therefore no analytical development of 'BritCrit', but rather the deployment of intersectional analysis.

With respect to (neo-)Marxism, the same stipulation applies as in the case of Rollock's singly authored piece, namely, that while classism is important, 'intersectionality' tends to render class *exploitation* invisible when class is subsumed within a 'race', gender, class matrix, with each viewed as *identities* only.

BRITCRIT SINCE JANUARY 2012

It could be argued that the papers in the special issue of *REE* were published too early for there to be substantial development of a British CRT. However, this is to ignore the fact that CRT has had a presence in the UK, at least since 2005, when Gillborn's first CRT article was published (Gillborn 2005).

I begin the first part of this chapter with a discussion of the four UK-based articles published in *REE* between the special edition in January 2012 and January 2016. The subject matter of the papers is as follows: *Student Teacher Perceptions of Black and White Teacher Educators*; *Schools' Racist Perceptions of Parents of Color*; *Student Teachers' Understandings of Discourse of 'Race', Diversity and Inclusion*; and *The Militarisation of English Schools*. Following on from the last article, I then consider the concepts of 'white supremacy' and institutional racism, respectively, focusing on some further co-written work by its author Charlotte Chadderton.

Student Teacher Perceptions of Black and White
Teacher Educators

The first article is by Heather Jane Smith and Vini Lander, teacher educators, one of whom is black and one of whom is white. In line with CRT's call for counter-storytelling, the black teacher educator maintained detailed diaries of her teaching experiences over the years (Smith and Lander 2012, p. 332), while the white teacher educator 'taught diversity and equality on a postgraduate initial teacher education course with a specific focus on critical whiteness studies' (p. 332)

From their research, they argue that the black teacher educator 'is expected to be knowledgeable about equality in general due to her "authentic" relationship with the issues' (p. 337). As they go on, crucially this does not automatically imply an 'intellectual' knowledge of the issues, since the focus is on experiential knowledge (p. 337).

A related consequence, they explain, 'of the perceived primacy of experiential knowledge is an assumption that Black teacher educators should be interested in teaching about educational equality and that this should be their main teaching/research interest' (p. 337). Perversely, they go on, 'this could also lead to a perception that only Black teachers should be interested in this subject area, leading to a concomitant marginalisation of the subject area itself' (p. 337).

In sharp contrast to all of this, they point out, the 'race' of the white teacher educator generally goes unmarked, and students have no reason 'to assume either the existence of experiential knowledge or a lack of intellectual knowledge' (p. 337). Moreover, even if they do notice the white teacher educator's 'race' (e.g. in questioning her interest in this subject area), an assumption of her likely lack of experiential knowledge may lead them 'to presuppose an intellectual knowledge' (p. 338).

Thus, they go on, the black teacher educator 'is perceived as legitimate in her role as a teacher of this subject area in terms of her experiential understanding', while the white teacher educator 'is perceived as a legitimate teacher educator because of her academic grounding in the subject area' (p. 338).

In addition, unlike the white teacher educator's experience of overt objections to her assumed political bias in teaching against racism, which is viewed as unfortunate but forgivable and which does not relate to her skin colour, the disreputable motive of racial bias is now assigned to the black teacher educator (p. 343). As one of the black teacher educator's students put it, in a somewhat perverse use of the phrase, 'she was play-ing the race card',[9] while one of the white teacher educator's students remarked, 'I don't mind having an argument with you because I feel you're like you're going to be unbiased in your opinions. If I detect that you might be more, obviously you're passionate about your subject, but I think there's a difference between being passionate and being personal' (pp. 343–344). In other words, the white teacher educator is viewed as an ardent intellectual, while the black teacher educator is viewed as having an 'agenda'—'an indoctrinator rather than a teacher' (p. 344). As one of the students explained of the latter: 'Gradually during the lecture I felt as if she was on a personal mission to change the way she was treated in the past' (p. 344).

This is a well-resourced, well-argued paper which underlines the insti-tutional racism in the UK education system, first *officially* acknowledged by Macpherson in the Stephen Lawrence Inquiry Report in 1999 (see the next section of this chapter). However, as the authors themselves note, there is nothing surprising in their findings, and once again, this article does not develop 'BritCrit'.

Schools' Racist Perceptions of Parents of Colour

Thandeka Chapman and Kalwant Bhopal (2013) examine how common sense understandings of 'parenting' paint parents of colour as inattentive and non-participatory actors in public (state) school settings in the USA (Chapman) and the UK (Bhopal). Their conclusion is that because of the white middle class framework of 'good parenting', the ongoing efforts of women of colour (men are not expected to participate in the same way as women) as fully engaged parents go unrecognized and underestimated which facilitates the blaming of failing schools within the family structures of people of colour, thus exonerating 'the systemic processes that maintain inequitable schooling' (Chapman and Bhopal 2013, p. 581).

It is informative here to dwell on 'common sense' from a neo-Marxist perspective. Gramsci made a distinction between 'common sense' and good sense. 'Common sense' refers to thoughts and reflections that are felt to be the product of years of knowing what is right and necessary, but really mirror the interests of the ruling class. 'Common sense', then, is 'based on surface appearances and information, and does not reach deeper to give a systemic explanation for the disparities that exist in soci-ety' (Taylor 2011, p. 7). Engels described this is as 'false consciousness':

> Ideology is a process accomplished by the so-called thinker consciously, indeed, but with a false consciousness. The real motives impelling him remain unknown to him...Hence he imagines false or apparent motives... He works with mere thought material which he accepts without examination as the product of thought, he does not investigate further for a more remote process.[10]

'Common sense' connects racialization with popular consciousness. Thus, we might pick up in the street, read in a tabloid or hear from a politician, 'it's only common sense to restrict immigration to this small island', or 'become an official member of the Common Sense Campaign...[and] win back America'.[11]

'Common sense' also works to reinforce racist stereotypes. Most pertinent to Chapman and Bhopal's article, political activist and Marxist academic Keeanga-Yamahtta Taylor gives the example of African Americans (although this can usually be applied to racialized groups in general) who, because of their worse housing, schooling, shorter life span and generally worse conditions, are perceived to be inferior—'they caused all this themselves'—which reinforces racism and racialization (Taylor 2011, p. 7).

Good sense, on the other hand, for Gramsci, is informed by a real political and economic awareness of capitalism, exemplified by Marxism and obtained by reading Marx. As educationalist Diana Coben (1999) has argued, good sense 'may be created out of common sense through an educative Marxist politics'. Good sense then would reveal that racialized groups are living in worse conditions because of racism, racialization and their structural location in capitalist society.

Chapman and Bhopal's analysis draws to a large extent on intersectionality and to a lesser extent on 'white privilege', the latter predating CRT (founded in 1989) and most associated with the work of Peggy McIntosh (1988).[12] Thus this paper may be viewed as a development in the theorization of transatlantic intersectionality and white privilege rather than 'BritCrit'.

Student Teachers' Understandings of Discourse of 'Race', Diversity and Inclusion

Kalwant Bhopal and Jasmine Rhamie (2014, p. 311) examine how students in Initial Teacher Training courses understand and conceptualize discourses of 'race', diversity and inclusion, focusing on racialized identities.

They claim that 'Critical Race Theory (CRT) underpinned the theoretical approach to the data analysis', since 'CRT acknowledges and foregrounds race suggesting that Whiteness is normalised in society and others are positioned in relation to this norm' (Bhopal and Rhamie (2014, p. 311) (CRT is only mentioned this once). However, their approach could more accurately be described as grounded in and developing intersectionality (mentioned twice in their account) rather than CRT. This is reflected in the worthwhile recommendations they make at the end which are:

- Initial Teacher Education (ITE) providers should provide explicit teaching on how to manage racism in schools with specific strategies and information on policy guidance.
- Opportunities should be provided for students to engage in discussions of their identities and how these may impact on their teaching.
- Issues of identity should be embedded across the whole of ITE provision ensuring that tutors themselves critically engage with their own identities drawing on this to support interactions with students.
- Further research in this area is needed, particularly the impact of the Equalities Act 2010 and how it affects the training of student teachers (Bhopal and Rhamie 2014, p. 322).

From a Marxist perspective, student teachers could usefully also explore how these identities position them in a racialized (and gendered) class-based neoliberal capitalist society, particularly in its current austerity/immiseration mode (see chapter 6 of this volume for a discussion).

The Militarization of English Schools

Finally in my consideration of 'BritCrit', I analyse an article that definitively informs the ongoing theoretical debate between CRT and Marxism, but, in my view, develops the latter at the expense of the former. The paper by Charlotte Chadderton, herself co-author of the article Preston and Chadderton (2012) singled out in chapter 3 of this volume for its contribution to the debate, is entitled 'The militarisation of English schools: Troops to Teaching and the implications for Initial Teacher Education and race equality' (Chadderton 2014). It utilizes both CRT (specifically the way it uses the idea of 'white supremacy') and neo-Marxism (in the form of Louis Althusser's concept of Ideological and Repressive State Apparatuses—ISAs and RSAs) (Althusser 1971).

She points out that the *Troops to Teachers* (*TtT*) initiative in E
schools combines the army RSA with the education ISA (Chadder
2014, p. 409), and, following Judith Butler (2004) and Enora Brow
(2011), suggests that we are currently undergoing a shift towards the
RSAs as the dominant form of social control, exemplified by a growing
culture of militarization (Chadderton 2014, pp. 408–409). From an
Althusserian perspective, she concludes, the linking of the RSA with the
ISA encourages the lowliest workers to 'accept their position' in capitalist
society (Chadderton 2014, p. 413). As she puts it, describing the realities
of austerity/immiseration capitalism:

> As the government withdraws its support for the welfare of the population
> and turns increasingly to profit and away from democratic practice, it makes
> sense that it will need ever more repressive apparatuses to ensure the com-
> pliance of the population and prevent revolt. The most likely to revolt are
> the disadvantaged or 'disposable' youth, as seen in the UK's 2011 riots…
> It should come as no surprise that those in power combine traditional RSAs
> and ISAs: schools and the army, to help achieve this. (Chadderton 2014,
> p. 418)

While her assertion that the UK government 'turns *increasingly* to profit'
(my emphasis) is rather bizarre in that capitalist governments always
prioritize profit-making, Chadderton's argument is quintessentially
neo-Marxist.

Chadderton also develops neo-Marxist analysis by linking neoliberal
capitalism to racism and generating the concept of a 'military–industrial–
education complex' in the guise of *TtT*, which Chadderton (2014, p. 407)
convincingly argues seeks to contain and police young people who are
marginalized along the lines of 'race' and class, and which contributes to a
wider move to increase ideological support for foreign wars in the context
of neoliberal objectives and increasing social inequalities.

Chadderton quite rightly notes how *TtT* targets economically deprived
working class children, theorized with an interesting application of (neo-)
Marxist concepts. However, it is difficult to see how the incorporation
of the CRT concept of 'white supremacy' aids the analysis of racialized
working class children. Indeed, I would argue that it actually detracts from
it. While, as I have argued, 'white supremacy' is not useful to describe
'colour-coded racism', it is even less well-equipped to understand non-
colour-coded racism. Racialized children on the receiving end of *TtT* will

sian and Minority Ethnic (BAME) children, but also
l sons of white Eastern European migrant workers,
d Traveller children and the children of refugees and
re on the receiving end of what I have referred to as
n which can be colour-coded or non-colour-coded).

'White Supremacy' or Institutional Racism?

As noted in chapter 2 of this volume, I critique the concept of 'white supremacy' at length in Cole (2017, p. 35). More recently (Cole 2016, pp. 13–20) I have updated this critique, identifying at least seven problematics with the CRT usage of 'white supremacy. In summary, I argue that 'white supremacy':

- directs attention away from capitalist economics and politics
- homogenizes all white people
- inadequately explains non-colour-coded racism
- does not explain newer hybridist racism
- does not explain racism that is 'not white' against 'not white'
- is historically and contemporaneously associated with beliefs and values which are not *necessarily* associated with 'everyday racism'; and historically and contemporaneously connects to fascism whereas racism and fascism need to be differentiated[13]
- is counterproductive in rallying against racism (Cole 2016).

Chadderton and Casey Edmonds have amplified their use of the concept of 'white supremacy'. They begin by stating that it is synonymous with 'white privilege' (Chadderton and Edmonds 2015, p. 140), whereas it would be more accurate to describe 'white supremacy' as the (perceived by Critical Race Theorists) *system* of oppression and 'white privilege' as the *benefits* that accrue from that system of oppression. It is worth recalling, as discussed in Cole (2017, p. 36), that according to Charles Mills (1997, p. 1) 'white supremacy' is 'the basic political system that has shaped the world for the past several hundred years' and 'the most important political system of recent global history', while the racial contract[14] 'designates Europeans as the privileged race' (Mills 1997, p. 33) To underline the point that he sees 'white supremacy' as a political system in its own right, and that the racial contract is both 'real' and 'global' (1997, p. 20) Mills asserts:

> Global white supremacy...is *itself* a political system, a particular power structure of formal or informal rule, socioeconomic privilege, and norms for the differential distribution of material wealth and opportunities, benefits and burdens, rights and duties. (Mills 1997, p. 3)

The term 'white supremacy', thus, for Critical Race Theorists, at least *implicates* all white people as part of some hegemonic bloc of 'whiteness'. From a Marxist perspective 'the basic political system' is more accurately described as a system that upholds and supports racialized (and gendered) neoliberal capitalism, now in austerity/immiseration mode, and accompanying imperialism promoted by some of the major powers (see chapter 6 of this volume for a discussion).

In the context of a discussion about 'white supremacy' and 'white privilege' in mainland Europe, Chadderton and Edmonds (2015, p. 141) write about anti-Polish racism in Germany both before and during the Nazi era. This may well be an accurate description of 'white supremacy' in its conventional usage, with the fascists forefronting the so-called Aryan 'race' as superior to all others. However, even if, as is the case with Chadderton and Edmonds, David Roediger is invoked (Roediger, e.g. 2005, argued that in the USA perceptions of 'whiteness' can change over time), 'white supremacy' and 'white privilege' do not explain 'white against white' anti-Polish and anti-Eastern European racism in general in the UK today. To understand this variant of racism—xeno-racism—we need to link the racialization process with the political and economic realities of neoliberal capitalism in the UK, and the economics and politics of the European Union. An abstract theory of global white supremacy does not explain xeno-racism in the UK in the second decade of the twenty-first century.

In a response to arguments by Alpesh Maisuria and myself (Cole and Maisuria 2007) that 'white supremacy' is not appropriate to analyse the experiences of refugees, some of whom are phenotypically white, Chadderton and Edmonds (2015, p. 142) state that white privilege does not refer to skin colour, but rather to 'a system of structural discrimination' which positions 'northern and western Europeans as superior to eastern and southern Europeans and the Irish, as well Jews'. This, they conclude, is particularly important to consider when examining refugees with respect to skin colour. While, this is, of course, true, it is also true as I have argued that racism is non-colour-coded. This is not only the case with certain Europeans, the Irish and Jewish peoples, but also the case with Gypsy, Roma and Traveller communities. In the UK, for example, many Gypsies have white skin, and racism directed at them is endemic. Finally, Islamophobia, rampant throughout the world, is also a form of racism that is based on modes or dress rather than skin colour.

To be blunt, is there really any purchase in trying to incorporate non-colour-coded racism (which includes not just xeno-racism, but anti-Irish racism and antisemitism—both acknowledged by Chadderton and Edmonds 2015, p. 141, as forms of racism) or hybridist racism (anti-refugee and anti-asylum-seeker racism and Islamophobia) under the banner of 'white supremacy' or 'white privilege'? What is the *point* of so doing?

The standard CRT defence of the use of 'white supremacy' as a descriptor of everyday racism is that 'whiteness' is fluid and minority ethnic groups slip in and out of its parameters in different geographical locations, and/or different historical periods. However, I am not convinced that 'white supremacy' is at all useful.

If Critical Race Theorists want to stress how extreme and all-pervasive racism is, how it is not aberrant, how it saturates society, if Critical Race Theorists want to demonstrate that 'institutions which claim, and appear to be, race neutral and equitable, such as education and training, actual reproduce racial inequality' (Chadderton and Edmonds 2015, p. 140), why not use a less ambiguous term like, for example, 'institutional racism' as does Housee in her article discussed above? Chadderton (2014, p. 408 states that 'white supremacy' shows that racism can be 'unwitting', which was, in fact, part of the Macpherson (1999) definition of 'institutional racism,' which, as noted earlier, was recognized officially in the UK in 1999 after the Stephen Lawrence Inquiry Report (Macpherson 1999). It needs to be stressed, however, that the practical implications of this recognition in the form of remedial action in institutional practices in the UK have virtually disappeared. Institutional racism is defined in the report as:

> The collective failure of an organisation to provide an appropriate and professional service to people because of their colour, culture, or ethnic origin. It can be seen or detected in processes, attitudes and behaviour which amount to discrimination through unwitting prejudice, ignorance, thoughtlessness and racist stereotyping which disadvantage minority ethnic people. (Macpherson 1999, 6.37, para 11.3)

From a Marxist viewpoint, the nebulous and ahistorical definition of institutional racism provided by Macpherson needs to have historical, economic and political foci. The definition also requires enhancement by the neo-Marxist concept of racialization. Last but not the least, I would also want to add intentional as well as unintentional or unwitting racism. I thus reformulate institutional racism as follows:

> Collective acts and/or procedures in an institution or institutions (locally, nationwide, continent-wide or globally) that intentionally or unintentionally have the effect of racializing, via 'common sense', certain populations or groups of people, through a process of interpellation.[15] This racialization process cannot be understood without reference to economic and political factors related to developments and changes, historically and contemporaneously, in national, continent-wide and global capitalism. Hegemony describes the ongoing attempts by the ruling class to consolidate a racist consensus.

Such a formulation, I would argue, provides better means to understand multifarious forms of racism in UK and US institutions today than 'white supremacy'. It also needs stressing, of course, that racism also takes place on an individual and/or personal basis, either face-to-face or mediated by phone, text or social media. It is not surprising that people who are socialized in institutionally racist societies are racist in their everyday interactions with other people.

Using the Marxist concept of endemic systemic all-pervasive institutional racism and stressing that the racialization of groups through history and geopolitically is not dependent on skin colour is less ambiguous and more straightforward than reducing racism to 'whiteness' and stressing that who is perceived as 'white' can change. Racialization, unlike 'white supremacy' and 'white privilege', makes this point articulately, and crucially also provides links with capitalist economic systems which, as we have seen, many Critical Race Theorists have to go outside CRT to theorize.

CONCLUSION

In this chapter, I looked at the remaining six articles on CRT in a British context (BritCrit) published in the special edition of *REE* (January, 2012) and at those published since January 2012, to assess, first, to what extent they develop BritCrit, and, second, whether they contribute to the debate between CRT and (neo-)Marxism. I found that there was little, if any, substantive development of 'BritCrit', and that, apart from 'counter-story' and 'counter- narrative', many of the articles employed theories other than CRT, including intersectionality, 'student voice', poststructuralism, 'white privilege' and (neo-)Marxism, as additional explanatory theories. Many did not use CRT as the main frame of reference, except in the sense of stressing the importance of 'race' (but this was often in the context of intersectionality). Most of the articles, I argued, could be enhanced by (neo-)Marxist analysis. Arguably then, it would appear that, with the important exception of Chadderton (2014) (which is more neo-Marxist that CRTist) and Preston and Chadderton (2012) (the focus of chapter 3 of this volume), *if these articles are representative of the field in the UK*, which I believe they are, CRT has yet to realize the potential envisaged for it in the UK, and the debate between CRT and Marxism has not further developed.

NOTES

1. UK-based CRT articles have been published in journals other than *REE* since January 2012, and there have also been CRT book chapters and books. However, given Gillborn's reputation on both sides of the Atlantic (in 2012, he was given the Derrick Bell Legacy Award from the Critical Race Studies in Education Association 'for his groundbreaking work on critical race theory' [Institute of Education/UCL 2012]); the status of *REE* in CRT circles and the stature and high profile within CRT of the authors I discuss, I would argue that the articles that are discussed in this chapter are representative of the field as it now stands. Moreover, I have supplemented some of the articles with other publications by the same author(s) where they illuminate or develop the point(s) being argued.

2. I have not included those articles where CRT is not claimed to be the main line of analysis, nor where it is merely referred to briefly.

3. On July 7, 2005 (7/7), a coordinated attack was made by Islamist suicide bombers on London's public transport system during the morning rush hour.

4. As Ambalavaner Sivanandan (cited in Fekete, 2001) notes, in Europe xeno-racism is 'racism in substance, but "xeno" in form'. While my concerns in this book are with xeno-racism in the UK context (I have, in my work, tended to limit xeno-racism to that directed at Eastern European migrant workers and their families), xeno-racism directed at 'foreigners' may, given the explicitly racist form that such hatred takes, in the modern world as a whole be more generally accurate as a descriptor than xenophobia.

5. Her deployment of the notion of 'buried alive' is derived from psychoanalysis and takes on different connotations: life in the

womb; horror stories; eternal life imprisonment; as well as the main theme of Chakrabarty's chapter—the experiences of racialized existence.

6. BME is one of two standard official nomenclatures in the UK. The other is BAME (Black, Asian and Minority Ethnic). They are roughly the equivalent of 'people of color' in the USA.

7. In contemporary South Africa there is also 'black on black racism', which can itself be partly explained by 'white supremacy' in its conventional sense, and is outside the remit of CRT. Such racism is a direct result of centuries of white against black violence and oppression, which normalized violence, and made it a way of life for black and other racialized workers, constantly on the receiving end of brutality from the repressive apparatuses of the state. Today with the connivance of the ideological apparatus of the state in the form of the media, black African immigrants are portrayed as 'foreigners', and thus a legitimate target for racialized black workers, while white foreigners as viewed as tourists or expats (Chengu 2015).

8. The Socialist Equality Party that publishes on the World Socialist Web Site (WSWS) is an example of an organization with a reductionist view of Marxism. While I find their analyses of neoliberal and austerity/immiseration capitalism enlightening and most insightful, and make use of it throughout this book, I would take issue with their frequent marginalization of issues other than social class.

9. 'Playing the "race" card' generally refers to white politicians using racism to get votes.

10. Marx–Engels correspondence 1893: Engels to Franz Mehring. Source: *Marx and Engels Correspondence*, International Publishers (1968) www.marxists.org/archive/marx/works/1893/letters/93_07_14.htm.

11. This is actually part of a real campaign by the Tea Party, a very right-wing faction in the US Republican Party (Common Sense Campaign [n.d.] http://commonsensecampaign.org/site/index.php/home-page/about-us.html), leading lights of which adopt a 'deport them all' stance on immigration (C. Vargas (2015) 'On immigration, will the Tea Party dominate the new Congress?' The Hill, 7 January, http://thehill.com/blogs/pundits-blog/immigration/228723-on-immigration-will-the-tea-party-dominate-the-new-congress).

12. McIntosh and 'white privilege' are discussed in Cole (2017, pp. 39–40).

13. Blanket use of the term 'white supremacy' by Critical Race Theorists to describe everyday racism rather than just the views of convinced racists and fascists in organisations such as the BNP in the UK and the Ku Klux Klan and other Hate Groups in the USA is particularly problematic in the era of Donald Trump, where traditional 'white supremacy' is simmering just below the mainstream surface. Compounding Trump's own up-front racism, in the sidelines is the American Freedom Party (AFP) whose goal is to make America a 'white ethnostate, a project that begins with electing Donald Trump' (Bhattacharya, 2016). Its plan for prominence and recognition, according to Chairman [sic] William Johnson, is to 'lobby … [and] put our people in there' in the wake of the departure of establishment Republicans following a Trump victory (p. 23). According to Johnson, the Plum Book (used to identify presidentially appointed positions within the Federal Government) lists 20,000 jobs 'that are open to a new administration' (cited in Bhattacharya, 2016). His aim is to identify all AFP members with a college degree as potential members of a Trump administration. As another AFP member puts it, 'We are the new GOP [Grand Old Party or Republican Party]' (cited in ibid.). Johnson flinches at the term 'white supremacist' or 'racist' preferring 'race realist' (Bhattacharya, 2016).

Eric enjoys reading *The Daily Stormer*, a leading alt-right (a segment of right-wing ideologies that reject mainstream conservatism) news site: 'Today is the anniversary of the birth of Adolf Hitler. In his lifetime he was a remarkable and misunderstood man' (Chief Editor, Colin Liddell 2015). Both Johnson and Eric believe in the 'looming extinction of the white race' and that 'diversity equals white genocide' (Battacharya, 2016, p. 25). As Eric concludes, 'Our civilisation is at war and we need to secure our people. We must seize power and take control. And the idea that we can do this peacefully is probably not realistic' (cited in Bhattacharya, 2016).

14. Mills's 'racial contract' refers to his belief that racism is at the core of the 'social contract', rather than being an unintended result, because of human failing. Social contract theory, which is nearly as old as philosophy itself, is the view that people's moral and/or political obligations are dependent on a contract or agreement among them

to form the society in which they live (Internet Encyclopedia of Philosophy [IEP], www.iep.utm.edu/soc-cont/).

15. See endnote 3 of the Introduction to this volume for a definition of interpellation.

REFERENCES

Althusser, L. (1971). Ideology and ideological state apparatuses. In *Lenin and philosophy and other essays*. London: New Left Books. http://www.marx2mao.com/Other/LPOE70NB.html

Bhattacharya, S. (2016, October 9). 'Call me a racist, but don't say I'm a Buddhist': Meet America's alt right. *The Guardian*. https://www.theguardian.com/world/2016/oct/09/call-me-a-racist-but-dont-say-im-a-buddhist-meet-the-alt-right

Bhopal, K., & Rhamie, J. (2014). Initial teacher training: Understanding 'race,' diversity and inclusion. *Race, Ethnicity and Education, 17*(3), 304–325.

Brown, E. (2011). Freedom for some, discipline for 'others'. In K. Saltmanand & D. Gabbard (Eds.), *Education as enforcement. The militarisation and corporatization of schools* (2nd ed.). New York/London: Routledge.

Butler, J. (2004). *Precarious life: The powers of mourning and violence*. London/New York: Verso.

Chadderton, C. (2014). The militarisation of English schools: Troops to teaching and the implications for Initial Teacher Education and race equality. *Race, Ethnicity and Education, 17*(3), 407–428.

Chadderton, C., & Edmonds, C. (2015). Refugees and access to vocational education and training across Europe: A case of protection of white privilege? *Journal of Vocational Education & Training, 67*(2), 136–152.

Chakrabarty, N. (2012). Buried alive: The psychoanalysis of racial absence in preparedness/education. *Race, Ethnicity and Education, 15*(1), 43–63.

Chakrabarty, N., Roberts, L., & Preston, J. (2012). Critical race theory in England. *Race, Ethnicity and Education, 15*(1), 1–3.

Chapman, T. K., & Bhopal, K. (2013). Countering common-sense understandings of "good parenting:" Women of color advocating for their children. *Race, Ethnicity and Education, 16*(4). doi:10.1080/13613324.2013.817773.

Chengu, G. (2015, April 20). Xenophobia in South Africa: The apartheid legacy of racism and "White Corporate Capitalism". *Global Research*. http://www.globalresearch.ca/xenophobia-in-south-africa-the-apartheid-legacy-of-racism-and-white-corporate-capitalism/5443965

Coben, D. (1999). Common sense or good sense: Ethnomathematics and the prospects for a Gramscian politics of adults' mathematics education. In M. van Groenestijn & D. Coben (Eds.), *Mathematics as part of lifelong learning. The fifth international conference of Adults Learning Maths – A Research Forum,* *ALM-5* (pp. 204–209). London: Goldsmiths College, University of London, in association with ALM. http://www.almonline.net/images/ALM/confer-ences/ALM05/proceedings/ALM05-proceedings-p204-209.pdf?7c979684e 0c0237f91974aa8acb4dc29=36f0is6pst9523pt8acs48p337

Cole, M. (2016). *Racism: A critical analysis.* London/Chicago: Pluto Press/ University of Chicago Press.

Cole, M. (2017). *Critical race theory and education: A Marxist response* (2nd ed.). New York/London: Palgrave Macmillan.

Cole, M., & Maisuria, A. (2007) 'Shut the F*** Up', 'You have no rights here': Citical race theory and racialisation in post-7/7 racist Britain. *Journal for Critical Education Policy Studies,* 5(1).

Collins, P. H. (1995). The social construction of black feminist thought. In B. Guy-Sheftall (Ed.), *Words of fire: An anthology of African-American feminist thought.* New York: The New Press.

Crenshaw, K. W. (1989). Demarginalizing the intersection of race and sex: A black feminist critique of antidiscrimination doctrine, feminist theory and antiracist politics. *Chicago Legal Forum, special issue: Feminism in the Law: Theory, Practice and Criticism* (University of Chicago).

Fekete, L. (2009). *A suitable enemy: Racism, migration and Islamophobia in Europe.* London: Pluto.

Fine, R. (1990). The antimonies of Neo-Marxism: A critique of Harold Wolpe's *Race, Class and the Apartheid State. Transformation,* 11, 1–118.

Gillborn, D. (2005). Education policy as an act of white supremacy: Whiteness, critical race theory and education reform. *Journal of Education Policy,* 20(4), 485–505.

Gillborn, D. (2008). *Racism and education: Coincidence or conspiracy?* London: Routledge.

Gillborn, D., Rollock, N., Vincent, C., & Ball, S. J. (2012). 'You got a pass, so what more do you want?': Race, class and gender intersections in the educa-tional experiences of the black middle class. *Race Ethnicity and Education,* 15(1), 121–139. doi:10.1080/13613324.2012.638869

Greenfields, M. (2006). Stopping places. In C. Clark & M. Greenfields (Eds.), *Here to stay: The gypsies and travellers of Britain.* Hatfield: University of Hertfordshire Press.

Grosvenor, I. (1987). A different reality: Education and the racialisation of the black child. *History of Education,* 16(4), 299–308.

Grosvenor, I. (1989). Teacher racism and the construction of black underachieve-ment. In R. Lowe (Ed.), *The changing secondary school.* Lewes: Falmer.

Housee, S. (2012). What's the point? Anti-racism and students' voices against Islamophobia. *Race, Ethnicity and Education,* 15(1), 101–120.

Hylton, K. (2012). Talk the talk, walk the walk: Defining critical race theory in research. *Race, Ethnicity and Education, 15*(1), 23–41. doi:10.1080/1361332 4.2012.638862.

Institute of Education/UCL. (2012, June 6). *Professor David Gillborn given an award for achievements in race theory.* http://www.ioe.ac.uk/64517.html

Macpherson, W. (1999). *The Stephen Lawrence enquiry, Report of an enquiry by Sir William Macpherson.* London: HMSO. https://www.gov.uk/government/uploads/system/uploads/attachment_data/file/277111/4262.pdf

McIntosh, P. (1988). *White privilege and male privilege: A personal account of coming to see correspondences through work in women's studies* (Working paper No. 189). Wellesley: Wellesley College Center for Research on Women.

Mills, C. W. (1997). *The racial contract.* New York: Cornell University Press.

Mitchell, E. (2013). I am a woman and a human: A Marxist feminist critique of intersectionality theory. The Charnel-House, September 12. https://thecharnel-house.org/2014/02/07/a-marxist-feminist-critique-of-intersectionalitytheory/

Poynting, S., & Mason, V. (2007). The resistible rise of Islamophobia: Anti-Muslim racism in the UK and Australia before 11 September 2001. *Journal of Sociology, 43*(1), 61–86.

Preston, J., & Chadderton, C. (2012). "Race traitor": Towards a critical race theory informed public pedagogy. *Race, Ethnicity and Education, 15*(1), 85.

Rectenwald, M. (2013). What's wrong with identity politics (and intersectionality theory)? A response to Mark Fisher's 'Exiting the Vampire Castle' (and its critics). *The North Star* http://www.thenorthstar.info/?p=11411

Rollock, N. (2012). The invisibility of race: Intersectional reflections on the liminal space of alterity. *Race, Ethnicity and Education, 15*(1), 65–84.

San Juan, Jr., E. (2003). Marxism and the race/class problematic: A re-articulation. *Cultural Logic.* http://clogic.eserver.org/2003/sanjuan.html

Sivanandan, A. (2001). Poverty is the new black. *Race and Class, 43*(2), 1–5.

Sivanandan, A. (2009). Foreword. In L. Fekete (Ed.), *A suitable enemy: Racism, migration and Islamophobia in Europe.* London: Pluto.

Smith, H. J., & Lander, V. (2012). Collusion or collision: Effects of teacher ethnicity in the teaching of critical whiteness. *Race, Ethnicity and Education, 15*(3). doi:10.1080/13613324.2011.585340.

Smith, S. (2013/14). Black feminism and intersectionality. *International Socialist Review* (91). http://isreview.org/issue/91/black-feminism-and-intersectionality

Solórzano, D., & Yosso, T. (2009). Counter-storytelling as an analytical framework for educational research. In E. Taylor, D. Gillborn, & G. Ladson-Billings (Eds.), *Foundations of critical race theory in education.* Abingdon: Routledge.

Taylor, Keeanga-Yamahtta. (2011, January 4). Race, class and Marxism. *socialistworker.org.* https://socialistworker.org/2011/01/04/race-class-and-marxism

Warmington, P. (2012). "A tradition in ceaseless motion": Critical race theory and black British intellectual spaces. *Race, Ethnicity and Education, 15*(1). doi:10.1 080/13613324.2012.638861

Wolpe, H. (1988). *Race, class and the apartheid state.* London: James Currey, with OAU, UNESCO.

Yuval-Davis, N. (2011). *Power, intersectionality and the politics of belonging.* Aalborg: Institut for Kultur og Global Studier, Aaloborg Universitet, Denmark. http://vbn.aau.dk/files/58024503/FREIA_wp_75.pdf

CHAPTER 5

Transatlantic Theoretical Developments: CRT in the USA

Introduction

In this chapter, I turn my attention to articles in *REE* on the USA, where of course Critical Race Theory (CRT) is much more firmly rooted (see Cole 2009, **2nd edition**, 2017), and interrogate the debate on that side of the pond.

My initial scan of the papers in *REE* between the special edition (*REE* 15, 1, 2012) and the latest edition at the time of writing (*REE*, 19, 4, 2016), for inclusion in this chapter indicated very few 'BritCrit' articles. For that reason, I did a thorough check of all the British articles to make sure that I had captured all of them, and had not missed any, before I concentrated on the four discussed in the first part of this chapter.

While there was a paucity of 'BritCrit' articles (just over 2 % of the total articles published), there was an abundance of US-based contributions that appeared to feature CRT analysis (41 or almost 25 % of the total). With respect to these US-based articles. I began by including only those that had CRT or CRT-associated words in the title, abstract or keywords. This brought the total down to 33. I then selected all those that had CRT as the only or main focus of analysis. This brought the numbers down to 24. Given that my remit is to look at current developments, I then omitted four historical accounts. Finally, since there were two on microaggression and two on mixed 'race' issues; I eliminated one each of these. This left 18, which I then read thoroughly. I now consider each in turn. They deal with the following issues:

© The Author(s) 2017
M. Cole, *New Developments in Critical Race Theory and Education*,
DOI 10.1057/978-1-137-53540-5_5

HMONG AMERICANS: 'CULTURE CLASH OR 'WHITENESS AS PROPERTY?

Christin DePouw (2012, pp. 223–224) examines Hmong American education, contrasting the media 'explanation' of Hmong peoples' 'racial exclusion and subordination' as resulting from 'culture clash' with what she describes as 'a more useful and humanizing approach to understanding Hmong American communities'. Drawing on the Marxist writer Etienne Balibar (1991) and the post-colonialist Edward Said (1978), DePouw argues that 'culture clash' draws on 'Orientalist conceptualizations of non-Western cultures as bounded, fixed, homogenous, hierarchical and located in the past' (DePouw 2012, p. 224).

She uses the CRT concept of 'whiteness as property' ('the rights to use and enjoyment and the absolute right to exclude'; see Ladson-Billings and Tate 1995, p. 59) to theorize how education ensures that 'Whiteness' is racially and culturally represented in the curriculum and is protected from negative or low expectations of academic 'ability' based on 'race' and makes sure that 'White needs', interests and concerns stay at the centre of institutional initiatives (Grillo and Wildman 1997, cited in DePouw 2012, p. 226).

DePouw (2012, p. 227) is right to argue that racism experienced by Hmong peoples 'is a logical outcome of the long history of anti-Asian and anti-immigrant sentiment and action within the United States'. I would also agree with DePouw (2012, pp. 227–228) that media depictions of 'the Hmong' as 'primitive' 'are located within deeper histories of colonial paternalism in relation to Indigenous peoples around the world' (see Cole 2016).

Just as is the case with the location of Warmington's discussion of black British intellectuals in the UK's plethora of forms of racism as addressed at the beginning of chapter 4 of this volume, it is informative here to position DePouw's analysis in the context of racism in the USA as a whole. Racism there needs to be seen in the context of 500 years of institutional racism, beginning with the 1492 Spanish invasion (Columbus's first 'voyage') and the subsequent attempted genocide of the Indigenous Peoples, the consequences of which reverberates piercingly in the twenty-first century. To comprehend the racism experienced by African Americans today, it is necessary to know about slavery and segregation, both of which still exist de facto today, the former in the guise of the prison–industrial complex, the latter clearly visible in the major cities of the USA. In addition, in order to understand anti-Latina/o racism we need to grasp the history of Mexicans and Mexican Americans, and of Puerto Ricans and Puerto Rican Americans. There is a self-evident and urgent need to address escalating Islamophobia as well as antisemitism; and the proliferation of Hate Groups (Cole 2016, chapter 2).

As well as Hmong Americans, anti-Asian racism has affected and continues to affect a wide constituency of other Asian Americans, such as Asian American and Pacific Islanders; Cambodian Americans; Chinese Americans; Filipina/o Americans; Indian Americans; Japanese Americans; Korean Americans; Laotian Americans; Pakistani and Bangladeshi Americans; Taiwanese Americans; and Vietnamese Americans.

DePouw's paper contains some interesting fieldwork, in which she informs us about a white student who asked her for help because she is required to create a slideshow on diversity and is 'really interested in doing the Hmong Student Association' (personal communication to DePouw, 5/10/10, cited in DePouw 2012, pp. 229–230). Such remarks come as no surprise to those of us who have over a period of many years (e.g. Cole 1986, 2014) have argued against this type of superficial multiculturalism. As DePouw (2012, p. 231) points out, recalling another aspect of superficial multiculturalism whereby white middle class teachers 'teach' other people's cultures, she is treated as if she is 'an expert on and go-between with Hmong Americans communities; an Orientalist insider/outsider whose authority on all things Hmong is only compounded by the presumed objectivity of [her] Whiteness' (DePouw 2012, p. 231) (cf. the article by Smith and Lander (2012) discussed in chapter 4 of this volume).

DePouw (2012, p. 233) uses the CRT concept of 'interest convergence' to explain how 'White interests' are served when (1) white institutions are seen as benevolent and antiracist; (2) when disenfranchising or excluding Hmong Americans from political, economic or social participation is rationalized; (3) when racist verbal or physical violence is rationalized; or (4) when US history is revised and purified. While I can understand how (1) and (4) could encapsulate interest convergence, I am not sure how Hmong Americans' interest could converge with whites with respect to (2) and (3). Perhaps it depends on the extent to which the schools, to use DePouw's terminology, 'Whiten Hmong American students' in order to:

> raise their numbers of enrolled students of color, promote a public image of 'diversity' and inclusion, create interracial contact and experiences for White students on campus, and perform exotic and symbolic versions of traditional Hmong culture for the use and enjoyment of Whites on campus. (DePouw 2012, p. 233)
>
> or 'Blacken' them:
>
> when they advocate for more meaningful inclusion in campus decision-making and push for more Hmong-related course offerings or Hmong faculty; when they request concomitant funding for these initiatives and attempt to institutionalize access to these resources; when Hmong American students expose and demand recourse for their experiences of racism on campus, particularly at the hands of White faculty and staff; and when Hmong American students' academic performance is not at parity with their White peers. (DePouw 2012, p. 233)

DePouw (2012, p. 237) concludes that 'race has played and continues to play a significant role in the lives of Hmong American youth and their families'. I would prefer to use the Marxist concept of racialization in place of DePouw's use of both 'Blacken' and 'race'. Deploying racialization, as argued throughout this volume, we can more clearly see how collective acts and/or procedures in the institution intentionally or unintentionally have the effect of racializing, via 'common sense', the Hmong students, through a process of interpellation (via the media, for example), which in turn explains *why* and *how* the white students acquire their racist views. This racialization process can then be connected to economic and political factors related to developments and changes, historically (the real history of the US ruling class's interventions in South East Asia) and contemporaneously (racism in the context of immiseration/immiseration capitalism and imperialism—see chapter 6 of this volume) and the ongoing attempts by the ruling class to consolidate a racist consensus.

As emphasized earlier, racism also, of course, takes place on an individual and/or personal basis, either face-to-face or mediated by phone, text or social media. The white students in DePouw's study will have been socialized into racist views not just in the education ideological state apparatus (ISA), but in the other racist institutions of the society, including the family. As also noted earlier in the chapter, it is hardly surprising that in institutionally racist societies, individuals, including the white students in DePouw's study, are racist in their everyday interactions with others, either on a one-to-one basis or collectively. This included 'being bullied, ignored, stereotyped, and racially threatened in school' (DePouw 2012, p. 234), and was often ignored by white school personnel, or made out as an isolated incident not related to racism (DePouw 2012, p. 234).

With respect to the long history of racism facing Asian Americans in general, it is imperative to challenge the 'model minority myth', which as noted earlier in this volume, is a stereotype that generalizes Asian Americans by depicting them as the perfect example of a totally successful minority ethnic group, a myth which of course DePouw is challenging, although she makes no mention of the myth.

DePouw's closing comments are:

> a critical race consciousness can support more active cultural and academic engagement for Hmong American students by providing them with the tools they need to develop affirming racial and cultural identities, which in

turn can empower Hmong American students to take meaningful action toward the betterment of their lives and of the communities in which they live. (DePouw 2012, p. 237)

(Neo-)Marxism can supplement this. It can provide an explanation of Hmong American students' location along with other racialized Americans in twenty-first-century racialized neoliberal capitalism and imperialism. The multiple forms of US racism need to be related to ongoing economic and political developments in US capitalism (Cole 2011, chapter 3, Cole 2016, chapter 2), now in its austerity/immiseration mode (see chapter 6 of this volume).

(Neo-)Marxism can also equip racialized Americans with the tools not just to develop their identities, but to empower them to take action for the betterment of their lives and communities, and also for the betterment of the US working class in general, racialized or not, and indeed for the progress of humankind worldwide. Marxism can empower people to challenge the very economic system in which they are exploited and oppressed. To be specific, twenty-first-century socialism provides a vision for what life in the USA and beyond *could* be like (see chapter 7 of this volume).

'RACIAL MICROAGGRESSIONS' DIRECTED AT PEOPLE OF COLOR

Rita Kohli and Daniel G Solórzano (2012) use a CRT framework and qualitative data to explore 'racial microaggressions'—subtle daily racist insults that support a racial and cultural hierarchy of minority inferiority—directed at black, Latina/o, Asian American, Pacific Islander and mixed 'race' participants, with respect to their names (Kohli and Solórzano 2012, p. 441). Kohli and Soórzano state that they are guided by five CRT tenets: the centrality of 'race' and racism; challenging dominant narratives; a commitment to social justice; valuing experiential knowledge and being interdisciplinary (2012, p. 445).

In the course of their paper, Kohli and Solórzano provide a number of examples of the effects of incorrect name pronunciations, whether the result of unintentional or intentional, overt or covert racism. These micro-aggressions devalue people's cultural heritage and result in anxiety and resentment. The examples given include two South Asian respondents, a man and a woman. The teacher of the man Nitin couldn't pronounce Nitin's name, and therefore, just like a slave master (though he was probably not aware of the connection), named Nitin after himself. By the time Nitin had graduated he had internalized his new 'name' to such an extent that he introduced himself as 'Frank' to everyone, including other South Asians (Kohli and Solórzano 2012, pp. 451–452).

The South Asian woman Nirupama was nicknamed 'Ghandi' by her classmates for the whole of the year, after the teacher asked her how to pronounce her name, followed by explaining that he wouldn't want to call her 'Ghandi' by accident (Kohli and Solórzano 2012, p. 452). As Kohli and Solórzano (2012, p. 452) point out, her peers were non-white and therefore would possibly have also encountered racial slights in their own schooling, but, nevertheless, contributed to the microaggression. It is worth noting here that it is difficult to see how this non-white on non-white racism could be explained by the CRT concept of 'white supremacy', a concept not referred to in Kohli and Solórzano' analysis.

Another respondent, a Chinese American woman, ended up changing her name to 'Anita' after her name was laughed at by a vice principal and members of the audience at an honours ceremony prior to graduation, which resulted in her not going on stage to receive the award (Kohli and Solórzano 2012, p. 453).

Chiamaka, whose name is Nigerian and means 'God is beautiful', and another Nigerian American in a different part of the USA, Oyekunle, both shared severe teasing of their names and recall how they were called 'African Booty Scratcher' (a brutal derogatory term for African Americans) with rare intervention from teachers (Kohli and Solórzano 2012, p. 454), while Maythee, a Latina American, tells how she had many bad experiences with teachers, and felt like an outsider.

Two final examples from the many in the article are two African American women, with Nigerian names, Shaquana and Dajenee, the former being made to feel uncomfortable with her name for many years, while the latter insisted her teacher call her D. because her teachers got it wrong and she grew to hate her name.

This is a very good important paper which provides useful insights into the consequences of regular severe microaggression towards people of colour in the USA. I would make four comments. First, as Kohli and Solórzano point out, the concept of 'microaggression' was coined by Chester Pierce. It needs to be added that Pierce first used the term in 1970 (Pierce 1970), which was actually before the birth of CRT, which had its origins in the 1980s (see Cole 2017, pp. 15–19). This is significant because, while the notion of 'microaggression' is an important one, it is difficult to see how CRT has a monopoly in explaining daily racism insults which occur in institutionally racist societies. Indeed, microaggression is not intrinsically linked to any theoretical position.

Second, microaggression needs to be viewed in the context of an institutionally racist society, as defined earlier in this chapter. Third, microaggression can also be generalized to other institutionally racist societies like the UK. Fourth, it needs to be stressed that microaggressions take place in societies, including the UK and the USA, that exhibit macroaggressions towards racialized peoples (Cole 2016).

African American Undergraduates: 'Achievement Gap' or 'Opportunity Gap'?

Robin Nicole Johnson-Ahorlu (2012) reveals how racism and stereotypes obstruct the academic success of black students, focusing on 'campus racism', and the way in which it impacts on their achievement potential and their behaviour and emotional well-being. As she puts it, 'the difference in grade performance between black and white students is not solely a reflection of individual achievement, but differences in opportunity', and these differences are largely related to unequal school conditions and resources, whereby African American students are 'robbed of the opportunity to perform and excel to the best of their ability'. She therefore refers to an 'opportunity gap' as opposed to an 'achievement gap' (Johnson-Ahorlu 2012, p. 635).

Johnson-Ahorlu (2012, p.636) refers to the five CRT tenets identified by Kohli and Soórzano (2012) and referred to immediately above, and states that she is guided by all these tenets in her paper in that it centralizes racism and stereotypes in investigating factors that impede opportunities for African American undergraduates; she challenges the dominant discourse that African Americans are deficit; values the experiential knowledge of African American students; has a social justice agenda for black students; and combines the disciplines of Education, Sociology and Psychology (Johnson-Ahorlu 2012, pp. 636–637).

Johnson-Ahorlu (2012, p. 641) shares one particularly poignant story about Howard who is described as 'a bright African American student', whose essay was singled out by his professor as 'a model piece of work'. Howard's prideful moment came abruptly to an end as the professor stated 'good job Howard' walked past him and promptly handed his paper to the only white student in the class. When Howard indicated that it was his essay, the professor, who had assumed that only the white student was capable of such quality, 'was in complete shock'.

Johnson-Ahorlu (2012, p. 642) also writes about stereotypes—'African American students are lazy' and how even African American faculty can harbour negative views about African American students, because of racism they have internalized about their own 'racial' group.

Penultimately, she refers to 'stereotype threat', where there is 'anxiety or stress triggered by the fear that one might fulfil or be associated with a relevant stereotype', with participants seeming most sensitive to being stereotyped as 'unintelligent', and students not wanting others to interpret their need for help or support as evidence of this (Johnson-Ahorlu 2012, p. 644) and feeling guilty or frustrated if they make a wrong move and perhaps reinforce a stereotype for the 'race' as a whole (Johnson-Ahorlu 2012, p. 645) As one student put it, '[n]ot validating the stereotype [is] more important...at times...more important than me getting a good grade' (cited in Johnson-Ahorlu 2012, p. 645).

Finally, she recounts lack of support, when almost all of the students in the focus groups felt that many faculty members were not supportive of African American students (Johnson-Ahorlu 2012, p. 646).

Johnson-Ahorlu (2012, p. 649) concludes that:

> research on the black–white 'achievement gap' can benefit from an examination of the 'opportunity gap' between black and white undergraduates. When such research only focuses on factors like standardized test scores, socio-economic status, and high school GPA, there is no room to consider structural or environmental factors in college that can hinder student achievement.

Once again, this is a valuable and perceptive indictment of institutional racism (Johnson-Ahorlu doesn't use this concept but does refer to 'institutional inequalities' [p.635]) in the USA, which is also applicable to the UK.

In her section of 'Racism and Stereotypes', Johnson-Ahorlu (2012, p. 637) gives a somewhat limited definition of racism, derived from Solórzano, Allen and Carroll (2002, p. 24), stating that it is the combination and interaction of three factors: one group believes itself to be superior; that group has power to carry out racist behaviour; and racism affects multiple 'racial/ethnic groups'.

In Cole (2017, pp. 55–57) I suggest a more wide-ranging definition of racism which includes feelings of superiority and difference based on cultural as well as biological racism. I also stress that racism can be intentional as well as unintentional; that 'seemingly positive' attributes will probably ultimately have racist implications and therefore need to considered as well as obvious negative racism. I also include in my definition dominative racism (direct and oppressive) as opposed to aversive racism (exclusion and cold-shouldering) (cf. Kovel 1988) and overt as well as covert racism. Finally, I insist, as stressed before in this volume, that racism can be non-colour-coded. All of these forms of racism can be individual or personal, and they can be occasioned by certain stimuli. These various forms of racism can also take institutional forms and there can, of course, be permutations among them. I would argue, therefore, that, in order to encompass the multifaceted nature of contemporary racism, it is important to adopt a broad concept and definition of racism, rather than a narrow one, based, as it was in the days of the British Empire, or pre–civil rights USA, for example, on notions of overt biological inferiority, even though there may also have been implications of cultural inferiority. I believe that the above conception and definition of racism both theoretically and practically better depicts racism in contemporary Britain (and elsewhere) than CRT notions of 'white supremacy'. From a Marxist perspective, in order to understand and combat racism, however, we must relate it to historical, economic and political factors. As I argue throughout this volume, it is my contention that the neo-Marxist concept of racialization which makes the connection between racism and capitalist modes of production and is thus is able to relate to these factors, namely, the real material contexts of struggle. While the extraction of surplus value defines the whole capitalist process (see the appendix to chapter 9 of Cole 2017), permutations of these factors vary greatly, and it is for this reason that the definition of racism has to be wide-ranging.

MAJORITARIAN STORIES IN THE EDUCATION OF SECONDARY MULTILINGUAL LEARNERS

Kara Mitchell (2013, p. 339) states at the outset that she believes that institutional racism is a foundational feature of US society and that its culture operates off 'white normativity'. Citing Rosina Lippi-Green (2006, p. 292) and illustrating the intersection of racism and linguicism (discrimination based on the language one speaks) she argues that, while most people would be surprised, if not shocked if an employer or teacher turned away and individual on the basis of skin colour, most would find nothing unusual or indeed wrong if a teacher viewed her Puerto Rican students as a problem to be solved.

In preparing for a very thorough and comprehensive paper on multilingual learners, Mitchell analysed about 100 empirical and conceptual studies through the lens of CRT. She identifies four common majoritarian stories, which, she explains, stand in contrast to CRT's tenets, tenets which she names as centralizing 'race'; challenging meritocracy, objectivity, neutrality, and ahistoricism; emphasizing experiential knowledge; and supporting interdisciplinarity (Mitchell 2013, p. 342, following Matsuda et al. 1993).

The majoritarian stories are *there is no story about 'race'; difference is seen as deficit; meritocracy is viewed as appropriate;* and *English is all the matters* (Mitchell 2013, pp. 345–358). The first is based on the premise that 'race' is simply no longer a significant issue in the USA; the second blames students, families and communities for student failure rather than mainstream schooling and that a successful student of colour is an assimilated student of colour (Solórzano and Yosso 2002, p. 31, cited in Mitchell 2013, p. 342); the third, against much of the literature which shows that this is a myth, positions public (state) schools as the great equalizers; the fourth, more about the targeted eradication of languages other than English from the public sphere, supports the notion that teaching multilingual learners is just good teaching (Mitchell 2013, pp. 345–358).

Mitchell notes that 'some of the racialization that multilingual learners encounter comes from tensions and conflicts that exist among and between various immigrant groups' (Mitchell 2013, p. 347). She goes on to point out that these issues may focus on language, culture and nationality, but there are also 'significant conflicts...between Chicana/o students and their newly arrived peers from Mexico, or between Puerto Rican students and those from the Dominican Republic'. As a Critical Race Theorist, Mitchell subscribes to 'white privilege' and 'white supremacy' (Mitchell 2013, pp. 345–346), so I would want to question once again the efficacy of the CRT concept and use of 'white supremacy' to understand the complexities of racism in the modern world, in this case racism that is non-white on non-white.

Derrick Bell and Fighting Racism Even If the Prospects for Change Are Bleak

REE 16 (4) is a special issue on the legacy of Derrick Bell, and the first article I consider is by Zeus Leonardo and Angela Harris (2013). They focus on a dualism in Bell's writing between what they describe as 'racial realism' (abandoning 'notions of one day ending racism') and 'ethical idealism' (inviting intellectuals 'to join him in fighting racism even if the prospects for change are sometimes bleak') (Leonardo and Harris 2013, p. 470). For them, '[o]ne cannot imagine Critical Race Theory in education without him' (p. 483). They describe how Bell used storytelling (Geneva Crenshaw, both fictitious and an allegory of real events in black history) to undermine majoritarian accounts of 'race relations' (Leonardo and Harris 2013, p. 473), specifically to 'fight fire with fire' (Bell 2005, p. 53, cited in Leonardo and Harris 2013, p. 473).

Commenting on Bell's ethics, Leonardo and Harris (2013, p. 475) argue that Bell inverted the philosopher Immanuel Kant's prioritizing respect for persons (in reality, given Kant's ethnocentricity, white Europeans) by blackening Kantian or putting 'Kant's system on its racial feet.' Just as Marx replaced Hegel's idealism with materialism[1] and the realities of class struggle, they argue, Bell replaced this idealism with the realities of racism and the struggle against 'white supremacy' (Leonardo and Harris 2013, p. 475). As Geneva Crenshaw puts it, commenting on the material investment in 'white supremacy', '[m]ost whites pay a tremendous price for their unthinking and often unconscious racism, but they are less willing to make direct payments for the privilege' (Bell 2005, p. 53, cited in Leonardo and Harris 2013, p. 475). As Bell puts it, '[s]lavery is, as an example of what white American has done, a constant reminder of what white America might do' (Bell 1992, p. 12, cited Leonardo and Harris 2013, pp. 475–476).

As Leonardo and Harris (2013, p. 480) make clear 'Bell has always been a "race man", seeing the world in black and white', being 'resolutely focused on African Americans' and Leonardo and Harris's article underlines the horrors and indeed the sadness and heartbreak of anti-black racism, both historically and today, thus confirming Bell's worst fears about its resilience. As Bell puts it in the conclusion to 'The Chronicle of the Space Traders' (Bell 1992, p. 194, cited in Leonardo and Harris 2013, p. 480), on Martin Luther King, Jr., Day, January 17, 2000, '[h]eads bowed, arms now linked by slender chains, black people left the New World as their forbears had arrived'. Elsewhere he writes of the dignity and enduring legacy of the enslaved:

> As the slave singers raised their voices to freedom, they must have known that there was no escape, no way out—in this world. The lyrics of their songs dreamed of 'A City Called Heaven', but while they lived, they continued to engage themselves in the creation of humanity. Here is our model. We need do no more—and surely must do no less—than seek to emulate what they have done. (Bell 1994, p. 164, cited in Leonardo and Harris 2013, p. 486)

While no one can deny the atrocious obscenity of slavery, other Critical Race Theorists, as Leonardo and Harris (2013, p. 480) point out, have deplored the exclusivity of the black–white binary (see chapter 3 of this volume, pp. 49–50), or black exceptionalism (as noted in chapter 2, p. 15 of this volume), the view that African American history is so distinctive that placing it at the centre of analysis is warranted (Delgago and Stefancic 2001, p. 69; see also Cole 2016, p. 87), and have incorporated 'indigenous peoples and Asian and Latino immigrants into their theories of race' (to Indigenous Peoples, Asian Americans and Latina/o peoples, I would add Muslims and Islamophobia; see Cole 2016, chapter 2).

While Bell often repeated his 'racism is permanent' thesis, he also issued an ethical invitation for blacks and whites alike to fight against racism, 'untethered by the hope that it will one day subside' (Leonardo and Harris 2013, p. 476). Leonardo and Harris (2013, p. 482) argue that Bell's dualism represents 'the two ends of one arc'. However, given that Bell had no vision of a future society without exploitation by social class or oppression by 'race', such a future society is left untheorized (see chapter 7 of this volume for a discussion of twenty-first-century socialism as a model for the future).

Bell and Educational Leadership

In the second tribute to Bell, Muhammad Khalifa, Christopher Dunbar and Ty-Ron Douglas (2013, p. 490) use his theories in an attempt to understand current practices in school leadership and the impact on students.

For example, they argue that an alarming example of interest convergence in current schooling practice is 'standardized high-stakes testing policy and requirements, and the ensuing business opportunities' (Khalifa et al. 2013, p. 493). Achievement gaps have actually widened in recent years between white and black and Latina/o students, while businesses have made profits out of the testing regimes.

They go on to explain the standardized testing and neoliberalism are totally at odds with what racialized Americans actually need, and how the cycle of neoliberalism perpetuates itself:

> Poor Black and Brown students attain low standardized test scores, and so neoliberal practices at their schools are intensified, and then since their curriculum has become even more scripted, the students are not able to receive the culturally-specific pedagogy and leadership needed, so their

scores worsen on the high-stakes tests, and the cycle continues. (Khalifa et al. 2013, p. 503)

Gloria Ladson-Billings' (1994, p. 339), they note, captures this very occurrence, when she writes:

These are also the schools most subject to a narrow, test-driven curriculum at a time when the students urgently need an education that helps them struggle against oppression and critique the new social inequalities enveloping their lives. (cited in Khalifa et al., p. 503)

Following Bell's (1995) counsel to 'include traditionally excluded views', they argue that this means not only hearing the voices of community leaders, but '*seeing*...community-based spaces...as existent, relevant, and resources for potential solutions' (Khalifa et al. 2013, p. 508). They are referring to the need for school leaders to draw from 'educative networks in non-school based contexts' (Khalifa et al. 2013, p. 507).

From a twenty-first-century socialist perspective, we can look to Latin America where such networks opposed to neoliberal capitalism and linked to revolutionary transformation can be found (Motta and Cole (eds) 2013; Motta and Cole 2014). In particular, Venezuela provides an excellent example of enduring self-education of the people from the late 1960s, prior to the election of socialist Hugo Chavez and the establishment of the Bolivarian Republic (Ciccariello-Maher 2013; Cole 2013; see also chapter 7 of this volume).

Finally, on a note of accuracy, Khalifa, Dunbar and Douglas (2013, p. 491) write:

CRT often allied with CLS, rejects the prevailing orthodoxy that scholarship could be or should be 'neutral' and 'objective' Crenshaw et al. (1995). The CLS group, of whom the most prominent associates are Derrick Bell, Patricia Williams, Richard Delgado, and Kimberlé Crenshaw, are marked by their utilization of developments in postmodern and poststructural scholarship, especially the focus on liminal or 'marginalized' communities and the use of alternative methodology in the expression of theoretical work. Most notable is their use of 'narratives' and other literary techniques (Dunbar 2008).

In fact, CRT is a critical response to Critical Legal Studies (CLS) and the scholars mentioned are associated with the founding of CRT, not with

CLS, and are allied with its materialist rather than its idealist, postmodern/ poststructural wing. Indeed, Richard Delagado has specifically argued that CRT needs to 'go back to class' (Delgado 2003).

BELL AND LATINA/O EDUCATION: A CRT TESTIMONIO

In analysing some articles, one struggles to find anything to write; in others the challenge is to decide what to leave out. Luis Urrieta Jr.'s and Sofia Villenas' (2013) paper falls squarely in the latter category. In the paper they demonstrate how Bell, along with Latina/o Studies and Latina/ Chicana feminist thought, has influenced their lives since they were graduate students. If Bell primarily viewed racism in terms of black and white, his influence outside the binary is not in question. By way of a testimonio co-creado (a co-created testimony), which equally values mind, body and spirit as sources of knowledge, creating a 'space of reclamation' (Delgado Bernal et al. 2012, p. 366, cited in Urrieta Jr. and Villenas 2013, p. 516), the authors validate their experiences as marginalized members of the academy (Urrieta Jr. and Villenas 2013, p. 516).

Their daily lives, they explain, were exposed to two kinds of racism: that spurred by the Spanish invasion of Latin America and targeted at indigenous, African descent and mestizos (mixed 'race') peoples and that aimed at Latinas/os (especially immigrant Latinas/os) (Urrieta Jr. and Villenas 2013, p. 517). Both acknowledge the influence of Marxism on their understanding of their history, specifically the way in which a Marxist analysis of Latin American and Chicano/a history questioned US intervention in Latin America and invasion in the Southwest. Latin American history, they point out, also provided new perspectives to analyse class struggle (Urrieta Jr. and Villenas 2013, p. 518).

The paper contains examples of a number of 'microaggressions': how they were expected to be the voice of Latinas/os during their doctoral studies; how Villenas, already an experienced mature mother, was interviewed by a 20-year-old from the WIC (Women, Infants and Children Food and Nutrition Services) programme when at university in North Carolina, asking about her knowledge of nutrition and telling her how to improve her family's nutrition; how during the delivery of her daughter, the doctor never spoke to her, but just asked the nurses if she spoke English (p. 521).

Urrieta Jr.'s microaggressions ranged from 'morbid silence in class, to direct verbal confrontations, to anonymous hateful notes slipped under

[his] office door, to complaints to [his] dean' (p. 526). Called in by one of his administrators, he was told that the students didn't have issues with him as a person of colour or as their professor, but that *he* had issues with them being white (p. 526).

The article is also full of antiracist insights: the Chicana/o movement slogans—'We didn't cross the border, the border crossed us!' and 'Who's the illegal alien Pilgrim?!' (p. 518); the 'Abuelita (Grandmother) Factor'—honouring and drawing from the rich knowledge base of Mexican and Central American grandmothers, often caretakers for young children while parents worked extraordinary hours to support their families; the way in which Urrieta Jr. and Villenas redefined 'school readiness' to include this knowledge base (p. 519).

They conclude with a mention of Paulo Freire's centralizing of social class and Bell's recognition of feminism, and pledge their future commitment 'to work with frames of intersectionality' (p. 531), thus underlining an increasingly visible trend among Critical Race Theorists, and signifying a further break with the CRT notion of the primacy of 'race' over class.

Finally, several mentions are made in the article of the permanence of racism (pp. 515, 523, 527, 529).

A CRT Counter-Narrative for Teacher Education

In the fourth article in the special *REE* issue on Derrick Bell, H. Richard Milner IV and Tyrone C. Howard present a counter-narrative for teacher education to disrupt and refute 'six pervasive narratives common in teacher education' (p. 537). These include:

- Teacher education programmes (such as Teach for America—TFA) should select and recruit the 'best and brightest' students from the most 'prestigious' institutions into teaching.
- It is appropriate to recruit teachers into teaching for a short period of time to teach in high poverty, 'high-need' environments.
- Teacher candidates who show high proficiency on teacher entrance examinations are 'better' teachers.
- The lack of teacher racial diversity in P-12 [primary and secondary] schools is not a problem.
- The racial and ethnic makeup of teacher educators is not a problem in preparing teachers for the racial and ethnic diversity they (will) encounter in P-12 schools.

- Curriculum and instructional practices should mainly focus on subject matter knowledge to the exclusion of other aspects in learning to teach.

Drawing on the same five tenets of CRT identified by Kohli and Solórzano (2012), discussed earlier in this chapter, they begin by discussing narratives in educational research and the use of counter-narratives. 'Race' and racism, for Milner IV and Howard (2013, p. 542), are placed at the centre of analysis.

In opposition to the first narrative, they dispute the fact that students must be 'best and brightest' according to some predetermined set of static criteria to teach effectively, and point out that the institutions that TFA targets are rarely those that are not perceived prestigious, and these institutions 'often have low enrollment of people of color as well as those who have been economically disadvantaged' (Milner IV and Howard 2013, pp. 543–544).

The counter-narrative to the second narrative challenges a short-term investment, referring to this as a 'missionary' approach whereby teachers can feel that they have done a good deed, and can now move on (pp. 545–546).

With respect to narrative 3, they point out that the overwhelming majority of prospective teacher candidates who do not pass teacher entrance exams are people of colour and a counter-narrative would raise questions about the usefulness and reliability of many of such exams (p. 547).

As far as the lack of teacher 'racial' diversity not being a problem (narrative 4) is concerned, Milner IV and Howard argue that of course this is a problem, with a total disproportionately low number of teachers of colour compared to students of colour, with more than a third of the US's public (state) schools having no teachers of colour at all (pp. 548–549).

The counter-narrative to narrative 5 is that the lack of 'racial' and ethnic diversity of teacher educators has the potential to create a significant knowledge gap for teachers, and to narrative 6, teaching should not be restricted to sound knowledge of subject matter. Teachers need to be aware of the home and neighbourhood lives of their students, the critical role that families play and how sociopolitical factors shape their lives. Milner IV and Howard show awareness of such factors throughout the paper, often referring to political, economic and socioeconomic issues, to poverty and so on. In endnote 3 of the paper, Milner IV and Howard (2013, p. 556) make the case that 'race' is not a useful or valid concept, arguing that it 'is physically, socially, legally, and historically constructed', that the 'meanings, messages, results, and consequences of race are developed and constructed by human beings, not by some predetermined set of laws or genetics', and that '[g]enetically and biologically, individuals are more the same than they are different'.

This is very similar to my own views of 'race', which I will describe briefly here. In chapter 3, I state in passing that I believe that 'race' is a social construct, a belief echoed by some Critical Race Theorists including Gillborn. Following neuroscientist Steven Rose and sociologist Hilary Rose (2005), in Cole 2016 (pp. 1–2) I argue that 'race' as a scientific concept is past its sell-by date. As Rose and Rose note, in 1972 the evolutionary geneticist Richard Lewontin pointed out that 85 % of human genetic diversity occurred within rather than between populations, and only 6–10 % of diversity is associated with the broadly defined 'races'. Rose and Rose explain that most of this difference is accounted for by the readily visible genetic variation of skin colour, hair form and so on. The everyday business of seeing and acknowledging such difference is not the same as the project of genetics. For genetics, and more importantly, for the prospect of treating genetic diseases, the difference is important, since humans differ in their susceptibility to particular diseases, and genetics can have something to say about this. However, beyond medicine, the invocation of 'race' is increasingly suspect.

There has been a growing debate among geneticists about the utility of the term, and an entire issue of the influential journal *Nature Reviews Genetics* (Autumn 2004) was devoted to it. The geneticists agreed with most biological anthropologists that for human biology the term 'race' is an unhelpful leftover. Rose and Rose argue that '[w]hatever arbitrary boundaries one places on any population group for the purposes of genetic research, they do not match those of conventionally defined races' (Rose and Rose 2005). For example, the DNA of 'native' Britons contains traces of the multiple entries into the UK of occupiers and migrants. The popular political slogan 'one race, the human race' would appear to be accurate. 'Race' as a concept should be abandoned. For these reasons, following Robert Miles, if I need to use the term 'race' as an 'idea', as a social construct, I put it in inverted commas, and, as we have seen, use racialization for the false grouping of people into 'races'.

Milner IV and Howard's (2013) arguments would also indicate that they might favour using 'racialization' as a conceptual tool rather than 'race'. Surprisingly, therefore, they reiterate their point that 'race' needs to be at the centre of analysis, by concluding that Bell's focus on 'race' is 'the right thing to do' (Milner IV and Howard 2013, p. 555). From a Marxist perspective, the issues of racism in education are vital areas to discuss and challenge, but the issues need to be more focused on the workings of the capitalist economy, and the political and social processes by which the racialization of American citizens is perpetuated.

KNOWLEDGE WORTH KNOWING FOR/ABOUT YOUNG BLACK MEN

In the penultimate dedication to Bell, Theodora Regina Berry and David Stovall's paper (2013, p. 588) has three themes: a discussion about young African American men as a population and in context of the schooling experience; a consideration of the article's theoretical framework—CRT and Critical Race Feminism (CRF); and, in the form of a Derrick Bell-type counter-story, a re-storying of how things could have been for Trayvon Martin, a 17-year-old African American who was fatally shot by a neighbourhood watch volunteer, in Sanford, Florida, in 2012. Once again the CRT/CRF account is extended to encompass intersectionality, and again Berry and Stovall adopt five elements of CRT, like Kohli and Solórzano (2012). As they point out, outside of the confines of communities of color, men and women of colour are viewed with suspicion (Berry and Stovall 2013, p. 593). Like Milner IV and Howard discussed in the previous subsection of this chapter, they agree that 'race' is a social construct (p. 594), and, like Johnson-Ahorlu discussed earlier, give a very narrow definition of racism, based on belief in superiority and the right to dominance (Berry and Stovall 2013, pp. 594–595), although in the case of the relationship between black men and the police and others in authority (especially those who are part of the repressive apparatuses of the state), it is true. Finally, Bell's permanence of racism is attested (p. 595).

Their charge, as Critical Race Scholars, they state is to 'revolutionize the curriculum' (p. 596), their task being 'anti-essentialism' with respect to the multiple identities of young black men (p. 597) to which I would add, 'this needs to include discussions of different ways of running the world' (see chapter 7 of this volume for a discussion). Berry and Stovall (2013, pp. 599–600) conclude with a counter-narrative of how things might have been in an America that was not institutionally racist, in this case with respect to young black men.

It is informative to locate Berry and Stovell's analysis in the context of the New Racial Domain (NRD). As I argue in Cole (2017, pp. 60–61), Manning Marable (2004) has connected racialization of African Americans to modes of production, when he described the current era in the USA as the NRD, which, unlike earlier forms of 'racial' domination which were based primarily in the political economy of US capitalism, is driven and largely determined by transnational capitalism and state neoliberalism. In the NRD, oppressive structures are mass unemployment, mass incarceration and mass disenfranchisement, with each factor directly feeding and accelerating the others (Marable 2004, cited in Cole 2017, p. 60).

CRITICAL RACE PEDAGOGY

Finally, with respect to Bell's contribution to CRT, Marvyn Lynn, Michael Jennings and Sherick Hughes (2013, pp. 618–620) assess what we can learn from Critical Race Pedagogy (CRP) identifying its four components: it embraces intersectionality; it recognizes the importance of the understanding of power in US society and the importance of empowering students of colour; it emphasizes the value of self-reflection, or reflexivity, that is, exploration of one's 'place' in a stratified society; and it encourages an explicitly liberatory pedagogy for justice and equity.

Like Gillborn (see Cole 2017, pp. 125–131), Lynn et al. seem to be suspicious of 'white Marxists'. They cite a chronicle written by Lynn elsewhere (Lynn 2010, p. 200) where the Latino school principal warns the media:

> Keep the Marxists out of our schools! They don't give a damn about people of color and sure in hell don't give a rat's ass about what happens to kids that don't look like them! They are only here because they want to take over our movement!

They also approvingly quote Ricky Lee Allen who argues that the 'racial' composition and power structure within the community of critical pedagogues mirrors the racial hierarchy in Latin America: whites on top, mestizos in the middle and black and Indigenous People at the bottom:

> In the alliance between white and light-skinned mestizo leftists, the racial strategy, whether exercised consciously or not, is to divert attention from white supremacy and toward the capitalist class so that when revolutions occur, the problem of racial struggle is overlooked and the darker masses still have a lower status. (Allen 2006, p. 8, cited in Lynn et al. 2013, p. 615)

As Gillborn (2008, p. 37) says of Allen, he 'views contemporary academic Marxism as an exercise of White power'. Allen (2006, p. 9, cited in Gillborn 2008, p. 37) argues stridently against any alliance with Marxists.

Elsewhere Allen (2007, p. 65) has stated that critical educators need to create an environment which creates identity crises for white students. Allen's (2007) views on 'whiteness' include the following: 'whites do not possess [love of the oppressed and] we whites…are more likely to have disdain or pity, certainly not love, for people of color' (p. 57); '[t]he best a white person can be is a white anti-racist racist' (p. 62). While this is, of course, true of some white people, such blanket comments undermine our common humanity, denigrate vast numbers of white revolutionaries and militate against becoming 'more fully human' which is Allen's declared aim (Allen 2007, p. 57).

I would argue that Allen's views on white people in general and on 'white Marxists' should be massively contested not just by Marxists but by Critical Race Theorists too. They certainly do not accord with Derrick Bell's radical humanism, to which I can personally testify (I acknowledge him in Cole 2017 for his help with the first version of the book—Cole 2009). As the last Derrick Bell Fellow (2009–2010) Vinay Harpalani (2012) writes of the distortion of Bell, with whom he once shared an office, by the right-wing media, specifically that he was racist towards white people:

> those of us who saw Professor Bell teach know that nothing could be further from the truth. Many of the students who were closest to him were White, as were the majority of the Derrick Bell Fellows—whom he chose personally…Students of all racial and political backgrounds could speak to Professor Bell's warmth and kindness—the personal stories and life lessons he offered while teaching, and the general compassion he encouraged everyone to display. Professor Bell was 'radical' and would proudly embrace the term. But much more than his political views, his philosophy of encouraging student dissent, of treating everyone with respect, and of 'humanizing the law school experience'—as he liked to put—made him a 'radical humanist' whose legacy will have a lasting impact on all whom he touched.

WHITE MALE RACIST PRIVILEGE IN HIGHER EDUCATION

Nolan León Cabrera (2014, p. 31) describes a paucity of writing about racism among white men in higher education (HE), a constituency he refers to elsewhere (Cabrera 2011) as having 'racial hyperprivilege'—a disproportionate amount of power relative to women and people of colour.

Once again adopting the Solórzano definition of CRT, Cabrera discovers four interconnected themes from interview transcripts from his sample twelve white male HE students. These are (1) individualized definitions of racism; (2) minimization of issues or 'race'; (3) white victimization/ minority privilege; and (4) minimal change in 'racial' views while in college (Cabrera 2014, p. 41). Before looking briefly at each theme, for reasons outlined earlier in this chapter, I would again question a narrow definition of racism. In this case, Cabrera's adopts Beverly Daniel Tatum (1992, p. 3)'s very limited 'a system of advantage based on race'.

With respect to the first theme, with two exceptions (p. 45), the students failed to note 'systemic reality' (Cabrera 2014, p. 41), or what I (and others) have referred to as institutional racism (see my definition in chapter 4 of this volume), and instead viewed racism as intentional individual acts by other people (pp. 41–42). As far as minimization of issues of 'race' (theme 2) is concerned, the students attributed racism to other factors such as the over-sensitivity of people of colour; job firings because of poor performance not racism; lace of ambition among people of colour (pp. 42–44). Students talked of 'reverse racism' and multiculturalism victimizing whites; and of affirmative action fighting racism with more racism (pp. 45–46) (theme 3); while most admitted little or no change in their views while in HE (pp. 47–48) (theme 4).

At the beginning of the article, Cabrera (2014, p. 41) describes the four themes as 'related to white supremacy in higher education'. Reading the comments of his students, it would seem to me that 'white privilege' more accurately describes their ideological views on racism than 'white supremacy'. As Cabrera (2014, p. 47) himself notes, in his discussion of theme 3, 'when minorities make even minor advances, whites frequently confuse an erosion of privilege for racial oppression' (he also refers to 'privilege' throughout the article, and 'white privilege is one of his keywords). As I argue in Cole 2009, pp. 25–28), while 'white privilege' should not homogenize the social relations of all white people, when related to social class (as in Peggy McIntosh's [1988] 46 privileges) and, as in the case with Cabrera's sample, which 'tended to cluster at the upper end of the socioeconomic scale' (Cabrera 2014, p. 38), white privilege or hyperprivilege seems a more accurate label.

Were Cabrera's sample of 12 students 'white supremacists' in the conventional sense of the term in the USA, they would be united by hatred, not just of people of colour, but hatred directed towards the government.

They would be weapon-bearing; likely to have swastika or other Far-Right fascist tattoos. Being sympathetic to fascist and specifically Nazi ideology, they would also be antisemitic (in this respect, it is worth noting that one of the students was Jewish) believing that the US government is controlled by Jews, denoted by the acronym ZOG (Zionist Occupied Government). They would also use offensive and pejorative racist language and 'racial' terms for people of colour, and would likely view racist white supremacist attackers of people of colour, such as Dylann Roof, as heroes, although they might think murder in a church was bad publicity (BBC 2015).

Once again, underlying my disagreement with the CRT use of 'white supremacy' as a descriptor of everyday racism, it is difficult to see any of these attributes applying to Cabrera's sample of affluent white men from 'a public, doctoral/research university...[which is] academically selective' (Cabrera 2014, pp. 36–37).

RECRUITING AND RECLAIMING STUDENT TEACHERS OF COLOUR

Keffrelyn Brown's literature search on the need for the recruitment and retention of more student teachers (preservice teachers) yielded the themes of those student teachers' perspectives and voices about teaching; and their experiences in teacher education programmes (Brown 2014, p. 330). The search revealed the lack of preparation that they feel they receive about teaching effectively, both students from diverse backgrounds and across multiple school contexts. Specifically, teacher preparation programmes are not designed to nor actively seek to engage with the knowledge student teachers of colour possess. Thus such programmes 'are marginalizing, isolating and not culturally affirming'. Student teachers reported 'high levels of alienation, a disconnection from the larger program community and a sense of not "seeing themselves" in their programs' (Brown 2014, p. 334). The extent to which student teachers of colour recognized and name racism, however, varied across studies and across different student groups (Brown 2014, p. 335). As Brown concludes:

> Programs that wish to prepare teachers to teach in critical, socially just ways must take care to prepare all candidates—including those of color—to recognize and work effectively against racism. (Brown 2014, p. 336)

Brown's analysis is firmly centred on 'race'. Unlike a number of other articles discussed in this chapter, she does not include intersectionality in her description of CRT in Education. This is significant because there is also no mention of social class in the paper. 'It is necessary', she states, 'to place race at the center of social analysis.' This is because in the USA 'the sociocultural factor of race has played a primary role in organizing and maintaining inequitable societal relationships' (Brown 2014, p. 238).

Brown (2014, pp. 340–341) concludes:

> If teacher education programs want to take seriously the call for recruiting more teachers of color, this goal must be grounded in the fact that teachers of color need quality teacher education training that fully addresses the contextual needs of its participants. This requires first recognizing that teacher training does not occur in a race-neutral context. Race must be acknowledged and critically addressed if teachers of color are to truly operate in a space of equity within teacher education. Second, teachers of color must be recognized as both individuals and members of historic groups that likely possess knowledge and experiences that are different from but complementary to those found in the dominant society. And third, programs must take care not to essentialize preservice teachers of color but recognize that all teachers—regardless of their background or race—require appropriate and relevant teacher training if they are to acquire the skills, knowledge and dispositions needed to become teachers committed to relevant, responsive and socially just teaching.

For Brown, it is not, as Marxists would argue, racialized neoliberal capitalism, now in austerity/immiseration mode, and its associated state apparatuses—in this case the educational ISA—that exploits and oppresses people of colour, including student teachers of colour (see Chadderton's article discussed in chapter 4 of this volume). Rather, it is 'Whiteness, as a cultural, socio-political and economic hegemonic force' (p. 327), operating 'both nationally and globally' (p. 327–328). 'Whiteness' here recalls Mill's 'global white supremacy' discussed in chapter 4 of this volume, as 'the basic political system' that controls the world, rather than capitalism.

On the issue of the 'permanence' of racism, Brown argues that 'while CRT moves from a place of pessimism', this should not diminish the sincere and passionate effort devoted to uncovering and dismantling it (p. 329). This has parallels with structuralist and humanist Marxism, with respect to transcending capitalism and creating socialism, and can also be applied to challenging racism. The fundamental difference between these two forms of neo-Marxism is that the former reminds us of how powerful the constraining structures of capitalism are, while the latter emphasizes the power of the human will in breaking through the structures of capitalist society. We should over-emphasize neither structuralism (as this leads to determinism and defeatism) nor humanism (as this leads to idealism) (Cole 2016, p. 8). As the humanist neo-Marxist Antonio Gramsci put it, 'Pessimism of the intellect, optimism of the will.' A fundamental difference between Critical Race Theorists who accept the 'permanence of racism' (even while fighting against it) and Marxists is that the latter believe that a future society without capitalism and where antiracism is the norm is realizable. These arguments are developed in the Conclusion to this chapter.

Teachers of Color Unpacking Internalized Racism and Striving for Antiracism in Schools

Rita Kohli (2014, p. 367) analyses internalized racism among teachers of colour, by way of in-depth interviews and focus groups with four black, four Latina and four Asian American female teacher educators (the inclusion of Native Americans and Alaska Natives would have given an even more thorough insight). I will give a few examples. Ashley, a black teacher, was given the impression when she herself was at school that she was a 'model black student': 'Well, Ashley's different'; 'Ashley's very articulate'; or 'You're not ghetto'; or 'Your hair is nice'. Based on this experience, she 'internalized a superiority to her community' (cited in Kohli 2014, p. 368).

When she was at elementary school, another teacher Janet was tested for ESL when her teacher overheard her mother speaking to her in Spanish, even though she had been succeeding in class for the whole year (pp. 375–376). She describes how it made her feel:

> As a kid, you're kind of like, well, why do I have to take this stupid test? I speak English, just like all the other kids. I didn't look like all the other kids, but I spoke perfectly fine. I was doing really well, but I just remember not wanting to be there. (cited in Kohli 2014, p. 376)

Sonia, a Sikh, recalls how at school when a fellow student saw her grandfather wearing a turban said, 'who's that dude wearing underwear on his head?' She recalls that, already feeling that her culture was 'invisible' in the curriculum, she was unable to say anything to defend her community, feeling 'very powerless because I already didn't have pride for my community' (cited in Kohli 2014, p. 376).

Finally, Elaine, a Korean American, had many negative experiences at school where she was teased for her language and phenotypically East Asian appearance, with one teacher even saying 'there's nothing I can do' (cited in Kohli 2014, p. 377). The repeated racism experiences led Elaine to 'feel shame about both her language and her family' (Kohl 2014, p. 377).

As Kohli (2014, p. 378) explains, the women in her study worked to unlearn internalized racism in many ways that included 'joining cultural groups, learning the history of their people, and studying race and racism'. She concludes:

> Through the lenses of CRT and internalized racism, this study brings light to the racialized realities of a multiracial group of teachers of color, and emphasizes their strength to challenge racism and inequity within education. The narratives woven throughout this article allows us to see how teachers of color can build on their experiences to think about culturally relevant, racially conscious teaching strategies. When considering the preparation of pre-service teachers of color, we must learn from their stories, and recognize that they bring many tools and insights to the classroom that can aid in the challenge to social and racial injustice in the lives of students of color. (Kohli 2014, pp. 384–385)

Kohli provides the standard definition of CRT as in many of the previous articles under discussion in this chapter, which here includes intersectionality, stated as including a number of factors including class and gender (p. 369). However, there are only two further passing references to social class. In the first (p. 371) she quotes Jeannie Oakes (2002) as noting that from five years old, children attend schools that are fraught with inequalities across 'racial' and class lines, and on p. 377, where Kohli mentions that one of the teachers of colour grew up in a working class Latina/o neighbourhood. Also, there is no further mention of gender, even though all her sample are women.

Like Brown (2014), in focusing on 'race', Kohli's analysis misses a contextualization within the wider framework of racialized (and gendered) neoliberal capitalism and the educational ISA within which schooling takes place.

A CRT Perspective on the Experiences of Mixed Race Persons in 'Post-racial' America

Celia Rousseau Anderson (2015) has written a very thought-provoking and moving account of the realities of being 'mixed "race"' in a country considered by some to be 'post-racial'. Support for this erroneous notion derives from both the presidency of Barack Obama, considered by many to be black (but technically mixed 'race'), and the growing number of 'mixed "race"' persons in the USA (pp. 1–2).

Anderson's paper is backed up by a CRT fictionalized narrative or vignette about fraternal twins, one of whom develops physical features that more closely mirror those of his African American father, while the other twin's physical features are more like his non-black mother. While Anderson's vignette serves to highlight the absurdity of 'race' as a meaningful way to categorize human beings,[2] she is right, I believe, to insist that in racist societies, such as the USA, teacher educators should be attuned to and helped to understand how to deal with issues of 'mixed "race"' as well as to the fact that the USA is a multicultural society (Anderson 2015, p. 14). As she points out, racism as well as the meaninglessness of 'race' is particularly obvious to people of 'mixed "race"' since their 'racial' classification is not a given (Senna 1998, p. 21, cited in Anderson 2015, p. 4).

Following Delgado (2001, pp. 2283, 2282), Anderson distinguishes between a materialist CRT which explains how racism systematically allocates privilege, status and wealth, and an idealist one that views racism as to do with thinking, attitude, categorization and discourse (Anderson 2015, p. 7). Anderson concludes that in order to explore the materialist and idealist manifestations of 'race' in the education of 'mixed "race"' students, we must use both forms of CRT in order to look squarely at issues of 'race' and inequality, to confront racism head on and to obviate the need to ask 'what are you?' (p. 16).

While I fully support the overall tenor of Anderson's arguments, I would like to make some comments from the perspective of Marxism and twenty-first-century democratic socialism. While I agree that racism takes on both materialist and idealist forms, I believe that US society needs to be seen, as I would stress once again, in the context of racialized neoliberal capitalism. In the final episode of the vignette, the father's reply to one of the twin's questions as to who made all the rules and laws is 'White people' (p. 15). Following on from this, we are left with the implication that *white people* are still in charge, despite Obama's presidency. It is more accurate, I would argue, to say that Obama's presidency has not really changed the ownership of the US's vast business wealth which remains in the hands of a *small corporate elite of overwhelmingly white capitalists.* As to the twins' father's final thoughts that other 'lessons on power and who is "in charge" would have to wait for another day' (p. 15), such discussions from a socialist father (of colour, of 'mixed "race"', or white) would entail a conversation about neoliberal capitalism, including its current austerity/immiseration mode, and the way this impacts on all working and middle class Americans, but particularly those of colour, and of 'mixed "race"'. It would also involve a consideration of alternative ways to run US society, such as an examination of the possibilities of sharing the vast wealth of the USA between the country's citizens, people of colour, 'mixed "race" people' and white people alike, rather than retaining it in the hands of a few. Different ways to exercise power such as participatory democracy as well as or rather than representative democracy would also be part of the agenda. In chapter 7 of this volume, I address these substantive issues in more detail, as well as considering how racism might be eradicated as part of a process of democratic twenty-first-century socialist revolution.

Institutional Racism and Inertia: Black Female Candidates Applying for an Educational Leadership Program

Vonzell Agosto, Zorka Karanxha and Aarti Bellara (2015) refer to the lack of diversity in educational leadership and point out that most principals and superintendents continue to be white men (pp. 789–790). Following on from this, they note that there is little research that specifically and deliberately examines the institutional process of the selection of people of colour (p. 792). In the article, they illustrate how faculty in departments of educational leadership attempted to challenge institutional racism that impeded black women from entering an educational leadership preparation programme; and to describe how efforts to promote a 'race'-conscious policy was obstructed by inertia and faculty's unwillingness and/or skill to engage in dialogues involving 'race' and gender (p. 786).

In their local context (Florida's public [state] schools) they inform us that for each of the five years prior to fall 2009, relative to the number of applicants, black women were consistently rejected at higher rates than white women, and in three out of the five years at more than double the rate (Agosto et al. 2015, p. 792). They argue that in the selection cycle in the fall of 2009:

> The haphazardness by which the committee proceeded during that first opportunity to select applicants for recommendation into the program coupled with the tendency to cast 'no' votes for applicants of color (even those who had met the formal criteria we had established), suggested that dialogue and change were needed in order to secure policies and practices that would be more transparent and better aligned with the mission statement. (p. 798)

Agosto et al. (2015, p. 801) expected that a common social justice discourse around issues of concern to committee members, such as gender equity, language equity, an agreed upon mission statement and past scholarship of faculty describing the areas of improvement needed in the programme would provide the interest convergence to support changes to 'the processes affecting' the admission and selection of candidates into the programme. Instead, however, they encountered forms of resistance to developing a selection process that would reduce disproportionality in the rejection rates. Resistance to change, they conclude, only partially explains the dynamics and resulting fatigue. Interest *divergence* helps to explain the source of resistance and the barriers impeding 'race'-conscious discourse and social justice leadership praxis.

Their pedagogical recommendations are first that there should be 'values based recruitment, selection and sponsorship', whereby women and men in positions of power in educational systems deliberately mentor more women, and especially more women of colour (p. 805), and that those in power become more aggressive in sponsoring African American women as students and graduates aspiring towards administrative positions, which would entail in turn recruiting more black women faculty and students into their programmes (p. 806). Second, those in powerful positions should have the courage to take risks and engage in 'race'-conscious dialogues and the advocacy of antiracist leadership (p. 806).

There is little here that would provide grounds for disagreement from Marxists. Marxists support reform in the short run, while advocating major structural changes in the long run. In an institutionally racist society, white middle class leaders will try to maintain their power and privileges at the level of local educational institutions as evidenced in this chapter, just as the ruling class will do the same at the level of the state (I referred to the white corporate elite still in control of the US state and economy, in spite of Obama's election in my comments on the previous article earlier).

RACE AND OPPORTUNITY IN A PUBLIC ALTERNATIVE SCHOOL

Jessica Dunning-Lozano (2016) draws three important conclusions from her qualitative case study on the stratifying role of a public (state) alternative school. First, employing the CRT concept of 'whiteness as property', her data revealed that continuation high school (public secondary alternative education programme) teachers and other schooling figures integral to the student referral process used strategies that promoted and secured the property values of whiteness; second, the 'race' and district status of students were a common denominator in the referral process; third, her study showed how some school personnel drew upon the 'racial' ideology of merit to deracialize the mass transfer of predominantly non-white, mainly black, Latina/o and Southeast Asian students into a substandard school.

Using Bourdieu's concept of 'symbolic violence', Dunning-Lozano describes how students came to internalize categories and narratives of meritocratic promotion in schools that mask institutional racism and a pattern of 'self-condemnation' engaged by students (p. 455). Although, her theoretical orientation is primarily CRT, e.g. 'whiteness as property' and 'counterstory telling', in addition to Bourdieu, like other Critical Race Theorists Dunning-Lozano employs intersectionality (e.g. p. 435, 439).

As far as the debate between CRT and Marxism is concerned, Dunning-Lozano (2016, p. 435) refers to my own observations (Cole 2009, 2nd edition, 2017) on the problematic nature of the CRT concept of 'white supremacy' (see also the discussion in chapter 4 of this volume), in that it 'ignores significant class and ethnic heterogeneity' and to my insistence that racialized capitalism can be 'non-color-coded', which she describes as 'cogent and valid' (Dunning-Lozano 2016, p. 435). In a further nod towards Marxism, she acknowledges the process of capital accumulation with respect to 'genocidal campaigns against Native Americans' and slavery ('the degraded position of Blacks as property'; p. 439).

W.E.B. Du Bois and 'Race' and Class Analysis Today: Filipina/o Americans' Exposure Programmes in the Philippines

While Dunning-Lozano (2016) recognizes the importance of the CRT/ Marxism debate, Michael Viola's (2016) article configures that debate as his primary focus. Viola's brief is to assess the contribution of the work of W.E.B. Du Bois as a whole to an understanding of racialized neoliberal capitalism or 'global apartheid' (Marable 2008).

For the Marxist side of the argument, Viola cites revolutionary critical pedagogy (RCP), associated with the work of Peter McLaren and others.[3] Specifically, Viola commends Du Bois's conceptualization of a 'guiding hundredth', whereby Du Bois urged historically subjugated groups in the USA to not only have a 'clear vision of present world conditions and dangers', but also to assist in forging alliances 'with cultural groups in Europe, America, Asia and Africa, and [others] looking toward a new world culture' (Du Bois 1948, cited in Viola 2016, p. 510) as having 'important implications for contemporary theorization of race relations in an epoch of neoliberal globalization' (Viola 2016, p. 510). Viola argues that 'RCP is well positioned to build upon Du Bois's application of historical materialism to matters of learning, labour, and living within the contexts and experiences of racialized groups', but that no interchange has taken place (Viola 2016, p. 503).

Critical Race Theorists, on the other hand, are 'inaudible' to Du Bois's internationalism and Marxism (p. 507) and learning from it 'can only enhance CRT's theoretical acumen as well as widen its ability to offer global counter-narratives' (pp. 501–502).

Viola also examines how such global awareness can facilitate an understanding of 'hypersegregated, racialized urban ghettos' around the world as well as in the USA (Marable 2008, p. 3, cited in Viola 2016, p. 501). It can plant the seeds for liberation from global apartheid—the 'racialized division and stratification of resources, wealth, and power that separates Europe, North America, and Japan from the billions of mostly black, brown, indigenous, undocumented immigrant and poor people across the planet' (Marable 2008, p. 4, cited in Viola 2016, p. 501).

In the context of Viola's article, liberation involves consideration of how 'collective visions for the future' and a 'new world' can be envisaged in the context of exposure of Filipina/o Americans to 'national democratic' sectors in the Philippines (political programmes that are anti-imperialist and based on national sovereignty, and include various democratic progressive forces such as labour organizers, women's organizations, young people, church people, educators, peasants, human rights advocates, indigenous activists, minority ethnic groups and cultural workers; Viola 2016, p. 512, pp. 519–520 note 4).[4]

Viola's discussion of a 'collective vision for the future' recalls developments in the Bolivarian Revolution of Venezuela. These developments and the realities and prospects for the twenty-first-century socialism today are discussed in chapter 7 of this volume.

Viola concludes by arguing that Du Bois's outline of a 'guiding hundredth' enables a generative application of 'race-class' concepts, and that the

> dismantling of global apartheid requires nothing less than an anti-racist pedagogical and political movement that is international in its orientation. The formation of a global counter-hegemonic bloc must offer possibilities of an alternative future to the present conditions facing people of color not only within the US but also the racialized peoples of the periphery who consist of 80% of the world's population. (Viola 2016, p. 517)

I would argue that Viola's and Du Bois's insights on racialized peoples can he enhanced by neo-Marxist analysis (e.g. Cole 2011, 2016). For example, in order to understand racism, racialization and their connections with the capitalist mode of production and imperialism, use can be made of a number of Marxist and neo-Marxist concepts, primarily the work of Gramsci and Althusser as discussed earlier in this volume.

Finally, Viola (2016, p. 519) is right that there are 'a multitude of dominated and exploited groups struggling to create a "new world"'. While the majority of such groups are racialized people of colour, white workers too are exploited by neoliberal global capitalism, and also 'have nothing to lose but their chains [and] a world to win' (Marx and Engels 1848 (1977), p. 63).

PRIVATE CATHOLIC SCHOOLING, RACISM AND PRIMARILY NON-CATHOLIC AFRICAN AMERICAN STUDENTS

In the last article under consideration here, Kevin Burke and Brian Gilbert (2016, p. 525), as with other articles discussed in this chapter, use theories other than CRT, in this case: cultural studies (based on the work of Stuart

Hall (e.g. Hall 1992); discourse analysis (derived from Foucault); postco-lonial theory (p. 530) and 'Whiteness Studies', with 'whiteness' defined primarily 'by what it is not' (Moreton-Robinson 2004, p. 74, cited in Burke and Gilbert 2016, p. 531).

In an analysis drawn from the memories of Burke growing up in Chicago in the 1980s, and 1990s with journalistic sources to paint a recent histori-cal picture of segregation tied to Catholic schools, along with Gilbert's experiences as a teacher in the South Side of Chicago from 2008 to 2014 and conversations on doctoral classes between 2012 and 2014, they argue 'that the discourse of Catholic schooling ... has become inflected (infected?) with commonsense racial undertones' (p. 525). These under-tones 'are propagated in a number of truly troubling ways', and while there 'have been reams written about the racialized (and genocidal) moves made by missioning whites the world over; less has been said about the ongoing shape of missionary work or long-established religious schools, serving [or in their case] refusing to serve, new populations' (Note 1, p. 539). Religion-as-tradition, according to Burke and Gilbert (2016, note 1, p. 539), is used 'as a bulwark to support white dominance'. In 'a bricolage of qualitative and interpretive research' (p. 527), they provide instances of overt biological racism against black students from parents: '[t]he school is spending all of their time recruiting these fucking monkeys from the ghetto' (p. 534); and from students who 'mimed gorillas'(p. 535), and stated that 'calling another student a "ni**er" is ok as long as you tell the Dean you were just joking' (p. 537). Moreover, a liturgical director was told by one of the school's religious order to 'keep that ni**er shit out of here' (p. 530). There are also references to nooses hanging from an office door (p. 530) and around a black student's neck (p. 535).

When it comes to bullying, the attitude tends to be that they 'usually bring it on themselves', as one school administrator put it. 'The students we think my be bullies were usually provoked by the other guy' (cited in Burke and Gilbert 2016, p. 537).

In the light of all this, Catholic educational leaders, they conclude, 'have a moral obligation—indeed a spiritual one—to begin to impose a theological cudgel to the structured racism upon which many parishes and schools have relied for their survival' (Burke and Gilbert 2016, p. 539).

A counter to the conservatism and racism, as described by Burke and Gilbert, is a current within the Catholic Church known as liberation the-ology (this is not referred to by them), which I briefly mentioned in the context of the RCP of Peter McLaren and others in endnote 53 in the discussion of Viola in the previous section of this chapter. The RCP is itself a theoretical development from critical pedagogy, the founder of which is generally acknowledged to be Paulo Freire, a Latin American socialist born in Brazil, and himself a self-described Marxist and liberation theologian. Exemplifying this, in an online video (Freire 2007; Freire actually died in 1997), he makes reference to his belief in Marx with respect to the world and Christ as far as the 'transcendental' is concerned. McLaren has recently gone beyond what Lilia Monzó (writing an afterword to McLaren's *Pedagogy of Insurrection: From Resurrection to Revolution* (McLaren 2015)) refers to as the 'righteous call of liberation theology to make the plight of the poor "the preferential option"'. McLaren's brief, Monzó argues, is to make the fight against poverty and exploitation, following Jesus, 'not merely an option but an obligation' (Monzó 2015, p. 441). As we saw in chapter 2 of this volume, McLaren is not afraid to change his theoretical orientation. Acknowledging this, Monzó states: while many Left radicals 'may ... remain sceptical of [his] alliance with the Bible', they will 'undoubtedly admire McLaren's penchant for constantly challenging himself to develop new avenues to bring forth a socialist revolution' (Monzó 2015, p. 441).

If Monzó (2015, p. 441) is right that 'millions of new disciples from the Christian faith' could be enlisted in the revolutionary struggle (remember there are already millions of socialist Catholics in Latin America), this would indeed provide a powerful antidote to the reactionary racist Catholics that feature in Burke and Gilbert (2016).

On a final note, like Dunning-Lozano, Burke and Gilbert (2016, p. 532, note 4, p. 540) appear to accept the existence of the concept of non-colour-coded racism when they compare the racist attitudes of the particular Irish Catholics in the USA that they analysed to anti-traveller racism back in Ireland. However, unlike Dunning-Lozano, it is not named as such. It is worth stressing at this point the long-standing anti-Irish racism, not just in the USA, but in the UK (as discussed in chapter 4 of this volume; see also Cole 2016, chapter 1), Australia (Cole 2016, chapter 3) and elsewhere.

CONCLUSION

In this chapter, I analysed a number of US-based CRT articles. In these, as in the UK-based articles, we also witness the deployment of theories other than CRT, here: intersectionality, 'Whiteness Studies', neo-Marxism, *[handwritten margin notes: "+ racial", "micro.", "aggression", "(one word)"]*

post-colonialism, discourse analysis and cultural studies. There is, however, a greater use of CRT concepts than in the UK articles: 'whiteness as property'; 'interest convergence'; 'interest divergence'; the 'model minority myth' (though not mentioned as such); 'counter-story', 'counter-narrative' and 'fictionalized narrative'; 'critical race pedagogy'; and 'critical race feminism'. As with the UK articles, I indicate throughout how the papers could be enhanced by (neo-)Marxism. Again, with respect to the debate between CRT and (neo-)Marxism, with the exception of Viola (2016) who, as we have seen, makes the case for the relevance of Dubois's Marxism to CRT, and his concept of the 'guiding hundredth' to RCP, there is no real indication that the US-based articles have moved this forward.

In both UK and US CRT, I noted a discernible trend (back) towards intersectionality. In the light of this trend, it is worth pondering whether we might be witnessing a relaxing of the CRT insistency of 'race' over class and a more enduring embracing of intersectionality, but with the use of class as an oppressed *identity*, along with other oppressed identities, rather than seen in addition as Marxists would see it, as axiomatic in capitalist *exploitation*.

The other main tenet of CRT, the problematic concept 'white supremacy' on the whole remains prominent in CRT analysis, and I indicate throughout the chapter what I consider to be its major problematics.

Both UK and US papers, I suggest, need to be contextualized in terms of the multifarious forms of racism in both countries, which both need a wide-based rather than a narrow definition of racism.

In CRT, in general, there is a continuing insistence, following Derrick Bell, on the permanency of racism (albeit with a parallel insistence to continue challenging it). From a Marxist perspective, nothing is permanent, except socialist thinking and perhaps revolution. Marxists argue for the need for class consciousness, while Critical Race Theorists often refer to 'race consciousness'. As I argue in chapter 7 of this volume, a twenty-first-century socialist consciousness includes a consciousness of all forms of oppression, including racism, accompanied by a commitment to eradicate all oppression and exploitation. This is not to advocate some kind of utopia, where no one ever has racist (or sexist or homophobic or transphobic or disablist or ageist) thoughts or never enacts such thoughts, but rather to call for a change of overall consciousness, whereby socialism and anti-oppression in general guide our thoughts and actions, where while some racist (and other oppressive) thoughts and actions remain, we all learn how to handle them and work to eliminate them.

NOTES

1. In opposition to Georg Wilhelm Friedrich Hegel's dialectics whereby continuous change is the expression of the world spirit, realizing itself in nature and in human society, for Marx and Engels change was inherent in the nature of the material world: out of the opposing forces in feudal society, capitalism was created which in turn created its own contradictory classes—workers and capitalists—and out of the ensuing class struggle, socialism became possible. Whereas Hegel tried to deduce the actual course of events from the 'principles of dialectics', for Marx and Engels, the principles must be inferred from the events.
2. In a very real sense, we are probably all 'mixed "race"', having a common ancestry in Africa (Hetherington and Reid 2010; Oppenheimer 2012; Pakendorf and Stoneking 2005; Siverwright 2015).
3. Viola cites my work (Cole, 2008, 2009) as an example of RCP. While I have some political sympathy with RCP because it *is* essentially Marxist (it also includes liberation theology: see the next section of this chapter on Burke and Gilbert, 2016), I have never identified myself as a Revolutionary Critical Pedagogy scholar, nor entered into any depth in the kind of Freireian (based on the works of Paulo Freire) analysis with which RCP tends to be associated, except in an attempt to understand the theoretical underpinnings of Bolivarian education in Venezuela (e.g. Cole 2011, pp. 160–164).
4. I would concur with Viola's concerns with the neglect of critical scholarship on Filipina/o American communities, and have addressed, albeit briefly, these communities elsewhere in the context of (neo-) Marxist analyses of racism (e.g. Cole 2011, pp. 99–100, 108–109, 2016, pp. 118–119).

REFERENCES

Agosto, V., Karanxha, Z., & Bellara, A. (2015). Battling inertia in educational leadership: CRT Praxis for race conscious dialogue. *Race, Ethnicity and Education, 18*(6), 785–812.
Allen, R. L. (2006). The race problem in the critical pedagogy community. In C. Rossatto, R. L. Allen, & M. Pruyn (Eds.), *Reinventing critical pedagogy: Widening the circle of anti-oppressive education* (pp. 3–20). Lanham: Rowman & Littlefield.
Allen, R. L. (2007). Whiteness and critical pedagogy. In Z. Leonardo (Ed.), *Critical pedagogy and race*. Oxford: Blackwell.

Anderson, C. R. (2015). What are you? A CRT perspective on the experiences of mixed race persons in 'postracial' America. *Race, Ethnicity and Education,* *18*(1), 1–19.

Balibar, E. (1991). Is there a 'neo-racism'? In E. Balibar & I. Wallerstein (Eds.), *Race, class, nation: Ambiguous identities.* New York: Verso Books.

BBC News. (2015, June 19). Charleston shooting: Who are US white supremacists? http://www.bbc.co.uk/news/world-us-canada-33198061

Bell, D. (1992). *Faces at the bottom of the well: The permanence of racism.* New York: Basic Books.

Bell, D. (1995). Serving two masters: Integration ideals and client interests in school desegregation litigation. In K. Crenshaw, N. Gotanda, G. Peller, & K. Thomas (Eds.), *Critical race theory: The key writings that formed the movement* (pp. 5–20). New York: The New Press.

Bell, D. (2005). In R. Delgado & J. Stefancic (Eds.), *The Derrick Bell reader.* New York: New York University Press.

Berry, T. R., & Stovall, D. O. (2013). Trayvon Martin and the curriculum of tragedy: Critical race lessons for education. *Race, Ethnicity and Education, 16*(4), 587–602.

Brown, K. D. (2014). Teaching in color: A critical race theory in education analysis of the literature on preservice teachers of color and teacher education in the US. *Race, Ethnicity and Education, 17*(3), 326–345.

Burke, K. J., & Gilbert, B. R. (2016). Racing tradition: Catholic schooling and the maintenance of boundaries. *Race, Ethnicity and Education, 19*(3), 524–545.

Cabrera, N. L. (2011). Using a sequential exploratory mixed-method design to examine racial hyperprivilege in higher education. In K. A. Griffin & S. D. Museus (Eds.), *Using mixed-methods approaches to study intersectionality in higher education* (New directions for institutional research, no. 151, pp. 77–91). San Francisco: Jossey.

Cabrera, N. L. (2014). Exposing whiteness in higher education: White male college students minimizing racism, claiming victimization, and recreating white supremacy. *Race, Ethnicity and Education, 17*(1), 30–55.

Ciccariello-Maher, G. (2013). *We created Cháccvez: A people's history of the Venezuelan revolution.* Durham/London: Duke University.

Cole, M. (1986). Teaching and learning about racism: A critique of multicultural education in Britain. In S. Modgil et al. (Eds.), *Multicultural education: The interminable debate.* Barcombe: The Falmer Press.

Cole, M. (2008, November 29). *Maintaining "the adequate continuance of the British race and British ideals in the world": Contemporary racism and the challenges for education.* Bishop Grosseteste University College Lincoln: Inaugural Professorial Lecture.

Cole, M. (2009). *Critical race theory and education: A Marxist response* (1st ed.). New York/London: Palgrave Macmillan.

Cole, M. (2011). *Racism and education in the U.K. and the U.S.: Towards a socialist alternative.* New York/London: Palgrave Macmillan.

Cole, M. (2013). Marxism. In P. L. Mason (Ed.), *Encyclopedia of race and racism* (2nd ed., Vol. 3, pp. 117–124). Detroit: Macmillan.

Cole, M. (2014). Racism and antiracist education. In D. C. Phillips (Ed.), *Encyclopedia of educational theory and philosophy.* London: Sage.

Cole, M. (2016). *Racism: A critical analysis.* London/Chicago: Pluto Press/ University of Chicago Press.

Cole, M. (2017). *Critical race theory and education: A Marxist response* (2nd ed.). New York/London: Palgrave Macmillan.

Delgado, R. (2001). Two ways to think about race: Ref lections on the Id, the ego, and other reformist theories of equal protection. *Georgetown Law Review, 89.* Available http://findarticles.com/p/articles/mi_qa3805/is_200107/ai_ n8985367/pg_2. Accessed 26 Mar 2008.

Delgado, R. (2003). Crossroads and blind alleys: A critical examination of recent writing about race. *Texas Law Review, 82,* 121.

Delgado, R., & Stefancic, J. (2001). *Critical race theory: An introduction.* New York: New York University Press.

Delgado Bernal, D., Burciaga, R., & Flores Carmona, J. (2012). Chicana/Latina *Testimonios*: Mapping the Methodological, Pedagogical and Political. *Equity, Excellence and Education, 45*(3): 363–372.

DePouw, C. (2012). When culture implies deficit: Placing race at the center of Hmong American education. *Race, Ethnicity and Education, 15*(2), 223–239.

Du Bois, W. E. B. (1948). The talented tenth memorial address. *The Boule Journal, 15*(1). http://sigmapiphi.org/home/the-talented-tenth.php

Dunning-Lozano, J. L. (2016). Race and opportunity in a public alternative school. *Race, Ethnicity and Education, 19*(2), 433–460.

Freire, P. (2007, June 5). *Paulo Freire—Karl Marx* (subtitled), Video. http:// www.youtube.com/watch?v=pSyaZAWIr1I&feature=related

Gillborn, D. (2008). *Racism and education: Coincidence or conspiracy?* London: Routledge.

Grillo, T., & Wildman, S. M. (1997). Obscuring the importance of race. The implication of making comparisons between racism and sexism (or other isms). In A. K. Wing (Ed.), *Critical race feminism: A reader.* New York: New York University Press.

Hall, S. (1992). Cultural studies and its theoretical legacies. In L. Grossberg, C. Nelson, & P. Treichler (Eds.), *Cultural studies* (pp. 277–294). New York: Routledge.

Harpalani, V. (2012, March). Professor Derrick Bell: "Radical humanist". *The Black Commentator,* 464. http://www.blackcommentator.com/464/464_ bell_harpalani_guest_share.html

Hetherington, R., & Reid, G. B. R. (2010). *The climate connection: Climate change and modern human evolution.* Cambridge: Cambridge University Press.

Johnson-Ahorlu, R. N. (2012). The academic opportunity gap: How racism and stereotypes disrupt the education of African American undergraduates. *Race, Ethnicity and Education, 15*(5), 633–652.

Khalifa, M., Dunbar, C., & Douglas, T. (2013). Derrick Bell, CRT, and educational leadership 1995–present. *Race, Ethnicity and Education, 16*(4), 489–513.

Kohli, R. (2014). Unpacking internalized racism: Teachers of color striving for racially just classrooms. *Race Ethnicity and Education, 17*(3), 367–387. http://www.tandfonline.com/doi/full/10.1080/13613324.2013.832935

Kohli, R., & Solorzano, D. G. (2012). Teachers, please learn our names!: Racial microaggressions and the K-12 classroom. *Race, Ethnicity and Education, 15*(4), 441–462.

Kovel, J. (1988). *White racism: A psychohistory*. London: Free Association Books.

Ladson-Billings, G. (1994). What we can learn from multicultural education research. *Educational Leadership, 51*, 22–26.

Ladson-Billings, G., & Tate, W. F. (1995). Towards a critical race theory of education. *Teachers College Record, 97*(1), 47–68.

Leonardo, Z., & Harris, A. P. (2013). Living with racism in education and society: Derrick Bell's ethical idealism and political pragmatism. *Race, Ethnicity and Education, 16*(4), 470–488.

Lippi-Green, R. (2006). Language ideology and language prejudice. In E. Finegan & J. R. Rickford (Eds.), *Language in the USA*. Cambridge: Cambridge University Press.

Lynn, M. (2010). 'Exorcising critical race theory' again: Reflections on being an Angry Black Man in the academy. In S. Jackson & R. Johnson III (Eds.), *The black professoriat: Negotiating a habitable space in the academy* (pp. 199–214). New York: Peter Lang.

Lynn, M., Jennings, M. E., & Hughes, S. (2013). Critical race pedagogy 2.0: Lessons from Derrick Bell. *Race, Ethnicity and Education, 16*(4), 603–628.

Marable, M. (2004). Globalization and Racialization. *ZNET*. https://zcomm.org/znetarticle/globalization-andracialization-by-manning-marable/

Marable, M. (2008). Blackness beyond boundaries: Navigating the political economies of global inequality. In M. Marable & V. Agard-Jones (Eds.), *Transnational blackness: Navigating the global color line* (pp. 1–8). New York: Palgrave Macmillan.

Marx, K., & Engels, F. (1848 [1977]). Manifesto of the Communist Party. In *Marx and Engels selected works in one volume*. London: Lawrence and Wishart.

Matsuda, M., Lawrence, C., Delgado, R., & Crenshaw, K. W. (1993). *Words that wound: Critical race theory, assaultive speech and the first amendment*. Boulder: Westview Press.

McIntosh, P. (1988). *White privilege and male privilege: A personal account of coming to see correspondences through work in women's studies* (Working paper No. 189). Wellesley: Wellesley College Center for Research on Women.

McLaren, P. (2015). *Pedagogy of insurrection: From resurrection to revolution*. New York: Peter Lang.

Milner, H. R., IV, & Howard, T. C. (2013). Counter-narrative as method: Race, policy and research for teacher education. *Race, Ethnicity and Education, 16*(4), 536–561.

Mitchell, K. (2013). Race, difference, meritocracy, and English: Majoritarian stories in the education of secondary multilingual learners. *Race, Ethnicity and Education, 16*(3), 339–364.

Monzó, L. D. (2015). Afterword. In P. McLaren (Ed.), *Pedagogy of insurrection: From resurrection to revolution*. New York: Peter Lang.

Motta, S., & Cole, M. (Eds.). (2013). *Education and social change in Latin America*. New York/London: Palgrave Macmillan.

Motta, S., & Cole, M. (2014). *Constructing twenty-first century socialism in Latin America*. New York/London: Palgrave Macmillan.

Oppenheimer, S. (2012). A single southern exit of modern humans from Africa: Before or after Toba? *Quaternary International, 258*, 88–99.

Pakendorf, B., & Stoneking, M. (2005). Mitochondrial DNA and human evolution. *Annual Review of Genomics and Human Genetics, 6*, 165.

Pierce, C. (1970). Offensive mechanisms. In F. Barbour (Ed.), *The black seventies*. Boston: Porter Sargent.

Rose, S., & Rose, H. (2005, April 9). Why we should give up on race: As geneticists and biologists know, the term no longer has meaning. *The Guardian*. https://www.theguardian.com/world/2005/apr/09/race.science

Senna, D. (1998). The mulatto millenium. In C. O'Hearn (Ed.), *Half and half: Writers on growing up biracial and bicultural* (pp. 12–27). New York: Pantheon Books.

Siverwright, S. (2015, August 4). The "Real Eve". Scientist in Limbo. http://scientistinlimbo.com/2015/08/04/the-real-eve/

Smith, H. J., & Lander, V. (2012). Collusion or collision: Effects of teacher ethnicity in the teaching of critical whiteness. *Race, Ethnicity and Education, 15*(3). doi:10.1080/13613324.2011.585340.

Solórzano, D. G., & Yosso, T. J. (2002). Critical race methodology: Counter-storytelling as an analytical framework for education research. *Qualitative Inquiry, 8*(1), 23–44.

Solórzano, D., Allen, W. R., & Carroll, G. (2002). Keeping race in place. Racial microaggressions and campus racial climate at the University of California, Berkeley. *Chicano-Latino Law Review, 23*(15).

Tatum, B. D. (1992). Talking about race, learning about racism: The applications of racial identity development theory. *Harvard Educational Review, 62*(1), 1–25.

Urrieta, L., & Villlenas, S. A. (2013). The legacy of Derrick Bell and Latino/a education: A critical race testimonio. *Race, Ethnicity and Education, 16*(4), 514–535.

Viola, M. J. (2016). W.E.B. Du Bois and Filipino/a American exposure programs to the Philippines: Race class analysis in an epoch of 'global apartheid'. *Race, Ethnicity and Education, 19*(3), 500–523.

CHAPTER 6

Racialized Neoliberal Capitalism and Imperialism in the Era of Austerity and Immiseration

Introduction

In Cole (2017, chapter 7), I begin by explaining that capitalism, from a Marxist perspective, is, *by definition*, a system in which a minority (the capitalist class) exploits the majority (the working class) by extracting surplus value from their labour power (this is developed in chapter 8 of Cole 2017). I go on to point out that, in *The Communist Manifesto*, Marx and Engels (1848 [1977], pp. 37–39) argued that capitalism has an inbuilt tendency to constantly expand. In the twenty-first century, I go on, following Chris Harman (2008, p. 11), global capitalism rests on the unplanned interaction of thousands of multinationals and a small number of nation states, and resembles a traffic system with no lanes, signs, traffic lights, speed restrictions or even a code that everyone has to drive on the same side of the road.

As noted in chapter 2 of this volume, I then argue that global capitalism in the twenty-first century is pre-eminently neoliberal. Neoliberalism means the rule of the market; the cutting of public expenditure; reducing state regulation of the economy (deregulation); privatization; and replacing the concept of 'the public good' with 'individual responsibility' (Martinez and García 2000, cited in Cole 2017, p. 159).

The first experiment in applied neoliberal theory began on September 11, 1973, in Chile when a US-backed military coup resulted in the death of democratically elected socialist Salvador Allende and his replacement by the brutal dictatorship of General Augusto Pinochet. Within a five-

© The Author(s) 2017
M. Cole, *New Developments in Critical Race Theory and Education*,
DOI 10.1057/978-1-137-53540-5_6

year period (1970–1975), the Chilean economy shifted from a command economy (the state in control of major industries) to neoliberalism. As Jonathan Barton explains the military junta was crucial in this process, with harsh repression and the banning of trade unions making labour power very flexible with respect to wages and discipline (1999, p. 66, cited in Lawton 2012). As such, Chile became a haven for multinationals, and wealth disparities between the rich and poor increased.

As Thomas G. Clark (2012) points out, after the 'success' of the Chilean neoliberal experiment, the instillation and economic support of right-wing military dictatorships to impose neoliberal economic reforms became unofficial US foreign policy.

The first of the democratically elected neoliberals was Margaret Thatcher (herself a friend and great fan of Pinochet—in 1999 she thanked him for bringing 'democracy to Chile'—BBC 1999[1]) in the UK and Ronald Reagan in the USA, who both set about introducing ideo-logically driven neoliberal reforms, such as the complete withdrawal of capital controls by UK Tory Chancellor Geoffrey Howe and the deregu-lation of the US financial markets. By 1989 the ideology of neoliberalism was enshrined as the economic orthodoxy of the world as undemocratic Washington-based institutions such as the International Monetary Fund (IMF), the World Bank and the US Treasury Department signed up to a ten-point economic plan. This epitomized neoliberal ideology, and as such included trade liberalization, privatization, financial sector deregula-tion and tax cuts for the wealthy (Clark 2012). As Clark concludes, 'this agreement between anti-democratic organisations is misleadingly referred to as "The Washington Consensus"' (Clark 2012). The signing of the General Agreement on Trade in Services (GATS) in 1994 gave global neoliberalism a major boost by removing any restrictions and internal government regulations in the area of service delivery that were consid-ered 'barriers to trade'.

The word 'neoliberal' itself, however, did not enter the socioeconomic vocabulary until November 1999 with the momentous protest against the World Trade Organization in Seattle. As Chris Harman (2008) points out, it is not to be found in earlier works dealing with the same phenomenon, such as David Harvey's *The Condition of Postmodernity* (Harvey 1989), or Harman's own book (Harman 1995).

As noted in the Introduction to this volume, since neoliberal capital-ism is actively complicit in the destruction of the environment and given the fact that the survival of the planet and thus any existing or potential social and economic system is at stake, the ecosystem must be a consistent and constant focus for the Left, including twenty-first-century socialists. I therefore begin this chapter with a discussion of global environmental destruction

I go on to look at the consolidation and hegemony of imperialism and racialized world capitalism. I conclude with a consideration of the effects of austerity/immiseration on the working classes of the UK and the USA in general, and the racialized fractions of those classes in particular. (Neo-) Marxism, I would argue, is well-placed to analyse these interconnections.

GLOBAL ENVIRONMENTAL DESTRUCTION

The future of the planet must be seen in terms of possible global environmental destruction, and in Cole 2017 (pp. 160–162) I discuss the damage reeked on agricultural land, the destruction of the rain forests, genetic modification and global warming. With respect to this last crucial issue, upon which depends our very existence, not least as a human species, around the time of the 2015 United Nations Climate Change Conference in Paris in November/December, 2015. *Sky News* issued the following warning:

If the World Temperature Rises by Two Degrees Mountain glaciers and rivers will begin to disappear and mountainous regions will witness more landslides, as the permafrost (thick layer of soil beneath the surface that stays below freezing point) that held them together melts away.

By 2100, sea levels could rise by a metre, displacing 10 % of the world's population. Countries such as the Maldives will be submerged, and the Indian subcontinent left fighting for survival. People will also die in greater numbers as it gets hotter and hotter.

The ecosystem will collapse and a third of all life on earth will face extinction. Plant growth will first slow, and then stop. Plants do not absorb carbon dioxide very well so they will begin to emit it, making global warming worse.

The world's food centres will become barren and, within under 100 years, one-third of the planet will be without fresh water.

If the World's Temperature Rises by Two to Three Degrees Up to 40 % of the Amazon rainforest will be destroyed and warmer soil will kill vegetation and release more carbon.

Hurricanes will be stronger and cities in Asia, Australia and the southeast of the USA will face destruction. Holland will be torn apart by the North Sea.

Saltwater will creep upstream, poisoning the groundwater (water present beneath the Earth's surface), ruining the food supply.

If the World's Temperature Rises by Three to Four Degrees Millions of people will begin to flee from coastal areas, cities will begin to vanish and some will become islands.

The ice at both the South and the North Pole will vanish and this could see a rise in sea levels of as much as 50 m, although this may take hundreds or thousands of years.

China, a major producer of the world's rice, wheat and maize, could see its agriculture fail, needing to feed more than a billion people on two-thirds of its current harvest.

Summers will be longer and soaring temperatures will see forests turn to firewood, with the south of Britain's reaching 45°C. The increased demand on air-conditioning will put massive pressure on the country's power grid.

If the World's Temperature Increases by Six Degrees Rainforests will be deserts and massive numbers of migrants will flock to the few parts of the world they see as habitable.

Stagnant oceans mean more hydrogen sulphide, which kills the sea-life and, if the sea heats up enough, massive stores of methane hydrate under the sea will begin to escape. Methane is flammable and the smallest spark or lightning strike could see fireballs tearing across the sky. Explosions greater than a nuclear bomb could destroy life on earth entirely.

Sulphur dioxide in the atmosphere will continue to weaken the ozone layer, leaving all remaining life exposed to extreme levels of ultraviolet (UV) radiation, a major source of skin cancer (Sky News 2015).

As Penny Cole (2015) points out, the Paris climate talks ended with an agreement claiming a global commitment to a 1.5°C temperature rise under pressure from worldwide public opinion, including millions whose homes will disappear if action is not taken. The figure, she goes on, was pulled, like a rabbit out of a hat, to show that governments take this issue seriously. Moreover, Climate Action & Energy Commissioner Miguel Arias Cañete admitted that he has no idea such a figure will be achieved (cited in P. Cole 2015). All there is really is the figure and a commitment to come together again in 2018 to check progress and seek advice on doing more (P. Cole 2015). Cole explains that none of the commitments on emissions are legally- = binding, and, in reality we are still facing a rise of between 2.5°C and 3°C, which will have severe consequences if the *Sky News* figures are accurate.

Moreover, 2015 was the hottest year since records began in 1850, the average global temperature being 0.75°C higher than the long-term average between 1961 and 1990, and much higher than in 2014, which was itself a record. This, according to climatologists, shows that global warming is driving the world's climate into 'uncharted territory' and is indicative of the urgency to implement the carbon-cutting pledges (cited in Carrington 2016, p. 14). The temperature in 2015 was already 1°C higher than that agreed in Paris (Carrington 2016, p. 14).

Political leaders know they must act but are unable to do what is required:

> And that's because action—real action—to reduce emissions would require a break from capitalism, the unsustainable, growth-based, profit-driven system that has brought us to this disaster...[to a system]...community-led, democratically-decided, not-for-profit and based on renewables. (P. Cole 2015).

THE CONSOLIDATION AND HEGEMONY OF IMPERIALISM AND RACIALIZED WORLD CAPITALISM[2]

As Chris Marsden argues, for almost a quarter of a century since the dissolution of the Soviet Union and the reintroduction of capitalism in Russia and China world imperialism has been seeking to take advantage to bring about what President George Bush senior proclaimed in 1991 to be the 'new world order' (Marsden 2015). As Bush put it, the end of the 1990–1991 Gulf War against Iraq (when coalition forces from 34 countries led by the USA attacked Iraq in response to its invasion and annexation of Kuwait) would herald a world 'where diverse nations are drawn together in common cause to achieve the universal aspirations of mankind [sic]—peace and security, freedom, and the rule of law' (George Bush senior, cited in Marsden 2015).

Since Bush senior's pledge, the major imperialist powers have visited destruction and death on millions of people—overwhelmingly Muslims and people of colour—in wars in the Balkans, the Middle East, Central

Asia and Africa. In the words of the International Committee of the Fourth International (2014), '[t]ime and again they have proven their indifference to human suffering'. Shortly after 9/11 (September 11, 2001) George W. Bush junior declared the 'war on terror.' The purpose of this 'war,' as Chris Marsden (2015) argues, both in its international and in its domestic manifestations, is 'to provide a political rationale for the re-division of the world between the major imperialist powers'. Military interventions in Afghanistan, Iraq, Libya, Syria and elsewhere, he goes on, have taken place to install puppet regimes in order to secure control of oil, gas and other geostrategic resources, as part of an attempt at global hegemony. In the course of these bloody conflicts, the 'imperialist powers have rained down bombs on defenceless civilians, carried out torture and assassination, and committed war crimes. Entire countries have been ravaged' (Marsden 2015).

In the Iraq War (2003–2011) alone, according to a 2013 report by university researchers in the USA, Canada and Baghdad in cooperation with the Iraqi Ministry of Health, in stark contrast to Bush senior's promise of peace, security, freedom and the rule of law, nearly half a million people are estimated to have died from war-related causes in Iraq since the US-led invasion in 2003 (Sheridan 2013). According to lead author, Amy Hagopian, violence caused most of the deaths, but about a third were indirectly linked to the war, and these deaths have been left out of previous counts (cited in Sheridan 2013).

Imperialism's reach is boundless. All the imperialist powers, the International Committee of the Fourth International (2014) argues, including the USA and the UK, are taking a full role in the 'struggle for spheres of influence'. 'Every area of the globe', it goes on, 'is a source of bitter conflict: not only the former colonies and semi-colonies in the Middle East, Africa and Asia but also the Arctic, Antarctic and even outer space and cyberspace'.

With respect to racism at home and the predicament of minority and immigrant communities, Marsden states:

> No one can seriously believe...[imperialism's] actions do not have a profound impact on domestic political life. In a globalised world economy, where populations have become more ethnically and nationally diverse, the indignation created by imperialism's crimes knows no borders. This is especially the case within the minority and immigrant communities that have

borne the brunt of attacks on workers' living conditions, leaving millions without work and faced with conditions of desperate poverty. (Marsden 2015)

The orchestrated removal of socialism from the political agenda, Marsden concludes, 'has created conditions in which the most disoriented and desperate elements can be steered toward terrorism as a way of protesting the social, political and cultural oppression they face' (Marsden 2015). While the state has, of course, to respond to acts of terrorism perpetrated by racialized, exploited and oppressed minorities, its form of response, such as aggressive surveillance of Muslim communities, especially when accompanied by the ongoing 'war on terror,' often aids in the recruitment to fascistic organizations such as so-called 'Islamic State' ('IS'), which gives further impetus to the 'war on terror' and to clampdowns at home by the Repressive Apparatuses of the State. All this takes place within the context of global Islamophobia, itself intensified by the Ideological Apparatuses of the State, such as the media. Islamophobia itself leads to further recruitment to organizations like 'IS'.[3]

This analysis is not meant to imply a deterministic relationship whereby imperialism overseas and actions at home by capitalist states and their accompanying state apparatuses are alone responsible for organizations such as the so-called 'Islamic State', since IS's existence has to be seen as an entity in its own right that its supporters view as a coherent 'religious/political' belief system. Rather, it is to make the point that without a credible alternative to capitalism on the agenda, such as socialism, 'IS' and/or similar groups will continue to find alienated and disillusioned recruits, especially among the ranks of the racialized working classes.

With respect to the working class as a whole (racialized and non-racialized), while the 'war on terror' goes on and on overseas and at home, austerity/immiseration capitalism means that it 'would be a fundamental political error to believe that the vast repressive apparatus being assembled is to be used against only one section of the population', since everywhere, 'the working class is being reduced to penury as jobs are destroyed, wages slashed, exploitation ramped up and vital social services destroyed' (Marsden 2015).

Five years before Bush senior's promise of a 'new world order', Margaret Thatcher stated in 1986, '[p]opular capitalism is nothing less than a crusade to enfranchise the many in the economic life of the nation. We Conservatives are returning power to the people' (Thatcher 1986). Some 30 years later, there are no signs of economic enfranchisement empowering the people. In 2014/2015, the International Labour Organization (ILO) compiled the Global Wage Report. As Patrick Martin argues, perhaps the most devastating revelation in the report is the following statement: 'Overall, in the group of developed economies, real wage growth lagged behind labour productivity growth over the period 1999 to 2013.' This means, Martin points out, that throughout this 14-year period, the share of national income going to the working class declined, while the share of national income going to the tiny minority of capitalists steadily increased (Martin 2014).

All the world conflicts, the International Committee of the Fourth International (2014) argues, breed the tensions that lead to 'ethnic divisions' and communal fighting. The Committee refers to the fundamental contradictions of the capitalist system between the development of a global capitalist economy and the division of the world into antagonistic nation states, in which the private ownership of the means of production is rooted. Capitalism is not capable of organizing the world economy rationally:

> The collision of imperialist and national state interests expresses the impossibility, under capitalism, of organising a globally-integrated economy on a rational foundation and thus ensuring the harmonious development of the productive forces. However, the same contradictions driving imperialism to the brink provide the objective impulse for social revolution. The globalisation of production has led to a massive growth of the working class. Only this social force, which owes no allegiance to any nation, is capable of putting an end to the profit system, which is the root cause of war. (International Committee of the Fourth International 2014)

Commenting on calls from sections of the ruling class, such as the Coalition for Inclusive Capitalism, to be wary of escalating inequalities, Damon (2015) concludes: 'Warnings about the growth of inequality are rooted in fears within the financial aristocracy that the ever more obvious and repulsive gap between the super-rich and everyone else will have revolutionary consequences.' I return to a discussion of the potential of revolutionary socialism in the twenty-first century in chapter 7 of this volume.

AUSTERITY/IMMISERATION CAPITALISM
AND THE RACIALIZED WORKING CLASS

Critical Race Theory and Education: A Marxist Response (Cole 2009, **2nd edition**, 2017) was written before the effects of the global financial crisis of 2007/2008. In the UK, the USA and most other capitalist countries, the crisis was seized upon by the ruling class as an opportunity to bail out the bankers and the ruling class in general, and to make the working class pay for the crisis. Neoliberal capitalism in its austerity/immiseration mode has wreaked havoc on the working class in general, and on the racialized working class in particular.

The vast and growing gap between rich and poor was laid bare in an Oxfam Report early in 2016 showing that the 62 richest billionaires own as much wealth as the poorer half of the world's population (in 2010, it was the 388 richest owning as much, and in 2014, just 80), with 1 % owning more wealth than the other 99 % combined. In addition, the wealth of the poorest 50 % dropped by 41 % between 2010 and 2015, despite an increase in the global population of 400 m. In the same period, the wealth of the richest 62 people increased by $500 bn (£350 bn) to $1.76 tn (cited in Elliott 2016). The figures give credence to Thomas Piketty's (2014) warning of a drift back to the levels of wealth concentration of the nineteenth century.

Oxfam cited estimates that rich individuals have placed a total of $7.6 tn in offshore accounts, adding that if tax were paid on the income that this wealth generates, an extra $190 bn would be available to governments every year. Moreover, it is estimated that tax dodging by multinational corporations cost developing countries at least $100 bn a year (cited in Elliott 2016).

With respect to Africa, 30 % of all its financial wealth is thought to be held offshore. The estimated loss of $14 bn in tax revenues would be enough to pay for healthcare for mothers and children that could save 4 million children's lives a year and employ enough teachers to get every African child into school (cited in Elliott 2016).

This growth of inequality is, of course, directly related to the ruling class's response to 2007/2008 and the insolvency of major banks which were to pump some $12 tn dollars into the financial markets via bank bailouts, near-zero interest rates and central bank money-printing (known as quantitative easing) (Damon 2015). As Andre Damon puts it:

This virtually free cash was used to drive up the world's stock markets and corporate profits to record highs. The same governments and central banks pursued brutal austerity policies against the working class, driving tens of millions into poverty. (Damon 2015)

As Damon (2015) goes on, emblematic of the parasitism of global capital, 'the financial and insurance sector minted more billionaires than any other industry'.

Moreover, as Sandra Polaski, ILO's Deputy Director-General for Policy, explains, '[w]age growth has slowed to almost zero for the developed economies as a group in the last two years, with actual declines in wages in some' (cited in Martin 2014). To take the UK as a prime example, as Gerry Gold (2014) argues, 'the austerity we've seen so far [is] only the warm-up for the main event':

The scale of future cuts proposed by the Tories is so vast and almost unimaginable that it's impossible to envisage any government carrying them through without provoking massive social and civil unrest. In effect, the ConDems...[in December, 2014] declared all-out war on the people. Left unstated by chancellor George Osborne, the political choices are as stark as a further 60% reduction in the state's budget the chancellor set out in his autumn statement. Osborne was short on detail. No wonder. The Tories are talking about taking government spending back to the levels last seen in the 1930s, when a global slump prefigured a second world war. (Gold 2014)

As Gold (2014) continues, austerity is patently self-destructive—'of people's lives and livelihoods, jobs and services. But it's all capitalism can come up with.'

Martin notes that currently nearly 200 million workers are unemployed worldwide, and that another 400 million will enter the job market looking for work in the next decade. How, he asks, 'will capitalism provide 600 million new jobs under conditions of worldwide economic stagnation? What wages will be offered? What will be the working conditions? What will be the level of exploitation?' (Martin 2014).

Racialized Fractions of the Working Class in the UK

It is overwhelmingly the racialized fractions of the working classes of the UK and the USA whose resulting poverty is greatest. As far as the UK is concerned, Paul Fisher and Alita Nandi (2015) describe how the impact of the 2008 recession and subsequent austerity measures affected the economic well-being of different ethnic groups. The study conducted by the Joseph Rowntree Foundation compared household income, access to goods and services for achieving a reasonable standard of living and poverty status. Some of the main findings were as follows:

- Much higher rates of persistent poverty and material deprivation for the Pakistani and Bangladeshi groups, followed by Black African and Black Caribbean groups.
- Employment rates fell among both females and males in the Black Caribbean, Black African and Other White (a diverse collection of people with different countries of birth, religions and languages) groups. For the rest, employment rates fell for men but rose for women, particularly among Bangladeshis. As a result of this, the proportion of couples with both adults in paid work increased among Pakistani, Bangladeshi and Chinese groups by 7–15 percentage points. Unemployment rates increased, mostly for younger people. For older workers, the hours worked fell.
- Average incomes fell across all groups except Pakistanis, whose average household incomes increased slightly (after deducting housing costs). This can possibly be explained by the fact that Pakistani men's employment rate increased. Those seeing the largest relative falls in average income were Chinese (30 %) followed by Black African, Indian and Other White (10 %). For the white majority, Black Caribbean and Bangladeshi groups, incomes fell by 3–4 %.
- For most groups, drops in income from earnings and investments caused falls in household income.
- The safety net provided by social security benefits and tax credits helped to offset part of the fall in earnings. Falls in deductions (including taxes) had a similar effect.
- Housing costs increased most for the Chinese and Other White groups, who had the highest percentage of private renters (Fisher and Nandi 2015; see Cole 2016, chapter 1 for a discussion of colonialism and its legacy in the UK).

Racialized Fractions of the Working Class in the USA

As Rakesh Kochhar and Richard Fry (2014) argue, with respect to the USA, the 2007/2008 crises in the housing and financial markets fuelled what they describe as 'The Great Recession', a recession that 'was universally hard on the net worth of American families…[but]…wealth inequality has widened along racial and ethnic lines'. Referring to the Pew Research Center analysis of data from the Federal Reserve's Survey of Consumer Finances (Board of Governors of the Federal Reserve System 2013), they note that the wealth of white households was 13 times the median wealth of black households in 2013, compared with eight times the wealth in 2010. Likewise, the wealth of white households was then more than ten times the wealth of 'Hispanic households', compared with nine times the wealth in 2010.

The gap between blacks and whites, they go on, has reached its highest point since 1989, when whites had 17 times the wealth of black households, while the 'white-to-Hispanic' wealth ratio has reached a level not seen since 2001. (Asians and other 'racial' groups, they point out, are not separately identified in the public-use versions of the Federal Reserve's Survey) (Kochhar and Fry 2014).

The net worth of American families overall—the difference between the values of their assets and liabilities—stayed steady during the economic recovery, with the typical household having a net worth of $81,400 in 2013, almost the same as what it was in 2010, when the median net worth was $82,300 (values expressed in 2013 dollars). The stability in household wealth follows a dramatic drop during the Great Recession. From 2007 to 2010, the median net worth of American families decreased by 39.4 %, from $135,700 to $82,300. Rapidly plunging house prices and a stock market crash were the immediate contributors to this huge fall (Kochhar and Fry 2014).

The Pew Center's analysis of Federal Reserve data reveals, however, a stark divide in the experiences of white, black and 'Hispanic' households during the economic recovery. From 2010 to 2013, the median wealth of non-Hispanic white households increased from $138,600 to $141,900 (2.4 %), while the median wealth of non-Hispanic black households fell 33.7 %, from $16,600 in 2010 to $11,000 in 2013. Among 'Hispanics', median wealth went down by 14.3 %, from $16,000 to $13,700. For all families—white, black and Hispanic—median wealth is still less than its pre-recession level (Kochhar and Fry 2014).

A number of factors, they go on, seem to be responsible for the widening of the wealth gaps during the economic recovery. As the Board of Governors of the Federal Reserve System, (2013) notes, the median income of minority households (blacks, 'Hispanics' and other non-whites combined) fell 9 % from its 2010 to 2013 surveys, compared with a decrease of 1 % for non-Hispanic white households. The reasons for this are that minority households may not have replenished their savings as much as white households or they may have had to draw down their savings even more during the recovery.

In addition, financial assets, such as stocks, have recovered in value more quickly than housing since the recession ended. White households are much more likely than minority households to own stocks directly or indirectly through retirement accounts. Thus, they were in a better position to benefit from the recovery in financial markets. All American households since the recovery have started to reduce their ownership of key assets, such as homes, stocks and business equity. But the decrease in asset ownership tended to be proportionally greater among minority households. For example, the home ownership rate for non-Hispanic white households fell from 75.3 % in 2010 to 73.9 % in 2013, a percentage drop of 2 %. Meanwhile, the home ownership rate among minority households decreased from 50.6 % in 2010 to 47.4 % in 2013, a drop of 6.5 % (Kochhar and Fry 2014).

While the current wealth gaps are higher than at the beginning of the recession, they are not at their highest levels as recorded by the Board of Governors of the Federal Reserve System's survey. Peak values for the wealth ratios were recorded in the 1989 survey—17 for the white-to-black ratio and 14 for the white-to-Hispanic ratio. However, those values of the ratios may be anomalies driven by fluctuations in the wealth of the poorest—those with net worth less than $500. Otherwise, Kochhar and Fry (2014) conclude, the racial and ethnic wealth gaps in 2013 are at or about their highest levels observed in the 30 years for which we have data (see Cole 2016, chapter 2 for a discussion of historical and contemporaneous racism in the USA).

Mass inequality is of course a global product of racialized neoliberal capitalism and imperialism. Unless capitalism and imperialism are successfully challenged, the racialized workers and communities who bear the greatest brunt in the present will also bear the maximum burden in the future. Fearful of the response from workers worldwide, the 'ruling classes of the world are preparing accordingly, heaping up weapons, building armies of police, intensifying their attacks on democratic rights and spying on the entire population of the world'(Martin 2014). As argued earlier in this chapter, the 'war on terror' provides part of the justification for this.

CONCLUSION

As Corinna Lotz (2016) has argued, new contradictions have emerged in place of those set out by Lenin in the period of classic imperialism. For Lenin (1917 [2002], p. 85), imperialism was 'merely monopoly capitalism' and imperialist war was 'the eve of socialist revolution' (p. 89). Corporate-driven globalization means, however, that the capitalist state has shed most of its democratic façade. Where once national industries could be subjected to some form of state control, today the major corporations are transnational by ownership and operation (Lotz 2016). As Lotz puts it, these industries 'are effectively beyond the reach of the state. Traditional finance capital has given way to 24-hour electronic trading of bonds, derivatives, currencies and commodities.' 'The state in advanced capitalist countries like Britain', she concludes, 'has gone through a major transformation, moving from a representative democratic welfare state to a market-state corporatocracy', with the state's 'main function [being] to ensure conditions for the smooth running of global corporations'.

At the same time, imperialism has not given way to world social revolution, but has consolidated itself and brought death and misery to millions, mainly people of colour, for the profits and hegemony of the imperialist powers.

Having looked at the origins and nature of neoliberalism or neoliberal capitalism and the way it is complicit in the destruction of the environment and of how in its austerity/immiseration mode in particular it impacts transatlantically on workers in general, and on the racialized fractions of that class in particular, and at the consolidation and hegemony of imperialism and racialized world capitalism, in the last chapter I turn to a consideration of Critical Race Theory (CRT) and Marxist visions of the future.

NOTES

1. Thatcher's meeting with Pinochet in 1999 was broadcast live. A particularly chilling moment was when the former announced that she was now going to have a private meeting with the general. Goodness knows what was discussed behind closed doors.
2. This section of the chapter draws on the Conclusion to Cole (2016).

3. Socialists must be constantly vigilant against any attempt to legitimize Islamophobia as a reasonable response to threats to non-Muslim and Muslim communities alike, whether real (as with 'IS') or fabricated (as with Saddam Hussein's 'weapons of mass destruction').

REFERENCES

Barton, J. (1999). Chile. In J. Buxton & N. Phillips (Eds.), *Case studies in Latin American political economy*. Manchester: Manchester University Press.

Board of Governors of the Federal Reserve System. (2013). *2013 survey of consumer finances*. http://www.federalreserve.gov/econresdata/scf/scfindex.htm

Carrington, D. (2016, January 21). Global temperatures highest for 165 years. *The Guardian*.

Clark, T. G. (2012). What is neoliberalism? http://anotherangryvoice.blogspot.co.uk/2012/09/what-isneoliberalism-explained.html

Cole, M. (2009). *Critical race theory and education: A Marxist response* (1st ed.). New York/London: Palgrave Macmillan.

Cole, M. (2016). *Racism: A critical analysis*. London/Chicago: Pluto Press/University of Chicago Press.

Cole, M. (2017). *Critical race theory and education: A Marxist response* (2nd ed.). New York/London: Palgrave Macmillan.

Cole, P. (2015, December 15). Paris climate agreement is diplomatic fudge. *A World to Win*. http://www.aworldtowin.net/blog/Paris-climate-agreement-is-diplomatic-fudge.html

Damon, A. (2015, January 26). Oxfam: Richest one percent set to control more wealth than the bottom 99 percent. *World Socialist Web Site (WSWS)*. http://www.wsws.org/en/articles/2015/01/20/oxfa-j20.html

Elliott, L. (2016, January 18). Richest 62 people as wealthy as half world's population combined. *The Guardian*. http://www.theguardian.com/business/2016/jan/18/richest-62-billionaires-wealthy-half-world-population-combined?utm_source=esp&utm_medium=Email&utm_campaign=GU+Today+main+NEW+H&utm_term=151527&subid=14322859&CMP=EMCNEWEML6619I2

Fisher, P., & Nandi, A. (2015, March 25). *Poverty across ethnic groups through recession and austerity*. York: Joseph Rowntree Foundation. https://www.jrf.org.uk/report/poverty-across-ethnic-groups-through-recession-and-austerity

Gold, G. (2014, December 4). Osborne's declaration of war on the people. *A World to Win*. http://www.aworldtowin.net/blog/Osbornes-declaration-of-war-on-the-people.html

Harman, C. (1995). *Economics of the madhouse: Capitalism and the market today*. London: Bookmarks.

Harman, C. (2008). Theorising neoliberalism. *International Socialism, 117*(Winter). https://www.marxists.org/archive/harman/2008/xx/neolib.htm

Harvey, D. (1989). *The condition of postmodernity: An enquiry into the origins of cultural change.* Oxford: Blackwell.

International Committee of the Fourth International. (2014, July 3). Socialism and the fight against imperialist war. *World Socialist Web Site (WSWS)*. https://www.wsws.org/en/articles/2014/07/03/icfi-j03.html

Kochhar, R., & Fry, R. (2014, December 12). Wealth inequality has widened along racial, ethnic lines since end of Great Recession. *PewResearchCenter.* http://www.pewresearch.org/fact-tank/2014/12/12/racial-wealth-gaps-great-recession/

Lawton, L. (2012). Liam's Labrynth. https://liamos85.wordpress.com/2012/07/12/a-critical-assessment-ofthe-impact-of-neoliberalism-on-the-chilean-state-during-the-pinochet-regime-1973-1989/

Lenin, V. I. (1917) [2002]. *On Utopian and scientific socialism: Articles and speeches.* Amsterdam: Fredonia Books.

Lotz, C. (2016). Hello Lenin! *A World to Win.* http://www.aworldtowin.net/transition/helloLenin.html

Marsden, C. (2015, January 14). Imperialist war, the 'war on terror' and the end of democracy. *World Socialist Web Site (WSWS)*. https://www.wsws.org/en/articles/2015/01/14/pers-j14.html

Martin, P. (2014, December 6). The state of world capitalism: Labor productivity up, real wages down. *World Socialist Web Site (WSWS)*. https://www.wsws.org/en/articles/2014/12/06/pcrs-d06.html

Martinez, E., & García, A. (2000). What is "Neo-Liberalism" A brief definition. *Economy*, 101. http://www.globalexchange.org/campaigns/econ101/neoliberalDefined.html

Marx, K., & Engels, F. [1848] (1977). The Communist Manifesto. In K. Marx & F. Engels (Eds.), *Selected works in one volume.* London: Lawrence and Wishart.

Piketty, T. (2014). *Capital in the twenty-first century.* Cambridge, MA: Harvard University Press.

Sheridan, K. (2013, October 15). Iraq Death Toll Reaches 500,000 Since Start of U.S.-Led Invasion, New Study Says. *The World Post.* http://www.huffingtonpost.com/2013/10/15/iraq-death-toll_n_4102855.html

Sky News. (2015). *What will happen as the world gets warmer?* http://news.sky.com/story/1604441/what-will-happen-as-the-world-gets-warmer

Thatcher, M. (1986, October 10). Speech to Conservative Party Conference. *Margaret Thatcher Foundation.* http://www.margaretthatcher.org/document/106498

CHAPTER 7

CRT and Marxist Visions of the Future

INTRODUCTION

Having set the context, following *Critical Race Theory and Education: A Marxist Response* (Cole 2009, **2nd edition,** 2017), of this current volume on new developments in Critical Race Theory (CRT) and Education in chapter 2, I went on to focus on the 'Race Traitor' movement, assessing its relevance to CRT and Marxism in the twenty-first century (chapter 3). I then critically assessed transatlantic theoretical developments in CRT and education in the UK (chapter 4), and in the USA (chapter 5). Finally, in chapter 6, I considered racialized neoliberal capitalism and imperialism in the era of austerity. In this final chapter I look to CRT and Marxist visions of the future, contrasting the vagaries of CRT with some concrete twenty-first socialist ones. I begin by contrasting the CRT concept of 'race consciousness' with the Marxist theory of 'class consciousness'. I go on to look at CRT notions of 'race consciousness' and the Marxist formulation of 'class consciousness' before turning my attention to CRT and Marxist visions of the future. With respect to the latter, I then look at developments in the Bolivarian Republic of Venezuela, focusing on the promotion of antiracism in that country. I conclude with a consideration of the election of Jeremy Corbyn to the leadership of the UK Labour Party and the candidacy of Bernie Sanders in the 2016 US presidential election, posing the question, has socialism moved from the margins to the mainstream in the capitalist heartland?

© The Author(s) 2017
M. Cole, *New Developments in Critical Race Theory and Education*,
DOI 10.1057/978-1-137-53540-5_7

'RACE CONSCIOUSNESS' OR CLASS CONSCIOUSNESS

Some Critical Race Theorists discussed in this volume, such as Warmington (2012) and Agosto et al. (2015), make use of the concept of 'race consciousness'. What they mean by this seems to be one of the central tenets of CRT, namely, that we should always be conscious of the importance of 'race' and its centrality in any analysis of oppression; that we live in institutionally racist societies; and that 'colour-blind' approaches to social justice (ignoring skin colour) actually serve to exacerbate racism.

While *neo*-Marxists, as demonstrated throughout this volume and the previous one (Cole 2009, **2nd edition,** 2017), acknowledge institutional racism and reject colour-blind approaches, for neo-Marxists and for more traditional Marxists, the fundamental form of consciousness in capitalist society is 'class consciousness'. This is because, as I argued in chapter 2 of this volume (and in the previous volume), capitalism relies for its very existence on class exploitation. Marx (1845) argued that language, like consciousness, only arose from the need, the necessity, of interaction between human beings. As Robert Lanning (2007) explains, if language is more than merely speaking, consciousness is more than simply being awake. As far as *class* consciousness is concerned, he goes on, if we ask the question, '"What is class consciousness?" we might also ask, "How do we get it?" and "What do we do once we have it?"' The advantage of a Marxist answer to the first question, Lanning points out, is that it also answers the other two. Furthermore, in answering the first question we get a better understanding of what Marxists mean by class, namely, our relationship to the means of production: oversimplifying matters, there are those who sell their labour power in order to live (the working class) and the owners of the means of production who live off the products of that labour power (the capitalist class). It is the interests of the latter to exploit the former as much as is possible in given historical and material circumstances, and in the interests of the latter to resist this. As Marx (1845) put it, 'Separate individuals form a class only insofar as they have to carry on a common battle against another class.' It is this dimension of social class that differentiates it from its use in intersectionalist analyses by Critical Race Theorists, as discussed in chapter 4 of this volume, where class is employed *merely* as a form of identity among a number of others, such as 'race' and gender.

Bertell Ollman (1993, cited in Lanning 2007) identifies six features of class consciousness:

- Subjective and objective manifestations (how people view their class situation and their relationship to the means of production)
- An understanding of this objective inherently hostile relationship
- Where one fits into this relationship of exploitation and struggle
- Solidarity with other class members
- Rational hostility to the capitalist class who will extract as much labour power from the workers as they can get away with, irrespective of human cost
- Having a Vision of a different non-exploitative society

Bullet points 1–5 could be adapted to 'race consciousness,' substituting 'class' for 'race,' and swopping Marxist with CRT terminology. The sixth, however, cannot, since Critical Race Theorists have no vision of the future beyond rhetoric, albeit progressive rhetoric.

CRT VISIONS OF THE FUTURE

In chapter 2 of this volume, I point out that in Cole (2017, p. 240) I note how Critical Race Theorists are vague about what the future should entail, quoting Crenshaw et al. (1995) and Dixson and Rousseau (2006). The same degree of vagueness is apparent in many of the more recent developments in CRT theorizing as discussed in chapters 4 and 5 of this volume. Kevin Hylton (2012), for example, refers, as we have seen, to 'social justice'; 'a challenge to oppression and subordination'; 'praxis orientation'; 'activist scholarship'; 'a participatory approach'; and 'challenging the passive reproduction of established questions and practices', while Kara Mitchell (2013, p. 341) advocates, in a similar vein, disputing 'majoritarian stories' and encouraging 'transformative research and pedagogy, in order to agitate the status quo'. Neither discusses capitalist *exploitation* or makes links to the economic and political realities of austerity/immiseration capitalism, and neither articulates a vision of the future.

According to Christin DePouw (2012, p. 225): 'CRT is...activist in nature, insisting on critical race work that is part of broader movements toward social justice.' Moreover, she ends her article, as discussed in chapter 5 of this volume, by stating that a critical race consciousness can 'empower Hmong American students to take meaningful action toward the betterment of their lives and of the communities in which they live' (DePouw 2012, p. 237). But no indication is given of what 'betterment' will entail.

Muhammad Khalifa, Christopher Dunbar and Ty-Ron Douglas (2013, p. 507) quote Derrick Bell as stating that Critical Race Theorists 'strive for a specific, more egalitarian state of affairs' and for 'collective wisdom' (Bell 1995, p. 901, cited in Khalifa et al., p. 507). Khalifa et al. do not elaborate on what this 'specific' is. Bell (1982) is also cited by Marvin Lynn, Michael Jennings and Sherick Hughes when, addressing law students and comparing them to slaves, Bell urges them to 'revolt' against authority. Once again there are no indications of what this may contribute to revolutionary practices or what will follow the revolution.

Finally, Celia Rousseau Anderson (2015, p. 8), following Delgado and Stefancic (2001), argues that only colour-conscious efforts to change the 'ordinary business' of society will relieve 'racial' injustice and inequity. What form this relief will take is left unanswered.

Given that 'race' is a social construct, in place of 'race'-conscious, it might be better to use the term 'racialization-conscious', since, as stressed throughout this volume, the neo-Marxist concept of racialization connects to economic and political factors, and to the way in which different groups are racialized, or in the case of Eastern Europeans, xeno-racialized, in different historical conjunctures. We also need to be 'Islamophobia-conscious',[1] and aware of the way in which Islamophobia is related to imperialism and to the 'war on terror', as discussed in chapter 6 of this volume.[2]

MARXIST VISIONS OF THE FUTURE

While CRT visions of the future lack any degree of specificity, Marxist solutions to exploitation, oppression and inequality are unequivocal in the insistence on the need for a world beyond capitalism. What then should be the nature of such a world? It is a common misunderstanding that Marxists believe in 'an ideal world', in a utopia, a blueprint for the future. How often has one heard in response to the arguments of Marxists, the 'common sense' reply: 'it sounds all right in theory, but it won't work in practice'? Marxists are actually anti-utopia. Within socialist theorizing, utopianism is, in fact, the province of the eighteenth-/nineteenth-century utopian socialists such as Henri de Saint-Simon, Charles Fourier and Robert Owen rather than the scientific socialism of Marx and Engels.[3] While, as I argue at the end of this chapter, socialism has been given a boost in the UK by the election of Jeremy Corbyn to the leadership of the Labour Party, and in the USA by the candidacy of Bernie Sanders, we cannot envisage a precise outline of what socialism might look like in these two societies. It is, nevertheless, useful and informative to examine actually existing attempts to create socialism, and I will now look at one of the most successful. I have already stressed the needs for twenty-first-century socialism to distance itself from Stalinism, and to encompass all equality issues. The Bolivarian Republic of Venezuela, to which I have made a number of references in this volume, while under serious threat at the time of completing this volume (Spring 2016), has historically exhibited an awareness of these needs.

In Cole (2017, chapter 8), I discuss developments in Venezuela, which are supplemented by further analysis in chapter 2 of this volume (for a more comprehensive general analysis, see chapter 3 of Motta and Cole 2014). Here I will concentrate on antiracism there and what comes next for that country in the light of the December 2015 election results.

ANTIRACISM IN VENEZUELA

There have been many advances for the indigenous and Afro-descendant peoples since the first presidency of Chávez in 1999. Since then, while significant obstacles and problems remain, major strides have been made to enhance the rights of Venezuela's indigenous and Afro-descendant communities (see Martinez et al. 2010, pp. 193–219). These measures should serve as an example to all of antiracism in practice, in the context of socialism in the making.

As I noted in Cole (2009, **2nd edition**, 2017, p. 204), as Chávez himself put it:

> We've raised the flag of socialism, the flag of anti-imperialism, the flag of the black, the white and the Indian...I love Africa. I've said to the Venezuelans that until we recognise ourselves in Africa, we will not find our way...We have started a hard battle to bring equality to the African descendants, the whites and the indigenous people. In our constitution it shows that we're a multicultural, multiracial nation. (Chávez 2008, cited in Campbell 2008, p. 58)

Indigenous Peoples[4]

In September 2014, the Venezuelan chapter of the Indigenous Parliament of America completed final details of a report on the levels of inclusion of original peoples in Venezuela communities. Indigenous Peoples were excluded for more than 500 years following the arrival of the colonizers. The report was presented at the World Summit on Indigenous Peoples at the United Nations held in September in New York City.

The document systematized all the policies fostered by Chávez since 1999. Indigenous leader César Sanguinetti revealed the racist nature of the 1961 Constitution of Venezuela that had only one chapter on Indigenous Peoples and gave the State gradual responsibility for incorporating Indigenous Peoples into 'civilization' (cited in Telesur 2014). Now, however, reflected in the Constitution of 1999, each original people 'has its own cosmovision and its own culture'. Sanguinetti also stated that 'the revolutionary process has recognized the ancestral rights of the autochthonous communities and promoted their full inclusion'. During the 15 years of the Bolivarian Revolution, he concluded, actions taken to protect Indigenous People 'are not only included in the constitutional juridical framework, but have also been consolidated through the application of effective policies', an example of which is a Ministry with jurisdiction over the affairs of indigenous communities and peoples, one that is 'unique in Latin America' (cited in Telesur 2014).

Mision Guaicaipuro seeks to restore territorial titles and human rights to the numerous autochthonous settlements in the country and exists to consolidate the Bolivarian Republic as multi-ethnic and intercultural. Its objectives are to:

• Demarcate and title the habitat and lands of Indigenous Peoples and communities.
• Promote the harmonious and sustainable development of Indigenous Peoples, within a vision that respects their different ways of conceiving that development.
• Promote the integral development of Indigenous Peoples to ensure the effective enjoyment of their social rights (health, education, housing, water and sanitation), cultural, economic and political rights in the Constitution of the Bolivarian Republic of Venezuela.
• Promote, develop and implement policies to settle the historical debt to organized indigenous communities, and generate the greatest amount of happiness.

Mision Guaicaipuro provides comprehensive healthcare and implements organizational tools for project ideas, and for the demarcation of indigenous lands and the formation of community councils to promote socialism (Gobierno Bolivariano de Venezuela, undated).

With respect to language, while Spanish is Venezuela's primary language, indigenous languages are also used officially for Indigenous Peoples and must be respected throughout the Republic's territory. The 1999 constitution also affirms that exploitation by the state of natural resources must be subject to prior consultation with the native communities, that Indigenous Peoples have the right to an education system of an intercultural and bilingual nature and the right to control ancestral knowledge over 'native genetic resources' and biodiversity. Three indigenous representatives are ensured seats in the country's National Assembly.

In October 2014, to celebrate Indigenous Resistance Day, Maduro established a presidential council for Indigenous Peoples, formed as a result of elections held in over 2000 indigenous communities after the idea was discussed in over 1500 countrywide assemblies. Delia Gonzalez, a spokesperson for the Wayúu community of Zulia state, noted that the debates leading up to the council's creation were conducted with respect, tolerance and spirituality, with the aim of enabling diverse Indigenous Peoples to make significant contributions to the transition towards socialism (cited in Dutka 2014).

Maduro also handed over collective land titles to 14 original communities. From 2011 to 2013 the Committee for the Demarcation of Land and Habitat, of the indigenous ministry, signed 40 property titles for collective lands, including over 1.8 million hectares of land (Dutka 2014). In addition, he lowered the threshold age for indigenous pensions to age 50, compared nationally to women over 55 and men over 60 who live in family homes maintained by minimum wage workers (Dutka 2014).

Maduro further announced the creation of an institute to protect the country's 44 native languages. Cognizant of the loss of some indigenous languages, Maduro proclaimed: 'We should immediately found and motivate a team systematically [that can] permanently, scientifically, register, rescue and revive all indigenous languages that exist in Venezuelan territory' (cited in Dutka 2014). Finally, Maduro announced over four and a half million pound investment to address extreme poverty in nearly 400 indigenous communities, and also promised 5000 new homes of Indigenous Peoples to be built in 2015 via Mision Vivienda (Dutka 2014).

Demonstrating its commitment to indigenous Venezuelans, as at the beginning of 2015, the Ministry of People's Power for Indigenous Peoples had built over 3000 homes, granted over 50 common ownership land deeds, financed nearly 1500 socio-productive projects, given grants to 500 Indigenous Peoples to study through an agreement with Cuba and had completed over 250 public work projects. Overall, over half a million Indigenous People had benefited (Radio Nacional de Venezuela/ Prensa-Embaiada venezolana en EE UU 2015). In addition, the Ministry has opened public spaces for debate and people's participation, including the Indo-American Youth Congress, the Congress for Socialism and the Eradication of Poverty, the Indigenous Peoples Peace Conference, the Presidential Council on People's Government of Indigenous Peoples and Communities and Indigenous Mercosur—an offshoot of Mercosur (Common Market of the South). Indigenous Peoples have also enjoyed new opportunities in sports and culture, as with, for example, the National Indigenous Games, a sports event (Radio Nacional de Venezuela/Prensa-Embaiada venezolana en EE UU 2015).

This is not to say that all is well with respect to Indigenous Peoples in the Bolivarian Republic of Venezuela. As Lusbi Portillo, coordinator of an indigenous rights NGO, makes clear, while the government has repeatedly handed over titles, this has not always resulted in actual access and control of the land. He also expressed concern about the quality of land handed over, 98 % of which is in the mountains 'and the big growers do not want it anyways' (cited in Fischer-Hoffman 2014). Portillo is referring to the ongoing battles between Indigenous People and the wealthy who claim ownership of large amounts of land. In 2008, as Portillo points out, Chávez stated 'between the large estate owners and the Indians, this government is with the Indians' but despite an official policy of siding 'with the Indians', Portillo goes on, one of the main contemporary struggles of Indigenous Peoples is for acknowledged rights to land that has the capability of producing food and providing for habitat (cited in Fischer-Hoffman 2014). Moreover, as Cory Fischer-Hoffman (2014) explains, conflict between 'land owners' and Indigenous Peoples has resulted in murders of the latter. Fischer-Hoffman (2014) also points out that most of the land granted to Indigenous People has been granted to the Yukpa, while there are over 30 other indigenous nations in Venezuela, and some, like the Guajiro (also known as Wayúu), remain landless.

As Portillo explains, the Yukpa have used land occupations as a means of asserting their rights to the land, which has forced the government to the negotiating table, and has resulted in the transferring of titles specifically to Yukpa communities (cited in Fischer-Hoffman 2014). Portillo warned that, despite the fact that Chávez halted coal mining in indigenous territory as long ago as 2008, a mining company has been pushing to reopen the two mines that Chavez had shut down (cited in Fischer-Hoffman 2014). Finally, there are ongoing struggles against military bases on indigenous territory.

Despite all this, compared to the plight of indigenous Americans (see Cole 2016b, chapter 2), Venezuela has much for these countries to emulate. As Indigenous leader, former Minister for Indigenous Peoples and (ruling Socialist Party) PSUV Deputy in the 2016 National Assembly (2016) put it, 'before the Revolution, Indigenous Peoples were invisible'.

Afro-Venezuelan and Afro-Descendant Peoples

In 2005, Hugo Chávez declared May 10 as Día de la Afrovenezolanidad (Afro-Venezuelan Day), the anniversary of the insurrection of enslaved people led by Jose Leonardo Chirino in 1795. At a conference in Caracas to celebrate the day in 2014, Nirva Camacho, a spokesperson for the National Afro-Venezuelan Front, reiterated a theme expounded by many of the speakers—the racism and violence of the Venezuelan right—the Venezuelan allies of the United States whose aim, she argued, is to recolonize Venezuela. She then read from a manifesto that affirmed the Front's commitment to the struggle against colonialism, capitalism and imperialism, and in full support of President Maduro's executive actions and the Bolivarian process (Eisen 2014). Maduro noted that 'today's fascist ideas that attack society and attempt to impose a racist model of society are the same that have always denied the liberation of the peoples'. He argued that the reasoning of the Venezuelan right today is the same as those who opposed the liberation of enslaved people (Eisen 2014).

Camacho went on to call for a programme of action:

Considering that the Afro-Venezuelan and Afro-descendant population in general still confronts the lashes of racism and racial discrimination, which are incompatible with socialism and the revolution, we propose that together the state and social organizations undertake to:

1. Incorporate racism as an element of analysis in the different forums dedicated to the construction of peace, since as an ideology it is present in part of Venezuelan society, especially in the ultra right's close relation to fascism.

2. Revise communication policies in public and private media to eliminate racist bias, which would contribute to respect for our ethnic diversity...

3. Apply the organic Law against Racial Discrimination[5] to persons and/or groups who incite hatred and violence through racist demonstrations, like those expressed in the terrorism that recently has plagued Venezuelan society.

4. Design and execute a plan to identify and articulate the variable of Afro-descendant, considered in the Organic Law on Education[6] as a necessary step towards the eradication of racial discrimination in the Venezuelan educational system in order to achieve equality for future generations.

5. Encourage a cross section of ethnic perspectives as state policy, in all public and private institutions that give attention to the people.

6. Direct all levels of government and popular power from the Presidency of the Republic to those who administer government in the streets inside Afro-Venezuelan communities, at regional, municipal and grassroots levels to evaluate and respond to specific needs (housing, health, education and roads), which historically are a product of structural racism.

7. Implement an ambitious plan of constructing Camps for Peace and Life in Afro-Venezuelan communities, especially in the communities where narcotraffickers have manipulated our youth (cited in Eisen 2014).

These obstacles to indigenous and Afro-Venezuelan and Afro-descendant rights underline the crucial need for the ongoing struggle to decolonize. As Fischer-Hoffman concludes, the 'framework of decolonizing is a growing theme throughout the Americas' (Fischer-Hoffman 2014).[7]

In his closing speech to the conference, approving the principles of the manifesto, Maduro enthusiastically praised the various Venezuelan insurrections led by enslaved people as decisive turning points in Venezuela's anti-colonial, anti-imperial struggles. He declared the whole nation a 'cumbe of equality, peace and love' and went on to express admiration for cultures of resistance and happiness bred in the struggles of Afro-descendants in the Caribbean, Latin America and North America. He concluded that the government would invest an extra 550 million bolivars to strengthen systems of popular culture, especially in Afro and Indigenous communities (Eisen 2014).

Undocumented Workers

As Tamara Pearson (2014) has argued, while 'most first world and imperialist countries criminalise refugees and undocumented migrants, scapegoating them, promoting racism, and mistreating them, Venezuela welcomes migrants; and provides them with the same rights as Venezuelan citizens'. While there are some problems because of bureaucracy and racism, the Chávez and Maduro governments, she goes on, have never blamed the millions of migrants on Venezuelan soil for any of the problems the country faces. On the contrary, 'migrants—documented or not—are welcomed and receive health care, education, and other benefits' (Pearson 2014).

According to Article 13 of the Migration Law of 2003, enacted by the Chávez government, migrants 'have the same rights as nationals without any limitations' (Ley De Migración Y Extranjería, 2003, cited in Pearson 2014). Furthermore, in February of the following year, Chávez issued Presidential Decree 2,823, which instigated a national campaign to pay what he referred to as 'Venezuela's historical debt to migrants' (cited in Pearson 2014). Foreigners residing in Venezuela without documents could legalize their stay and become 'indefinite residents'. Police in Venezuela are obliged to help children without documents to get identification (Pearson 2014).

Ruben Dario, a general director at the National Experimental University for Security (UNES), a university for police officers that focuses on human rights, stated that Venezuela's migration policy 'is distinguished for being tolerant, without any kind of discrimination, solidarious, with complete respect for all migrant human rights, and for not criminalising migration' (cited in Pearson 2014).

Pearson (2014) points out that Venezuela has been taking concrete, though slow and small steps, towards a united Latin America based on cooperation between regions, and where borders either do not exist or are less prohibitive, and where no one is 'illegal'. She concludes:

> Venezuela [is] setting an example for first world countries: showing that humane treatment of all migrants, documented or not, is easy and possible. Further, that the most important thing is to not force migration: to remove borders, to have cooperative trade policies (rather than the US's

trade policies which impoverish people in Mexico, Haiti, and so on), and to not support the invasion and destruction of other countries, such as Iraq, thereby creating the refugees that countries like Australia and the US refuse to look after. (Pearson 2014)

Pearson could have added the UK to her reference to Australia and the USA as countries to whom the Bolivarian Republic of Venezuela is providing an example of compassion and humanity to all categories of migrants. Indeed, Venezuela's overall policy of interculturalism and intraculturalism, tied to decolonization, and of course to twenty-first-century socialism in the making, serves as an exemplar to the treatment of racialized minority groups per se worldwide.

The preceding analysis is not meant to idealize Venezuela as a multicultural paradise. Indeed, racism still exerts a significant blemish on society (Cole 2016a). What makes the country exceptional with respect to the combating of racism, and what totally distinguishes it from the UK, the USA and Australia, is that ever since the election of Chávez nearly 20 years ago, and continuing under Maduro, despite the 2015 election setback, the state apparatuses are consciously attempting to promote both the physical and mental welfare of racialized groups.

WHAT NEXT FOR VENEZUELA?

In a number of places, I have made references to Venezuela's uncertain future and impending challenges, following the parliamentary elections in December 2015. These elections resulted in the ruling socialist party (the PSUV) being decisively defeated by the opposition party, Democratic Unity Roundtable (MUD), for the first time since Chávez's first presidency in 1999, even though Maduro retains his presidency until 2019. Francisco Dominguez (2016) has responded to triumphalist reactions from the ruling class and its supporters that this heralds the end of the Bolivarian Revolution:

> The huge Right Wing majority in Venezuela's National Assembly has been mistakenly interpreted as having the constitutional power to dismantle the whole Bolivarian institutional and constitutional edifice that has been built over the last 17 years. This can be accomplished only if (a) it forces and wins a recall referendum against President Maduro, and/or, (b) it convenes a Constituent Assembly, which will involve the election of MPs to the

Assembly, for which it will need to win a majority and start the whole process from scratch.

Dominguez (2016) is optimistic that the revolution will continue, given that any neoliberal attempt to 'water down, undermine, reverse, or abolish any of the highly progressive gains of *Chavismo* since 1998' will highlight the stark contrasts between what has been achieved and what might lie ahead.

To reiterate, I believe that Venezuela is the best existing example of socialism *in the making*. James Suggett (2015) has reviewed five broad solutions for the Bolivarian Republic of Venezuela, in the wake of December 2015. These include 'neoliberalism, market-based reform, correction and maintenance of current policies, socialism with the state, and socialism without the state' (Suggett 2015).

Of these, it is only the last two that are worthy of consideration as progressive models by Marxists. By socialism with the state, Suggett means a continuation of the 'twenty-first century socialist model', inaugurated by Chávez. This consisted of a massive catalogue of social democratic reforms via the *misiones*, tens of social programmes targeted at the poor and providing food and nutrition, in the form of high-quality cheap products, and healthcare, which is comprehensive and free. They also ensure adequate housing—legitimating the dwellings in the barrios, as well as building new homes. The misiones give subsidies to low-income women and retirement benefits for the poor. In addition, the environment is protected; and there has been substantial rural development. Indigenous rights are secured, though there is still much work to be done, as there is with Afro-Venezuelans (see later in this chapter). All these innovations have taken place in the context of socioeconomic transformation (the promotion of production for social needs rather than profit) and the expropriation and redistribution of land.

Those misiones dealing specifically with education, all free of charge, include Mision Ribas, which provides evening remedial classes to high school dropouts; Mision Sucre, where ongoing higher education (HE) courses are given to adults; and Mision Robinson, where volunteers teach reading, writing and arithmetic also to adults. As a direct result of these education misiones, in 2005 UNESCO recognized Venezuela as country free of illiteracy. Mision Sucre caters for the university sector at the centre of which is Universidad Bolivariana de Venezuela.

Crucially, the cornerstones of socialism in the making—communal councils, communes and workplace democracy—also had the support of Chávez and continue to get backing from Maduro.[8] The specific possibilities for the 'socialism with the state' solution suggested by Suggett include:

- Progressive tax reform
- Nationalize foreign commerce
- Nationalize the banking sector
- Create a national plan for industrialization
- Reduce government waste and combat inefficiency
- Replace current council of ministers with movement leaders of demonstrated integrity
- Public audit of Petróleos de Venezuela, S.A., foreign debt and other government agencies
- Establish permanent independent auditing commission open to the public
- Protect labour with safeguards on wages, subcontracting and workplace security
- Gradually establish worker control of production, distribution and sale of goods
- Integrate a network of socialist enterprises and expand their scope to gradually take over the economy

Socialism without the state is the social movement-led alternative and entails:

- Gradually transfer control of political decisions and economic activity to organized communities
- Submit all government positions and functions to open public auditing and regular revision
- Promote cultural and political re-education to promote new socialist–humanist values
- Support occupations of factories, vacant and idle land, buildings, and other spaces by the dispossessed
- Assist in the growth and evolution of 'popular government' and fully participatory democratic economy (Suggett 2015)

Suggett (2015) concludes that what will actually happen will be a combination of all five approaches. From my own Marxist perspective, the best solution is a combination of socialism with the state and socialism without the state, but, given that socialism is a *process* rather than an event, with a progression from the former towards the latter.

Ciccariello-Maher (2016) explains why, whatever happens, the Bolivarian Revolution should be central to the Left. As he reminds us:

> There are hundreds of thousands of people in nearly 1,500 communes struggling to take control of their territories, their labor, and their lives... As the mainstream media howls about economic crisis and authoritarianism, there is little mention of the grassroots revolutionaries who have always been the backbone of the Bolivarian process. (Ciccariello-Maher 2016)

Ciccariello-Maher (2016) castigates those on the international Left 'whose dogmas and pieties creak and groan when confronted with a political process that doesn't fit, in which the state, oil, and a uniformed soldier have all played key roles'. '[N]owhere is communism pure', he goes on, 'and the challenges Venezuela's comuneros confront today are ones that we neglect at our own peril'. The revolutionary movements that 'created Chávez', he points out, 'did not simply stop there and stand back to admire their creation'. On the contrary, they 'continued their formative work in and on the world by building radically democratic and participatory self-government from the bottom-up' (Ciccariello-Maher 2016). The communes, Ciccariello-Maher informs us, are producing directly and democratically millions of tons annually of coffee, corn, plantains and bananas 'and straining upward for increased regional and national coordination'.

In an ideal scenario, long time militant and activist Roland Denis argues, 'the communes could create a productive capacity that begins to compete with capitalism, with its own internal rules and logic, and this could really progressively generate a non-state' (cited in Ciccariello-Maher 2016). 'There are some very interesting communes moving in this direction,' Denis concludes. Moreover, as former Commune Minister Reinaldo Iturriza points out, while communes need to produce, 'the commune is also something that is produced' (cited in Ciccariello-Maher 2016). Ciccariello-Maher (2016) concludes:

> As the crisis deepens and divides the state against itself, setting the opposition-controlled National Assembly against the Maduro government, anything is possible. The only certainty is that the tipping point is rushing forth to greet

us, and Chavismo will either move decisively to the left or retreat to the right. But retreat would be as cowardly as it is naïve—as goes the commune, so goes the Bolivarian Revolution as a whole. As Chávez himself often put it, the choice on the table is increasingly between *la comuna o nada*, the commune or nothing.

SOCIALISM IN THE CAPITALIST HEARTLAND: FROM THE MARGINS TO THE MAINSTREAM?

In chapter 6, I examined, from a (neo-)Marxist perspective, racialized neoliberal capitalism and imperialism in the era of austerity and immiseration. Lest the analysis in that chapter appears overly depressing and fatalistic, it is worth stressing the inherent fragility of capitalism as a system, a vulnerability on which Glenn Rikowski (2015) has elaborated (see also Holloway 2015). The election of socialist Jeremy Corbyn to the leadership of the British Labour Party is also an encouraging reminder of the fragility of the political superstructure that upholds capitalism.[9] Corbyn's campaign agent and Shadow Chancellor John McDonnell declared soon after Corbyn's victory that they had 'changed the world…changed the Labour Party and…opened up a whole opportunity now to change our country' (*Independent*, 12 September).

Corybyn's remarkable landslide victory (nearly 60 % at the first round of votes) has indeed changed the Labour Party. His policy commitments—renationalizing the railways; bringing back the 50 % tax rate for the top 1 % of earners; opposing Trident and wars generally; rent controls; a mandatory living wage; and scrapping tuition fees and reintroducing maintenance grants for university students—represent a renewed and revitalized social democratic politics, and a move away from austerity/immiseration capitalism (Corbyn's insistence that austerity and poverty are not inevitable itself signifies a major shift in Labour Party policy). If implemented, these initiatives, welcome to the public in general as they are to socialists (to be distinguished from social democrats), will further change the politics of the Labour Party, as they change the fundamental nature of British society.

Equally important for socialists is the fact that socialist arguments have now become mainstream, rather than the province of a tiny handful of revolutionaries. In its constituency parties as well as among a small handful of MPs, the Labour Party is now on course for the opening up of serious discussions about socialist transformation not just of Britain, but of the world. Such discussions will include the nationalization of the main levers of the economy, the large landed estates, the national and transnational monopolies and all the private banks, under the democratic control of the working class. For true socialism to become viable, there is a need for a fundamental transfer and redistribution of wealth from the rich to the poor—that which has been missing from the Bolivarian Revolution.

Corbyn's well-documented support for equal rights and equality for all, including a firm commitment to antiracism, is a standard tenet of twenty-first-century socialism, as opposed to its twentieth-century Stalinist incarnation which celebrated white working class heterosexual able-bodied men (see chapter 2 of this volume). In the course of his victory speech, Corbyn also made reference to another fundamental difference between twentieth- and twenty-first-century socialism—the foregrounding of ecology, what some have referred to as ecosocialism (see chapter 2 of this volume).[10]

For Corbyn, politics should not be primarily about charisma or the lack of it among party leaders, but power to the people. And this is what the ruling class fears most. Thus Michael Fallon, the defence secretary, was quick to warn of risks to economic security, weakening 'our defences', and, astonishingly, 'hurting working people'. Since his election to the leadership of the Labour Party, attacks on Corbyn from the ruling class and their supporters in parliamentary parties, including the Labour Party, and the media have continued unabated.

On the other side of the Atlantic, early in 2016, Democratic Presidential Candidate Bernie Sanders, who describes himself as a democratic social-ist,[11] gave a major speech in which he pledged:

> We will no longer tolerate an economy and a political system that has been rigged by Wall Street to benefit the wealthiest Americans in this country at the expense of everyone else…Our goal must be to create a financial system and an economy that works for all Americans, not just a handful of billion-aires. (Sanders 2016)

He went on to argue that the 'reality is that Congress doesn't regulate Wall Street. Wall Street, its lobbyists and their billions of dollars regulate Congress', that this must be changed and that as president he will change that reality (Sanders 2016).

'We live in a country today', he stated, that has an economy that is rigged, a campaign finance system which is corrupt and a criminal justice system which, too often, does not dispense justice.' 'Not one major Wall Street executive', he stressed, 'has been prosecuted for causing the near collapse of our entire economy.'

Like Corbyn Sanders favours people power. He concluded:

> Finally, let me tell you what no other candidate will tell you. No president… can effectively address the economic crises facing the working families of this country alone. The truth is that Wall Street, corporate America, the corporate media and wealthy campaign donors are just too powerful. What this campaign is about is building a political movement which revitalizes American democracy, which brings millions of people together—black and white, Latino, Asian-American, Native American—young and old, men and women, gay and straight, native born and immigrant, people of all religions. Yes. Wall Street has enormous economic and political power…They have an endless supply of money. But we have something they don't have. And that is that when millions of working families stand together, demanding fundamental changes in our financial system, we have the power to bring about that change. Yes, we can make our economy work for all Americans, not just a handful of wealthy speculators.

As with Corbyn, there is fear and panic among the ruling class.[12] The lead editorial in the January 20, 2016, *Wall Street Journal*, 'Taking Sanders Seriously,' warned:

> [I]t's no longer impossible to imagine the 74-year-old socialist as the Democratic nominee. Many Republicans claim to welcome a Sanders nomination on the assumption he'd be easy to beat. But don't be so sure, at least not this year…the possibility of an extreme election outcome is no longer unthinkable. (cited in Eley 2016)

As journalist David Millward (2015) points out, there were 'striking similarities in the Sanders and Corbyn campaigns…with both being regarded as rank outsiders when they entered their respective contests'. As Millward explains, it was assumed that both represented the views of a small minority of left-wingers, 'and most observers saw their candidacies as doing little more than widening the debate in the leadership elections':

> But their appeal appears to have caught 'establishment' candidates on both sides of the Atlantic by surprise as…[they ride] a tidal wave of grass roots support.

> In Britain, attempts by the Labour hierarchy to head off Mr Corbyn's rise to the party leadership proved completely ineffective. The lessons of what happened with the Labour Party are being digested in Washington where there are already signs of panic within the Democrat establishment as they see Mr Sanders' poll ratings soar.

The living project of twenty-first-century socialism—crucially bringing socialism from the margins to the mainstream—has no doubt been given a boost by the election of Jeremy Corbyn, and by the prominence given to Bernie Sanders, and, albeit in a small way, has changed the world.

As Tom Eley (2016) has argued:

> There is an objective significance to the growth of popular support for a candidate who inveighs against social inequality and calls himself a socialist in a country where anti-communism has for the better part of a century been a state religion in all but name. For decades, socialism has been politically quarantined in America. Socialist views have been excluded from political discourse in the corporate-controlled media. A battery of anti-democratic election laws make it virtually impossible for a socialist opponent of the two big business parties to obtain ballot status.

'That under such conditions', Eley goes on, 'Sanders has won a level of popular support that he, least of all, anticipated, reflects a broad shift to the left and political radicalization among working people and youth.' 'Tens of millions in America', he points out, 'are disgusted with the existing economic and political set-up and are looking for a radical alternative' (Eley 2016).

That the elevation of Sanders, irrespective of whether he gets the Democratic Party nomination, should be a cause for celebration for the Left is explored by Brad Bauerly and Ingar Solty (2016) in that his campaign 'politicized the usually completely depoliticized American presidential elections of neoliberal candidates of various shades vaguely promising "hope" and "change" and "conservative values"'. 'The Left has won', he goes on, 'by enforcing a debate about capitalism and its surface symptomology income and wealth inequality.' It is a victory for the Left since it has pulled out into the open:

> how this obscene inequality is corrupting liberal democracy, how it has created an oligarchic power structure and how only a comprehensive strategy of conflict-oriented social movements at all levels—the workplace, the

street, and the political/parliamentary system, i.e. a revolutionary realpolitik (Rosa Luxemburg) inside and against the state, which is aimed at shifting the balance of forces between capital and labour, can undo it. And it has won by clearly demarcating the divide between the left in the US and the neoliberal wing of the Democratic Party. (Bauerly and Solty 2016)

'Bernie', they go in, in an observation that could apply equally to the U.K. Labour Party, 'has opened up future possibilities by exposing the rift in the party. In fact, we quite possibly will look back at this as the moment of the break with neoliberalism of the party'.

'[T]he most remarkable achievement, the American left has won', they conclude, is the placing of 'Sanders' concrete left-wing social–democratic and/or transformative transition demands in the American political landscape and imagination', with the entire world 'watching how the anti-neoliberal left is now suddenly capable of building majorities around transformative transition programs', sending 'shivers down the spines of current and former third way social–democratic party leaders all across the core capitalist countries' and 'realistically posing the question of (political) power—and not only in the "imperialist chain's weakest links,"...such as Greece, but also in the very heart of the core capitalist countries and the American Empire' (Bauerly and Solty 2016).

I will conclude with a comment by Dan Baiz, the chief correspondent of the influential *Washington Post*, on the similarities in the Corbyn and Sanders campaigns:

In a time of economic insecurity and an anti-establishment mood among so many voters here and elsewhere, the unexpected is no longer unthinkable... If Clinton's problems and Sanders's success are part of a surprising summer of politics here, the Corbyn victory was even more unthinkable only a few months ago after Labour suffered a historic defeat in the general election. (Baiz, cited in Millward 2015).

In case, because of my positive comments about political developments in the UK and the US Labour and Democratic Parties, I am misinterpreted and/or misrepresented by some future socialist reviewer of this book as advocating a solution in social democratic politics, let me state categorically that I am not suggesting that either of these successes will create socialism in the UK or the USA, let alone the world. What they represent, however, is proof that the living project of twenty-first-century socialism is no longer at the margins of Western society.

NOTES

1. I would argue that we need to have a separate category of 'Islamophobia-conscious', since, though a hybridist form of *racism*, Islamophobia is primarily based on (perceived) religious affiliation, unlike antisemitism, for example, which is based on perceived 'racial' denigration as well as religion. Achieving 'racialization consciousness', and eliminating racialization also obviates the need for a category of 'mixed race persons'—the subject of Anderson's chapter.
2. As we saw in chapters 2 and 4, Critical Race Theorists Gillborn and Housee also show awareness of the relationship between the 'war on terror' and Islamophobia.
3. For Engels, Saint-Simon's major contribution to Marxism was his recognition of class struggle; Fourier's was dialectical thinking (see endnote 50); and Owen's was communism (living communally) and his dedication to workers' welfare. What the utopian socialists had in common was a belief that social change was to come about by 'peaceful means', by 'small experiments' and by 'force of example' (Marx and Engels 1977 [1847], p. 60). Marx and Engels, however, believed that socialism could only come about by the 'overthrow of all existing social conditions' (p. 63). The 'scientific socialism' of Marx and Engels is based on the materialist conception of history (all history with the exception of its most early stages— 'primitive communism', the original hunter-gatherer society of humanity—is the history of class struggles (Engels 1977 [1892], pp. 394–428) and on the Labour Theory of Value (the source of capitalists' profits is surplus value appropriated from workers who do not get the full fruits of their labour, with the worker getting only a fraction of the value that he/she creates (for a discussion of socialism and Marxist theory, see Cole 2008, chapter 2).
4. The following analysis of Indigenous Peoples, Afro-descendants and 'Undocumented Workers' draws on Cole (2016a).
5. This was passed in May 2011.
6. The objective of the 2009 law is 'to guarantee our people a free, accessible, liberatory, and secular education that definitively guarantees teacher stability and autonomy'. To accomplish this, the Law redefines the structure of the education system and its constituent parts. Specifically, Article 20 emphasizes the community role in education, including parents, teachers, administrative workers, labourers, and community organizations in the definition of

the educational community. Families are given the responsibility of instilling certain enumerated values and principles in their children as part of the joint education effort between families, schools, society, and the state (cited in Arnoldy 2010, p. 875).

7. Fischer-Hoffman notes that in 2014 the Seattle City council unanimously voted to change Columbus Day to 'Indigenous People's Day', becoming the first city in the USA to do so.

8. It should be pointed out that not all socialist groupings are supportive of Maduro. Marea Socialista (MS) left the PSUV in 2015. One of its members, César Romero, explains the organization's reasons. After the 'peace talks' in 2014 (negotiations between the government and key business leaders convened by Maduro) in response to the wave of protests by middle and upper class young people, following Chávez's death in 2013, Maduro was faced with a decision. He could either make alliances with the dominant groups or radicalize the process to preserve the support of its social base. According to Romero, he chose the former in order to stay in power. This resulted in new anti-popular measures such as tax cuts for business and new Special Economic Zones where companies do not have to abide by labour laws or pay any taxes. The main difference between the governments of Chávez and Maduro, Romero concludes, is that when there was a crisis under Chávez the workers never paid the consequences but under Maduro they do (María and Romero 2016).

9. The following analysis of the Corbyn victory is derived from Cole (2015).

10. This remark was made while thanking former leader Ed Miliband for his passion for defending the environment. At the same time Corbyn referred to Ed's 'late father the great Ralph Miliband', the Marxist academic. Corbyn was commenting on the dignified way Miliband junior responded to the vilification of his father by the right-wing media because of Miliband senior's Marxist politics, part of the personality politics that has dominated parliamentary elections and from which Corbyn has totally distanced himself. Personality politics is, of course, also a fundamental feature of the U.S. political landscape.

11. In an unfortunate incident, and in response to a Hilary Clinton email which linked him to Chávez, Sanders described three-times elected Chávez, who presided over an election process described

by ex-US president Jimmy Carter as 'the best in the world' (The Real News 2012) as 'a dead communist dictator' (Koerner 2015). Sanders' comments regarding the election of Corbyn were more enlightened: 'At a time of mass income and wealth inequality throughout the world, I am delighted to see that the British Labour Party has elected Jeremy Corbyn as its new leader. We need leadership in every country in the world which tells the billionaire class that they cannot have it all. We need economies that work for working families, not just the people on top' (Millward 2015).

12. As Tony Green has pointed out, this is by no means unanimous, with some sections of the ruling class viewing Corbyn's success as the final demise of the Labour Party (his comments on this volume).

REFERENCES

Anderson, C. R. (2015). What are you? A CRT perspective on the experiences of mixed race persons in 'postracial' America. *Race, Ethnicity and Education, 18*(1), 1–19.

Bauerly, B. A., & Solty, I. (2016, March 19). Sanders and the left after super tuesday—Why there is still hope and why the left should rejoice and push forward. *Links International Journal of Socialist Renewal*, reposted from *Socialist Project*. http://links.org.au/node/4645

Bell, D. (1982). One dean's perspective – The law student as slave. *Student Law, 11*, 18.

Bell, D. (1995). Serving two master: Integration ideals and client interests in school desegregation litigation. In K. Crenshaw et al. (Eds.), *Critical race theory: The key writings that formed the movement*. New York: New Press.

Ciccariello-Maher, G. (2016, March 23). Venezuela: ¡Comuna o Nada! *Links International Journal of Socialist Renewal*. Reposted from *ROAR Magazine* with permission. http://links.org.au/node/4646

Cole, M. (2008, November 29). *Maintaining "the adequate continuance of the British race and British ideals in the world": Contemporary racism and the challenges for education*. Bishop Grosseteste University College Lincoln: Inaugural Professorial Lecture.

Cole, M. (2009). *Critical race theory and education: A Marxist response* (1st ed.). New York/London: Palgrave Macmillan.

Cole, M. (2016a). Imperialism and racialised world capitalism or intercultural twenty-first century socialism. *Knowledge Cultures, 4*(6).

Cole, M. (2016b). *Racism: A critical analysis*. London/Chicago: Pluto Press/University of Chicago Press.

Cole, M. (2017). *Critical race theory and education: A Marxist response* (2nd ed.). New York/London: Palgrave Macmillan.

Crenshaw, K., Gotanda, N., Peller, G., & Thomas, K. (1995). Introduction. In K. Crenshaw, N. Gotanda, G. Peller, & K. Thomas (Eds.), *Critical race theory: The key writings the formed the movement.* New York: New Press.

Delgado, R., & Stefancic, J. (2001). *Critical race theory: An introduction.* New York: New York University Press.

DePouw, C. (2012). When culture implies deficit: Placing race at the center of Hmong American education. *Race, Ethnicity and Education, 15*(2), 223–239.

Dixson, A. D., & Rousseau, C. K. (2006). Introduction. In A. D. Dixson & C. K. Rousseau (Eds.), *Critical race theory in education: All god's children got a song.* New York: Routledge.

Dominguez, F. (2016, January 27). Right wing majority in Venezuela's National Assembly: The constitutional and political stakes. *The Huffington Post.* http://www.huffingtonpost.com/dr-francisco-dominguez/right-wing-majority-in-ve_b_9069350.html

Dutka, Z. C. (2014, October 15). Maduro Hands Over Land Titles to Indigenous Communities, Creates Institute to Protect Native Languages. *venezuelanalysis.com.* https://venezuelanalysis.com/news/10964Fischer-Hoffman is cited in an earlier chapter

Eisen, A. (2014, March 27). Racism Sin Vergüenza in the Venezuelan Counter-Revolution. *Venezuelanalysis.com.*

Eley, T. (2016, January 26). Growing support for Sanders highlights US political crisis. *World Socialist Web Site (WSWS).* http://www.wsws.org/en/articles/2016/01/26/dems-j26.html

Engels, F. (1977) [1892]. Socialism utopian and scientific. In K. Marx & F. Engels (Eds.), *Selected works in one volume.* London: Lawrence and Wishart.

Holloway, J. (2015). We are the fragility of the system, John Holloway interviewed by Fiona Jeffries. In F. Jeffries (Ed.), *Nothing to lose but our fear.* London: Zed Books.

Hylton, K. (2012). Talk the talk, walk the walk: Defining critical race theory in research. *Race, Ethnicity and Education, 15*(1), 23–41. doi:10.1080/13613324.2012.638862.

Khalifa, M., Dunbar, C., & Douglas, T. (2013). Derrick Bell, CRT, and educational leadership 1995–present. *Race, Ethnicity and Education, 16*(4), 489–513.

Koerner, L. (2015, September 17). US Presidential hopeful Bernie Sanders Slams Chávez in reposte to Clinton attack. *Venezuelanalysis.* http://venezuelanalysis.com/news/11511

Lanning, R. (2007, March). What is class consciousness. *Political Affairs, 86*(3). https://sites.google.com/site/lanningrd/what-is-class-consciousness-3

Ley De Migración Y Extranjería. (2003). http://www.derechos.org.ve/pw/wpcontent/uploads/ley_migraci%C3%B3n.pdf

María, E., & Romero, C. (2016, April 15). Chavismo from below. *Jacobin.* https://www.jacobinmag.com/2016/04/chavez-maduro-venezuela-mud-psuv/

Martinez, C., Fox, M., & Farrell, J. (2010). *Venezuela speaks!: Voices from the grass-roots.* Oakland: PM Press.

Marx, K. (1845). *The German ideology.* https://www.marxists.org/archive/marx/works/1845/german-ideology/ch01a.htm

Millward, D. (2015, September 14). Jeremy Corbyn backed by Bernie Sanders. *The Telegraph.* http://www.telegraph.co.uk/news/politics/Jeremy_Corbyn/11865090/Jeremy-Corbyn-backed-by-Bernie-Sanders.html

Motta, S., & Cole, M. (2014). *Constructing twenty-first century socialism in Latin America.* New York/London: Palgrave Macmillan.

Ollman, B. (1993). *Dialectical investigations.* New York: Routledge.

Pearson, T. (2014, April 10). Undocumented migrants in Venezuela have more rights than US citizens in the US. *venezuelanalysis.com.* https://venezuelanalysis.com/analysis/10599

Rikowski, G. (2015). *Crises, commodities and education: Disruptions, eruptions, interruptions and ruptions.* A paper prepared for the Research in critical Education Studies (RiCES) Seminar, School of Education, University of Lincoln, 19 November, online at Academia: http://www.academia.edu/18511424/Crises_Commodities_and_Education_Disruptions_Eruptions_Interruptions_and_Ruptions

Sanders, B. (2016). http://www.marketwatch.com/story/text-of-bernie-sanders-wall-street-and-economy-speech-2016-01-05

Suggett, J. (2015, December 27). Venezuela: Potential paths out of the economic crisis. *Venezuelanalysis.* http://venezuelanalysis.com/analysis/11790

Telesur. (2014, September 17). Venezuela to present report on indigenous rights at UN. *venezuelanalysis.com.* https://venezuelanalysis.com/news/10916

The Real News. (2012, October 5). *Jimmy Carter says: Election process in Venezuela is the best in the world.* http://therealnews.com/t2/?option=com_content&task=view&id=31&Itemid=74&jumival=8935

Warmington, P. (2012). "A tradition in ceaseless motion": Critical race theory and black British intellectual spaces. *Race, Ethnicity and Education, 15*(1). doi:10.1080/13613324.2012.638861

CHAPTER 8

Conclusion

In this volume, I began (chapter 2) with a retrospective look at my book *Critical Race Theory and Education: A Marxist Response* (2009; **2nd edition, 2017**), critiquing some of the book's contents, but also providing additional explanations.

I then addressed new developments in Critical Race Theory (CRT) across the pond, focusing, first, with respect to the ongoing debate between CRT and Marxism, on an important article on the 'Race Traitor' (RT) movement by leading UK Critical Race Theorists, John Preston and Charlotte Chadderton, concluding that despite their enthusiasm for the propagation of 'RT' in CRT and their claims of its relevance for Marxists, 'RT' has no future. This is not merely because the movement seems to have dwindled, but also on account of the fact that its co-founders have reverted unambiguously to Marxism (chapter 3).

Next I looked at attempts to develop a quintessentially British CRT or 'BritCrit' (chapter 4), before considering new work on CRT in the U.S (chapter 5). In chapter 4, I concluded that there is little, if any, significant development of 'BritCrit', and that many of the UK articles that I looked at employed other theories in addition to CRT, including Marxism. Most of the articles, I argued, could be enhanced by (neo-)Marxist analysis.

In the articles on the USA (chapter 5), I also witnessed the deployment of theories other than CRT, again including neo-Marxism. However, the US articles employ a greater use of CRT *concepts* than the UK ones. Again, like the UK articles, the US ones in general can be enriched by (neo-)

179

M. Cole, *New Developments in Critical Race Theory and Education*,
DOI 10.1057/978-1-137-53540-5_8

Marxism. While a few of the UK-based articles have contributed to the debate between CRT and Marxism, there is no real indication that the US ones have. In both the UK and US articles, I noted a discernible trend (back) towards intersectionality, which may herald a relaxing of the CRT insistence of 'race' over class, but with social class as an oppressed *identity* rather than as axiomatic in capitalist class exploitation.

The nature of this exploitation in the current era of austerity and immiseration is the subject of chapter 6, in which I traced the history of neoliberal capitalism, before moving on to its effects on global environmental destruction. I then looked at the consolidation of hegemony, imperialism and racialized world capitalism, before homing in on how austerity/immiseration capitalism adversely affects the racialized working classes generally, and of the UK and USA specifically.

In chapter 7, I looked at visions of the future with respect to Critical Race Theorists and Marxists. While I found those of the former vague and insubstantial, in the case of the latter I looked at twenty-first-century socialism in the Bolivarian Republic of Venezuela, focusing on antiracist initiatives there. I concluded the chapter with a consideration of the rise of Jeremy Corbyn in the UK and Bernie Sanders in the USA, in the context of the movement of twenty-first-century socialist ideas (as well as social democratic ones) from the margins to the mainstream of the capitalist heartland.

CRT can provide some useful insights about racism, as noted throughout this volume. However, in signifying 'the enemy' as 'white supremacy' (defined very broadly) or 'white powerholders', it fails to make connections to the capitalist economy, a linkage which is the strength of (neo-) Marxism.

CRT offers no vision of the future, no solution. A future without racialized (and gendered) neoliberal capitalism requires a revolution against that very system. The world is increasingly polarized between those who own the wealth and those that create it, particularly the racialized fractions of the latter, while the movement in the UK and the USA of twenty-first-century socialist ideas from the margins to the mainstream not only signifies the depth of the crisis in capitalism, but attests to the endurance and resilience of socialism.

While it is highly unlikely that the Corbyn phenomenon will have diminished by the time this volume is published, it is possible that Sanders will have been usurped by Hilary Clinton. While for most people on the Left, this would be most unfortunate, it should not be a cause for despair.

I will leave the last word, as I did in my chapter in my co-edited collection on education and social change in Latin America (Motta and Cole (eds) 2013) but, nevertheless, prescient to socialist revolutionaries everywhere, to one resident of the Caracas barrio of Baruto, who joined the hundreds of thousands of people, maybe a million, descending from the barrios around Caracas, successfully demanding the reinstatement of Chávez after the military coup in 2002. While the woman is referring specifically to Chávez, her words express the material base of socialist momentum and hope, are applicable to any social revolution and to any socialist leader and remind us of both the source and the indestructibility of socialist thinking. Here socialism is in its twenty-first-century mode, where women of colour feature prominently in what might be referred to as the ultimate counter-narrative—the 'good sense' of socialism as opposed to the 'common sense' that abounds in the capitalist ideological state apparatuses:

> We love our president, but this is not his revolution. This is our revolution and it will always be the revolution of the people. If President Chávez goes, we will miss him dearly but we will still be here. We are revolutionaries and we will always be here. We will never go back! (cited in Blough 2010)

References

Blough, L. (2010, April 14). Bolivarian republic of Venezuela: It is not Chávez. It is the people. *Axis of Logic.* http://axisoflogic.com/artman/publish/Article_59344.shtml

Cole, M. (2009). *Critical race theory and education: A Marxist response* (1st ed.). New York/London: Palgrave Macmillan.

Cole, M. (2017). *Critical race theory and education: A Marxist response* (2nd ed.). New York/London: Palgrave Macmillan.

Motta, S., & Cole, M. (Eds.). (2013). *Education and social change in Latin America*. New York/London: Palgrave Macmillan.

REFERENCES

Agosto, V., Karanxha, Z., & Bellara, A. (2015). Battling inertia in educational leadership: CRT Praxis for race conscious dialogue. *Race, Ethnicity and Education, 18*(6), 785–812.

Allen, R. L. (2006). The race problem in the critical pedagogy community. In C. Rossatto, R. L. Allen, & M. Pruyn (Eds.), *Reinventing critical pedagogy: Widening the circle of anti-oppressive education* (pp. 3–20). Lanham: Rowman & Littlefield.

Allen, R. L. (2007). Whiteness and critical pedagogy. In Z. Leonardo (Ed.), *Critical pedagogy and race*. Oxford: Blackwell.

Althusser, L. (1971). Ideology and ideological state apparatuses. In *Lenin and philosophy and other essays*. London: New Left Books. http://www.marx2mao.com/Other/LPOE70NB.html

Anderson, C. R. (2015). What are you? A CRT perspective on the experiences of mixed race persons in 'postracial' America. *Race, Ethnicity and Education, 18*(1), 1–19.

Balibar, E. (1991). Is there a 'neo-racism'? In E. Balibar & I. Wallerstein (Eds.), *Race, class, nation: Ambiguous identities*. New York: Verso Books.

Bartolovich, C. (2002). Introduction. In C. Bartolovich, & N. Lazarus (Eds.), *Marxism, modernity and postcolonial studies*. Cambridge: Cambridge University Press.

Barton, J. (1999). Chile. In J. Buxton & N. Phillips (Eds.), *Case studies in Latin American political economy*. Manchester: Manchester University Press.

Bauerly, B. A., & Solty, I. (2016, March 19). Sanders and the left after super tuesday—Why there is still hope and why the left should rejoice and push forward. *Links International Journal of Socialist Renewal*, reposted from *Socialist Project*. http://links.org.au/node/4645

© The Author(s) 2017

183

M. Cole, *New Developments in Critical Race Theory and Education*,
DOI 10.1057/978-1-137-53540-5

BBC News. (2015, June 19). Charleston shooting: Who are US white supremacists? *BBC News*. http://www.bbc.co.uk/news/world-us-canada-33198061

Bell, D. (1982). One dean's perspective – The law student as slave. *Student Law, 11*, 18.

Bell, D. (1985). Foreword: The civil rights chronicles (the Supreme Court, 1984 term). *Harvard Law Review, 99*, 4–83.

Bell, D. (1992). *Faces at the bottom of the well: The permanence of racism.* New York: Basic Books.

Bell, D. (1995). Serving two masters: Integration ideals and client interests in school desegregation litigation. In K. Crenshaw, N. Gotanda, G. Peller, & K. Thomas (Eds.), *Critical race theory: The key writings that formed the movement* (pp. 5–20). New York: The New Press.

Bell, D. (2005). In R. Delgado & J. Stefancic (Eds.), *The Derrick Bell reader.* New York: New York University Press.

Bell, S., & Cole, M. (2013). Qualitative research for antiracism: A feminist approach informed by Marxism. In T. M. Kress, C. Malott, & B. Porfilio (Eds.), *Challenging status quo retrenchment: New directions in critical research.* Charlotte: Information Age Publishing.

Beratan, G. (2008). The song remains the same: Transposition and the disproportionate representation of minority students in special education. *Race, Ethnicity and Education, 11*(4), 337–354.

Berry, T. R., & Stovall, D. O. (2013). Trayvon Martin and the curriculum of tragedy: Critical race lessons for education. *Race, Ethnicity and Education, 16*(4), 587–602.

Bhattacharya, S. (2016, October 9). 'Call me a racist, but don't say I'm a Buddhist': Meet America's alt right. *The Guardian.* https://www.theguardian.com/world/2016/oct/09/call-me-a-racist-but-dont-say-im-a-buddhist-meet-the-alt-right

Bhopal, K., & Rhamie, J. (2014). Initial teacher training: Understanding 'race,' diversity and inclusion. *Race, Ethnicity and Education, 17*(3), 304–325.

Blough, L. (2010, April 14). Bolivarian republic of Venezuela: It is not Chávez. It is the people. *Axis of Logic.* http://axisoflogic.com/artman/publish/Article_59344.shtml

Board of Governors of the Federal Reserve System. (2013). *2013 survey of consumer finances.* http://www.federalreserve.gov/econresdata/scf/scfindex.htm

Brown, E. (2011). Freedom for some, discipline for 'others'. In K. Saltmanand & D. Gabbard (Eds.), *Education as enforcement. The militarisation and corporatization of schools* (2nd ed.). New York/London: Routledge.

Brown, K. D. (2014). Teaching in color: A critical race theory in education analysis of the literature on preservice teachers of color and teacher education in the US. *Race, Ethnicity and Education, 17*(3), 326–345.

Burbach, R., & Piñero, C. (2007). Venezuela's participatory socialism. *Socialism and Democracy*, Online. http://sdonline.org/45/venezuela%e2%80%99s-participatory-socialism/

Burke, K. J., & Gilbert, B. R. (2016). Racing tradition: Catholic schooling and the maintenance of boundaries. *Race, Ethnicity and Education, 19*(3), 524–545.

Butler, J. (2004). *Precarious life: The powers of mourning and violence*. London/ New York: Verso.

Cabrera, N. L. (2011). Using a sequential exploratory mixed-method design to examine racial hyperprivilege in higher education. In K. A. Griffin & S. D. Museus (Eds.), *Using mixed-methods approaches to study intersectionality in higher education* (New directions for institutional research, no. 151, pp. 77–91). San Francisco: Jossey.

Cabrera, N. L. (2014). Exposing whiteness in higher education: White male college students minimizing racism, claiming victimization, and recreating white supremacy. *Race, Ethnicity and Education, 17*(1), 30–55.

Cameron, David. (2011, February 5). Speech on radicalisation and Islamic extremism, Munich. *New Statesman*. http://www.newstatesman.com/blogs/the-staggers/2011/02/terrorism-islam-ideology

Carrington, D. (2016, January 21). Global temperatures highest for 165 years. *The Guardian*.

CBS News. (2016, January 16). http://www.cbsnews.com/news/nh-poll-bernie-sanders-leads-every-major-voting-bloc/

Chadderton, C. (2014). The militarisation of English schools: Troops to teaching and the implications for Initial Teacher Education and race equality. *Race Ethnicity and Education, 17*(3), 407–428.

Chadderton, C., & Edmonds, C. (2015). Refugees and access to vocational education and training across Europe: A case of protection of white privilege? *Journal of Vocational Education & Training, 67*(2), 136–152.

Chakrabarty, N. (2012). Buried alive: The psychoanalysis of racial absence in preparedness/education. *Race, Ethnicity and Education, 15*(1). doi:10.1080/136 13324.2012.638863.

Chakrabarty, N., Roberts, L., & Preston, J. (2012). Critical race theory in England. *Race, Ethnicity and Education, 15*(1), 1–3.

Chapman, T. K., & Bhopal, K. (2013). Countering common-sense understandings of "good parenting:" Women of color advocating for their children. *Race, Ethnicity and Education, 16*(4). doi:10.1080/13613324.2013.817773.

Chengu, G. (2015, April 20). Xenophobia in South Africa: The apartheid legacy of racism and "White Corporate Capitalism". *Global Research*. http://www.globalresearch.ca/xenophobia-in-south-africa-the-apartheid-legacy-of-racism-and-white-corporate-capitalism/5443965

Ciccariello-Maher, G. (2013). *We created Cháccvez: A people's history of the Venezuelan revolution*. Durham/London: Duke University.

Ciccariello-Maher, G. (2016, March 23). Venezuela: ¡Comuna o Nada! *Links International Journal of Socialist Renewal*. Reposted from *ROAR Magazine* with permission. http://links.org.au/node/4646

Coben, D. (1999). Common sense or good sense: Ethnomathematics and the prospects for a Gramscian politics of adults' mathematics education. In M. van Groenestijn & D. Coben (Eds.), *Mathematics as part of lifelong learning. The fifth international conference of Adults Learning Maths – A Research Forum, ALM-5* (pp. 204–209). London: Goldsmiths College, University of London, in association with ALM. http://www.almonline.net/images/ALM/conferences/ALM05/proceedings/ALM05-proceedings-p204-209.pdf?7c979684e0c0237f91974aa8acb4dc29=36f0is6pst9523pt8acs48p337

Clark, T. G. (2012). What is neoliberalism? http://anotherangryvoice.blogspot.co.uk/2012/09/what-isneoliberalism-explained.html

Cole, M. (1986). Teaching and learning about racism: A critique of multicultural education in Britain. In S. Modgil et al. (Eds.), *Multicultural education: The interminable debate*. Barcombe: The Falmer Press.

Cole, M. (2005). The "inevitability of globalized capital" vs. the "ordeal of the undecidable": A Marxist critique. In M. Pruyn & L. M. Heurta-Charles (Eds.), *Teaching Peter McLaren: Paths of dissent*. New York: Peter Lang.

Cole, M. (2006). Imperialism and racialised world capitalism or intercultural twenty-first century socialism. *Knowledge Cultures, 4*(6).

Cole, M. (2008, November 29). *Maintaining "the adequate continuance of the British race and British ideals in the world": Contemporary racism and the challenges for education*. Bishop Grosseteste University College Lincoln: Inaugural Professorial Lecture.

Cole, M. (2009a). *Critical race theory and education: A Marxist response* (1st ed.). New York/London: Palgrave Macmillan.

Cole, M. (2009b). The color-line and the class struggle: A Marxist response to critical race theory in education as it arrives in the United Kingdom. *Power and Education, 1*(1), 111–124.

Cole, M. (2009c, April). On 'white supremacy' and caricaturing Marx and Marxism: A response to David Gillborn's 'who's afraid of critical race theory in education'. *Journal for Critical Education Policy Studies, 7*(1). http://www.jceps.com/index.php?pageID=article&articleID=143

Cole, M. (2009d). Critical race theory comes to the UK: A Marxist response. *Ethnicities, 9*(2), 246–269.

Cole, M. (2009e). A response to Charles mills. *Ethnicities, 9*(2), 281–284.

Cole, M. (2011a). The CRT concept of 'white supremacy' as applied to the U.K.: Eight major problematics and some educational implications. In K. Hylton, A. Pilkington, P. Warmington, & S. Housee (Eds.), *Atlantic crossings: International dialogues on critical race theory*. Birmingham: C-SAP, University of Birmingham.

Cole, M. (2011b). *Racism and education in the U.K. and the U.S.: Towards a socialist alternative*. New York/London: Palgrave Macmillan.

Cole, M. (2012a). Critical race theory in education, Marxism and abstract racial domination. *British Journal of Sociology of Education, 33*(2), 167–183.

Cole, M. (2012b). "Abolish the white race" or "transfer economic power to the people"? Some educational implications. *Journal for Critical Education Policy Studies, 10*(2). http://www.jceps.com/index.php?pageID=article&articleID=265

Cole, M. (2012c). Capitalist crisis and fascism: Issues for educational practice. In D. R. Cole (Ed.), *Surviving economic crises through education*. New York: Peter Lang.

Cole, M. (2013). Marxism. In P. L. Mason (Ed.), *Encyclopedia of race and racism* (2nd ed., Vol. 3, pp. 117–124). Detroit: Macmillan.

Cole, M. (2014a). Racism and antiracist education. In D. C. Phillips (Ed.), *Encyclopedia of educational theory and philosophy*. London: Sage.

Cole, M. (2014b). The Bolivarian Republic of Venezuela: Education and twenty-first-century socialism. In S. C. Motta & M. Cole, *Constructing twenty-first-century socialism in Latin America: The role of radical education*. New York/London: Palgrave Macmillan.

Cole, M. (2014c). Austerity/immiseration capitalism and Islamophobia; or twenty-first century multicultural socialism? *Policy Futures in Education, 12*(1), 79–92.

Cole, M. (2015a). *One small step for humankind*. http://www.huffingtonpost.co.uk/mike-cole/jeremy-corbyn_b_8130772.html

Cole, P. (2015b, December 15). Paris climate agreement is diplomatic fudge. *A World to Win*. http://www.aworldtowin.net/blog/Paris-climate-agreement-is-diplomatic-fudge.html

Cole, M. (2016a). *When I became aware of racism—Professor Mike Cole*. https://www.youtube.com/watch?v=3tKyRku12t8

Cole, M. (2016b). Critical race theory: A Marxist critique. In M. A. Peters (Ed.), *Encyclopedia of educational philosophy and theory*. Singapore: Springer.

Cole, M. (2016c). *Racism: A critical analysis*. London/Chicago: Pluto Press/University of Chicago Press.

Cole, M. (2017). *Critical race theory and education: A Marxist response* (2nd ed.). New York/London: Palgrave Macmillan.

Cole, M., & Maisuria, A. (2007) 'Shut the F*** Up', 'You have no rights here': Citical race theory and racialisation in post-7/7 racist Britain. *Journal for Critical Education Policy Studies, 5*(1).

Cole, M., & Motta, S. C. (2011, January 14). Opinion: The giant school's emancipatory lessons. *Times Higher Education Online*.

Collins, P. H. (1995). The social construction of black feminist thought. In B. Guy-Sheftall (Ed.), *Words of fire: An anthology of African-American feminist thought*. New York: The New Press.

Congreso Nacional de Educación. (2006). Especial: Congreso Nacional de Educación de Bolivia, July 3 (15).

Crenshaw, K. W. (1989). Demarginalizing the intersection of race and sex: A black feminist critique of antidiscrimination doctrine, feminist theory and antiracist politics. *Chicago Legal Forum, special issue: Feminism in the Law: Theory, Practice and Criticism* (University of Chicago).

Crenshaw, K., Gotanda, N., Peller, G., & Thomas, K. (1995). Introduction. In K. Crenshaw, N. Gotanda, G. Peller, & K. Thomas (Eds.), *Critical race theory: The key writings the formed the movement*. New York: New Press.

Curran, F. (2007). What happened to the global justice movement? Fighting neoliberalism—The view from Scotland. *International Viewpoint*. Available http://www.internationalviewpoint.org/spip.php?article1365

Damon, A. (2015, January 26). Oxfam: Richest one percent set to control more wealth than the bottom 99 percent. *World Socialist Web Site (WSWS)*. http://www.wsws.org/en/articles/2015/01/20/oxfa-j20.html

DeCuir-Gunby, J. T. (2006). "Proving your skin is white, you can have everything": Race, racial identity, and property rights in whiteness in the Supreme Court case of Josephine DeCuir. In A. D. Dixson & C. K. Rousseau (Eds.), *Critical race theory in education: All god's children got a song*. New York/London: Routledge.

Delgado, R. (1995). *The Rodrigo Chronicles: Conversations about America and race*. New York: New York University Press.

Delgado, R. (1998). Rodrigo's committee assignment: A sceptical look at judicial independence. *Southern California Law Review, 72*, 425.

Delgado, R. (2001). Two ways to think about race: Ref lections on the Id, the ego, and other reformist theories of equal protection. *Georgetown Law Review, 89*. Available http://findarticles.com/p/articles/mi_qa3805/is_200107/ai_n8985367/pg_2. Accessed 26 Mar 2008.

Delgado, R. (2003). Crossroads and blind alleys: A critical examination of recent writing about race. *Texas Law Review, 82*, 121.

Delgado, R., & Stefancic, J. (2001). *Critical race theory: An introduction*. New York: New York University Press.

Delgado Bernal, D., Burciaga, R., & Flores Carmona, J. (2012). Chicana/Latina *Testimonios*: Mapping the Methodological, Pedagogical and Political. *Equity, Excellence and Education, 45*(3): 363–372.

DePouw, C. (2012). When culture implies deficit: Placing race at the center of Hmong American education. *Race, Ethnicity and Education, 15*(2), 223–239.

Dixson, A. D., & Rousseau, C. K. (2006). Introduction. In A. D. Dixson & C. K. Rousseau (Eds.), *Critical race theory in education: All god's children got a song*. New York: Routledge.

Dominguez, F. (2016, January 27). Right wing majority in Venezuela's National Assembly: The constitutional and political stakes. *The Huffington Post*. http://www.huffingtonpost.com/dr-francisco-dominguez/right-wing-majority-in-ve_b_9069350.html

Du Bois, W. E. B. (1903). The forethought. In *The souls of black folk*. http://www.bartleby.com/114/100.html

Du Bois, W. E. B. (1948). The talented tenth memorial address. *The Boule Journal*, *15*(1). http://sigmapiphi.org/home/the-talented-tenth.php

Du Bois, W. E. B. (1996) [1900]. The present outlook for the darker races of mankind. In E. Sundquist (Ed.), *The Oxford W.E.B. Du Bois reader*. Oxford: Oxford University Press.

Dunning-Lozano, J. L. (2016). Race and opportunity in a public alternative school. *Race, Ethnicity and Education, 19*(2), 433–460.

Dussel, E. (1985). *La producción teórica de Marx. Un comentario a los Grundrisse*.

Dussel, E. (1988). *Hacia un Marx desconocido. Un comentario de los Manuscritos del 61–63*.

Dussel, E. (1990). *El último Marx (1863–1882) y la liberación latinoamericana: Un comentario a la tercera y cuarta redacción de "El Capital"*.

Dussel, E. (1994). *Las metáforas teológicas de Marx*.

Dussel, E. (2001). *Towards an unknown Marx: A commentary on the manuscripts of 1861–1863*. London: Routledge.

Dussel, E. (2003). *Beyond philosophy: History, Marxism, and liberation theology*. Maryland: Rowman and Littlefield.

Dutka, Z. C. (2014, October 15). Maduro Hands Over Land Titles to Indigenous Communities, Creates Institute to Protect Native Languages. *venezuelanalysis.com*. https://venezuelanalysis.com/news/10964Fischer-Hoffman is cited in an earlier chapter

Eisen, A. (2014, March 27). Racism Sin Vergüenza in the Venezuelan Counter-Revolution. *Venezuelanalysis.com*.

Eley, T. (2016, January 26). Growing support for Sanders highlights US political crisis. *World Socialist Web Site (WSWS)*. http://www.wsws.org/en/`articles/2016/01/26/dems-j26.html

Elliott, J. (2011). Judith Butler at Occupy Wall Street. *Salon*. http://www.salon.com/2011/10/24/judith_butler_at_occupy_wall_street/

Elliott, L. (2016, January 18). Richest 62 people as wealthy as half world's population combined. *The Guardian*. http://www.theguardian.com/business/2016/jan/18/richest-62-billionaires-wealthy-half-world-population-combined?utm_source=esp&utm_medium=Email&utm_campaign=GU+Today+m

ain+NEW+H&utm_term=151527&subid=14322859&CMP=EMCNEWEM
L661912

Engels, F. (1977) [1892]. Socialism utopian and scientific. In K. Marx & F. Engels
(Eds.), *Selected works in one volume*. London: Lawrence and Wishart.

Fekete, L. (2009). *A suitable enemy: Racism, migration and Islamophobia in
Europe*. London: Pluto.

Fine, R. (1990). The antimonies of Neo-Marxism: A critique of Harold Wolpe's
Race, Class and the Apartheid State. Transformation, 11, 1–118.

Fischer-Hoffman, C. (2014, October 14). Honoring indigenous resistance day in
Venezuela, the struggle continues. *venezuelanalysis*. https://venezuelanalysis.
com/news/10959

Fisher, P., & Nandi, A. (2015, March 25). *Poverty across ethnic groups through
recession and austerity*. York: Joseph Rowntree Foundation. https://www.jrf.
org.uk/report/poverty-across-ethnic-groups-through-recession-and-austerity

Freire, P. (2007, June 5). *Paulo Freire—Karl Marx* (subtitled), Video. http://
www.youtube.com/watch?v=pSyaZAWIr1I&feature=related

Garvey, J. (2015). No more missouri compromises. *Insurgent Notes, 11*. http://
insurgentnotes.com/2014/11/no-more-missouri-compromises/

Garvey, J., & Goldner, L. (2015). Ferguson and after: Where is this movement
going? Insurgent Notes Jan 24, http://insurgentnotes.com/2015/01/

Gillborn, D. (2005). Education policy as an act of white supremacy: Whiteness,
critical race theory and education reform. *Journal of Education Policy, 20*(4),
485–505.

Gillborn, D. (2008). *Racism and education: Coincidence or conspiracy?* London:
Routledge.

Gillborn, D. (2009). Who's afraid of critical race theory in education? A reply to
Mike Cole's "The color-line and the class struggle". *Power and Education,
1*(1), 125–131.

Gillborn, D. (2010). Full of sound and fury, signifying nothing? A reply to Dave
Hill's "Race and class in Britain: A critique of the statistical basis for critical race
theory in Britain". *Journal for Critical Education Policy Studies, 8*(1), 78–107.
http://www.jceps.com/?pageID=article&articleID=177

Gillborn, D. (2011). Once upon a time in the UK: Race, class, hope and whiteness
in the academy: Personal reflections on the birth of 'BritCrit'. In K. Hylton,
S. Housee, A. Pilkington, & P. Warmington (Eds.), *Atlantic crossings:
International dialogues on critical race theory*. Birmingham: C-SAP.

Gillborn, D. (2013). Interest-divergence and the colour of cutbacks: race, recession and the undeclared war on black children. *Discourse: Studies in the Cultural
Politics of Education, 34*(4), 477–491.

Gillborn, D. (2014). Racism as policy: A critical race analysis of education reforms
in the United States and England. *The Educational Forum, 78*(1), 26–41.

Gillborn, D., Rollock, N., Vincent, C., & Ball, S. J. (2012). 'You got a pass, so
what more do you want?': Race, class and gender intersections in the educational

experiences of the black middle class. *Race Ethnicity and Education, 15*(1), 121–139. doi:10.1080/13613324.2012.638869

Gilroy, P. (2004). *After empire: Multiculture or postcolonial Melancholia*. London: Routledge.

Gold, G. (2014, December 4). Osborne's declaration of war on the people. *A World to Win*. http://www.aworldtowin.net/blog/Osbornes-declaration-of-war-on-the-people.html

GOV.UK. (2011). PM's speech at Munich Security Conference, delivered on: 5 Feb. 2011. https://www.gov.uk/government/speeches/pms-speech-at-munich-security-conference

Greenfields, M. (2006). Stopping places. In C. Clark & M. Greenfields (Eds.), *Here to stay: The gypsies and travellers of Britain*. Hatfield: University of Hertfordshire Press.

Grillo, T., & Wildman, S. M. (1997). Obscuring the importance of race. The implication of making comparisons between racism and sexism (or other isms). In A. K. Wing (Ed.), *Critical race feminism: A reader*. New York: New York University Press.

Grosvenor, I. (1987). A different reality: Education and the racialisation of the black child. *History of Education, 16*(4), 299–308.

Grosvenor, I. (1989). Teacher racism and the construction of black underachievement. In R. Lowe (Ed.), *The changing secondary school*. Lewes: Falmer.

Hall, S. (1992). Cultural studies and its theoretical legacies. In L. Grossberg, C. Nelson, & P. Treichler (Eds.), *Cultural studies* (pp. 277–294). New York: Routledge.

Harman, C. (1995). *Economics of the madhouse: Capitalism and the market today*. London: Bookmarks.

Harman, C. (2008). Theorising neoliberalism. *International Socialism, 117*(Winter). https://www.marxists.org/archive/harman/2008/xx/neolib.htm

Harpalani, V. (2012, March). Professor Derrick Bell: "Radical humanist". *The Black Commentator*, 464. http://www.blackcommentator.com/464/464_bell_harpalani_guest_share.html

Harvey, D. (1989). *The condition of postmodernity: An enquiry into the origins of cultural change*. Oxford: Blackwell.

Hetherington, R., & Reid, G. B. R. (2010). *The climate connection: Climate change and modern human evolution*. Cambridge: Cambridge University Press.

Hill, D. (2009a, June 25–26). *Statistical skullduggery in the case for critical race theory: How statistical tables comparing "race" and class underachievement have been fiddled to prove CRT's point in England*. Paper delivered to *Critical race theory in the UK: What is to be learnt? What is to be done?* Conference organized by C-SAP, BSA, The Institute of Education, University of London.

Hill, D. (2009b). Race and class in Britain: A critique of the statistical basis for critical race theory in Britain; and some political implications. *Journal for Critical Education Policy Studies, 7*(2). http://www.jceps.com/?pageID=article&articleID=159

Hill, D., & Helavaara Robertson, L. (Eds.). (2011). *Equality in the primary school: Promoting good practice across the curriculum*. London: Continuum.

Holloway, J. (2015). We are the fragility of the system, John Holloway interviewed by Fiona Jeffries. In F. Jeffries (Ed.), *Nothing to lose but our fear*. London: Zed Books.

Housee, S. (2012). What's the point? Anti-racism and students' voices against Islamophobia. *Race, Ethnicity and Education, 15*(1), 101–120. doi:10.1080/1 3613324.2012.638867.

Hylton, K. (2012). Talk the talk, walk the walk: Defining critical race theory in research. *Race, Ethnicity and Education, 15*(1), 23–41. doi:10.1080/1361332 4.2012.638862.

Ignatiev, N. (2010). The world view of C.L.R. James. In N. Ignatiev (Ed.), *C.L.R. James a new notion: Two works by C.L.R. James: Every cook can govern and the invading socialist society*. Oakland: PM Press.

Ignatiev, N. (2011a). Noel Ignatiev at Occupy Boston: Video 1 of 2, November 15. Youtube: http://www.youtube.com/watch?v=BFj63NShxsw

Ignatiev, N. (2011b). Noel Ignatiev at Occupy Boston: Video 2 of 2, November 15. Youtube: http://www.youtube.com/watch?v=DSegN9I9y3Q

Ignatiev, N. (2015a). 'Comment' on 'Garvey, J. (2015). No more Missouri Compromises. *Insurgent Notes*, 11. http://insurgentnotes.com/2014/11/no-more-missouri-compromises/

Ignatiev, N. (2015b). Race or class? *PM Press*. http://www.pmpress.org/content/article.php/20150720120508552

Ignatiev, N., & Garvey, J. (Eds.). (1996). *Race traitor*. London: Routledge.

Illich, I. (1973). *Deschooling society*. Harmondsworth: Penguin.

Institute of Education/UCL. (2012, June 6). *Professor David Gillborn given an award for achievements in race theory*. http://www.ioe.ac.uk/64517.html

International Committee of the Fourth International. (2014, July 3). Socialism and the fight against imperialist war. *World Socialist Web Site (WSWS)*. https://www.wsws.org/en/articles/2014/07/03/icfi-j03.html

James, C. L. R. (1939). The SWP and Negro work. SWP New York Convention Resolutions, 11 July, http://www.marxists.org/archive/james-clr/works/1939/07/negro-work.htm

Johnson-Ahorlu, R. N. (2012). The academic opportunity gap: How racism and stereotypes disrupt the education of African American undergraduates. *Race, Ethnicity and Education, 15*(5), 633–652.

Karenga, M. (2003). Du Bois and the question of the color line: Race and class in the age of globalization. *Socialism and Democracy, 17*(1). http://sdonline.org/33/du-bois-and-the-question-of-the-color-line-race-and-class-in-the-age-of-globalization/.

Kennedy, D. (1982). Legal education and the reproduction of hierarchy. *Legal Education, 32*, 591–615.

Khalifa, M., Dunbar, C., & Douglas, T. (2013). Derrick Bell, CRT, and educational leadership 1995–present. *Race, Ethnicity and Education, 16*(4), 489–513.

Kochhar, R., & Fry, R. (2014, December 12). Wealth inequality has widened along racial, ethnic lines since end of Great Recession. *PewResearchCenter.* http://www.pewresearch.org/fact-tank/2014/12/12/racial-wealth-gaps-great-recession/

Koerner, L. (2015, September 17). US Presidential hopeful Bernie Sanders Slams Chávez in reposte to Clinton attack. *Venezuelanalysis.* http://venezuelanalysis.com/news/11511

Kohli, R. (2014). Unpacking internalized racism: Teachers of color striving for racially just classrooms. *Race Ethnicity and Education, 17*(3), 367–387. http://www.tandfonline.com/doi/full/10.1080/13613324.2013.832935

Kohli, R., & Solorzano, D. G. (2012). Teachers, please learn our names!: Racial microaggressions and the K-12 classroom. *Race, Ethnicity and Education, 15*(4), 441–462.

Kovel, J. (1988). *White racism: A psychohistory.* London: Free Association Books.

Kuo, R. (2015, April 2). 6 reasons we need to dismantle the model minority myth of those "hard-working' Asians". *Everyday Feminism.* http://everydayfeminism.com/2015/04/dismantle-model-minority-myth/

Ladson-Billings, G. (1994). What we can learn from multicultural education research. *Educational Leadership, 51,* 22–26.

Ladson-Billings, G. (1999). Just what is critical race theory and what's it doing in a nice field like education? In L. Parker, D. Deyhle, & S. Villenas (Eds.), *Race is… race isn't: Critical race theory and qualitative studies in education.* Boulder: Westview Press.

Ladson-Billings, G. (2006). Foreword they're trying to wash us away: The adolescence of critical race theory in education. In A. D. Dixson & C. K. Rousseau (Eds.), *Critical race theory in education: All god's children got a song.* New York: Routledge.

Ladson-Billings, G., & Tate, W. F. (1995). Towards a critical race theory of education. *Teachers College Record, 97*(1), 47–68.

Lanning, R. (2007, March). What is class consciousness. *Political Affairs, 86*(3). https://sites.google.com/site/lanningrd/what-is-class-consciousness-3

Lather, P. (1991). *Getting smart; feminist research and pedagogy with/in the postmodern.* New York: Routledge.

Lawton, L. (2012). Liam's Labrynth. https://liamos85.wordpress.com/2012/07/12/a-critical-assessment-ofthe-impact-of-neoliberalism-on-the-chilean-state-during-the-pinochet-regime-1973-1989/

Lenin, V. I. (1917) [2002]. *On Utopian and scientific socialism: Articles and speeches.* Amsterdam: Fredonia Books.

Leonardo, Z., & Harris, A. P. (2013). Living with racism in education and society: Derrick Bell's ethical idealism and political pragmatism. *Race, Ethnicity and Education, 16*(4), 470–488.

Ley De Migración Y Extranjería. (2003). http://www.derechos.org.ve/pw/wpcontent/uploads/ley_migraci%C3%B3n.pdf

Lippi-Green, R. (2006). Language ideology and language prejudice. In E. Finegan & J. R. Rickford (Eds.), *Language in the USA*. Cambridge: Cambridge University Press.

Lipsitz, G. (2011). *How racism takes place*. Philadelphia: Temple University Press.

Lopes Cardozo, M. (2013). *Future teachers and social change in Bolivia: Between decolonization and demonstration*. Delft: Uitgeverij Eburon.

Lotz, C. (2016). Hello Lenin! *A World to Win*. http://www.aworldtowin.net/transition/helloLenin.html

Lynn, M. (2010). 'Exorcising critical race theory' again: Reflections on being an Angry Black Man in the academy. In S. Jackson & R. Johnson III (Eds.), *The black professoriat: Negotiating a habitable space in the academy* (pp. 199–214). New York: Peter Lang.

Lynn, M., Jennings, M. E., & Hughes, S. (2013). Critical race pedagogy 2.0: Lessons from Derrick Bell. *Race, Ethnicity and Education, 16*(4), 603–628.

Macpherson, W. (1999). *The Stephen Lawrence enquiry, Report of an enquiry by Sir William Macpherson*. London: HMSO. https://www.gov.uk/government/uploads/system/uploads/attachment_data/file/277111/4262.pdf.

Marable, M. (2004). Globalization and Racialization. *ZNET*. https://zcomm.org/znetarticle/globalization-andracialization-by-manning-marable/

Marable, M. (2008). Blackness beyond boundaries: Navigating the political economies of global inequality. In M. Marable & V. Agard-Jones (Eds.), *Transnational blackness: Navigating the global color line* (pp. 1–8). New York: Palgrave Macmillan.

María, E., & Romero, C. (2016, April 15). Chavismo from below. *Jacobin*. https://www.jacobinmag.com/2016/04/chavez-maduro-venezuela-mud-psuv/

Marsden, C. (2015, January 14). Imperialist war, the 'war on terror' and the end of democracy. *World Socialist Web Site (WSWS)*. https://www.wsws.org/en/articles/2015/01/14/pers-j14.html

Martin, P. (2014, December 6). The state of world capitalism: Labor productivity up, real wages down. *World Socialist Web Site (WSWS)*. https://www.wsws.org/en/articles/2014/12/06/pers-d06.html

Martinez, E., & García, A. (2000). What is "Neo-Liberalism" A brief definition. *Economy*, 101. http://www.globalexchange.org/campaigns/econ101/neo-liberalDefined.html

Martinez, C., Fox, M., & Farrell, J. (2010). *Venezuela speaks!: Voices from the grassroots*. Oakland: PM Press.

Marx, K. (1845). *The German ideology.* https://www.marxists.org/archive/marx/works/1845/german-ideology/ch01a.htm

Marx, K., & Engels, F. [1848] (1977). The Communist Manifesto. In K. Marx & F. Engels (Eds.), *Selected works in one volume.* London: Lawrence and Wishart.

Matsuda, M., Lawrence, C., Delgado, R., & Crenshaw, K. W. (1993). *Words that wound: Critical race theory, assaultive speech and the first amendment.* Boulder: Westview Press.

McIntosh, P. (1988). *White privilege and male privilege: A personal account of coming to see correspondences through work in women's studies* (Working paper No. 189). Wellesley: Wellesley College Center for Research on Women.

McLaren, P. (1995). *Critical pedagogy and predatory culture: Oppositional politics in a postmodern era.* London/New York: Routldege.

McLaren, P. (2008). This fist called my heart. *Antipode, 40*(3), 472–481.

McLaren, P. (2015). *Pedagogy of insurrection: From resurrection to revolution.* New York: Peter Lang.

McLaren, P., & Farahmandpur, R. (2005). *Teaching against global capitalism and the new imperialism: A critical pedagogy.* Oxford: Rowman and Littlefield.

Mills, C. W. (1997). *The racial contract.* New York: Cornell University Press.

Mills, C. W. (2009). Critical race theory: A reply to Mike Cole. *Ethnicities, 9*(2), 270–281.

Millward, D. (2015, September 14). Jeremy Corbyn backed by Bernie Sanders. *The Telegraph.* http://www.telegraph.co.uk/news/politics/Jeremy_Corbyn/11865090/Jeremy-Corbyn-backed-by-Bernie-Sanders.html

Milner, H. R., IV, & Howard, T. C. (2013). Counter-narrative as method: Race, policy and research for teacher education. *Race, Ethnicity and Education, 16*(4), 536–561.

Mitchell, E. (2013a). I am a woman and a human: A Marxist feminist critique of intersectionality theory. The Charnel-House, September 12. https://thecharnel-house.org/2014/02/07/a-marxist-feminist-critique-of-intersectionalitytheory/

Mitchell, K. (2013b). Race, difference, meritocracy, and English: Majoritarian stories in the education of secondary multilingual learners. *Race, Ethnicity and Education, 16*(3), 339–364.

Monzó, L. D. (2015). Afterword. In P. McLaren (Ed.), *Pedagogy of insurrection: From resurrection to revolution.* New York: Peter Lang.

Motta, S., & Cole, M. (Eds.). (2013). *Education and social change in Latin America.* New York/London: Palgrave Macmillan.

Motta, S., & Cole, M. (2014). *Constructing twenty-first century socialism in Latin America.* New York/London: Palgrave Macmillan.

Nather, D. (2015, March 6). Obama on Ferguson: "They weren't just making it up". *Politico.* http://www.politico.com/story/2015/03/obama-ferguson-reaction-doj-115839.html

Núñez, A. (2016, March 18). *Speech to the briefing on developments in Venezuela*. London: Bolivar Hall.

Ollman, B. (1993). *Dialectical investigations*. New York: Routledge.

Oppenheimer, S. (2012). A single southern exit of modern humans from Africa: Before or after Toba? *Quaternary International, 258*, 88–99.

Pakendorf, B., & Stoneking, M. (2005). Mitochondrial DNA and human evolution. *Annual Review of Genomics and Human Genetics, 6*, 165.

Pearson, T. (2014, April 10). Undocumented migrants in Venezuela have more rights than US citizens in the US. *venezuelanalysis.com*. https://venezuelanalysis.com/analysis/10599

Pierce, C. (1970). Offensive mechanisms. In F. Barbour (Ed.), *The black seventies*. Boston: Porter Sargent.

Piketty, T. (2014). *Capital in the twenty-first century*. Cambridge, MA: Harvard University Press.

Piketty, T. (2014). *Capital in the twenty-first century hardcover*. Cambridge, MA: Harvard University Press.

Postel, D. (1997, January 1). An interview with Noel Ignatiev. *Z Magazine*. https://zcomm.org/zmagazine/an-interview-with-noel-ignatiev-by-danny-postel/

Poulantzas, N. (1978). *State, power, socialism*. London: NLB.

Poynting, S., & Mason, V. (2007). The resistible rise of Islamophobia: Anti-Muslim racism in the UK and Australia before 11 September 2001. *Journal of Sociology, 43*(1), 61–86.

Preston, J. (2007). *Whiteness and class in education*. Dordrecht: Springer.

Preston, J. (2010). Concrete and abstract racial domination. *Power and Education, 2*(2), 115–125.

Preston, J. (2013). *Whiteness in academia: Counter-stories of betrayal and resistance*. Newcastle upon Tyne: Cambridge Scholars Publishing.

Preston, J., & Chadderton, C. (2012). "Race traitor": Towards a critical race theory informed public pedagogy. *Race, Ethnicity and Education, 15*(1), 85.

Rectenwald, M. (2013). What's wrong with identity politics (and intersectionality theory)? A response to Mark Fisher's 'Exiting the Vampire Castle' (and its critics). *The North Star*. http://www.thenorthstar.info/?p=11411

Rikowski, G. (2015). *Crises, commodities and education: Disruptions, eruptions, interruptions and ruptions*. A paper prepared for the Research in critical Education Studies (RiCES) Seminar, School of Education, University of Lincoln, 19 November, online at Academia: http://www.academia.edu/18511424/Crises_Commodities_and_Education_Disruptions_Eruptions_Interruptions_and_Ruptions

Rollock, N. (2012). The invisibility of race: intersectional reflections on the liminal space of alterity. *Race, Ethnicity and Education, 15*(1). doi:10.1080/1361332 4.2012.638864.

Rose, S., & Rose, H. (2005, April 9). Why we should give up on race: As geneticists and biologists know, the term no longer has meaning. *The Guardian.* https://www.theguardian.com/world/2005/apr/09/race.science

Sanders, B. (2016). http://www.marketwatch.com/story/text-of-bernie-sanders-wall-street-and-economy-speech-2016-01-05

Sandlin, J., & Burdick, J. (2010). Inquiry as answerability: Toward a methodology of discomfort in researching critical public pedagogies. *Qualitative Inquiry, 16*(5), 349–360.

San Juan, Jr., E. (2003). Marxism and the race/class problematic: A re-articulation. *Cultural Logic.* http://clogic.eserver.org/2003/sanjuan.html

Sartre, J. P. (1960). *The search for method (1st part). Introduction to critique of dialectical reason.* http://www.marxists.org/reference/archive/sartre/works/critic/sartre1.htm

Scatamburlo-D'Annibale, V., & McLaren, P. (2010). Classifying race: The "compassionate" racism of the right and why class still matters. In Z. Leonardo (Ed.), *Handbook of cultural politics and education.* Boston: Sense Publishers.

Seidman, S. (1998). *Contested knowledge: Social theory in the postmodern era.* Oxford: Basil Blackwell.

Senna, D. (1998). The mulatto millenium. In C. O'Hearn (Ed.), *Half and half: Writers on growing up biracial and bicultural* (pp. 12–27). New York: Pantheon Books.

Sheridan, K. (2013, October 15). Iraq Death Toll Reaches 500,000 Since Start of U.S.-Led Invasion, New Study Says. *The World Post.* http://www.huffingtonpost.com/2013/10/15/iraq-death-toll_n_4102855.html

Sivanandan, A. (2001). Poverty is the new black. *Race and Class, 43*(2), 1–5.

Sivanandan, A. (2009). Foreword. In L. Fekete (Ed.), *A suitable enemy: Racism, migration and Islamophobia in Europe.* London: Pluto.

Siverwright, S. (2015, August 4). The "Real Eve". Scientist in Limbo. http://scientistinlimbo.com/2015/08/04/the-real-eve/

Sky News. (2015). *What will happen as the world gets warmer?* http://news.sky.com/story/1604441/what-will-happen-as-the-world-gets-warmer

Smith, D. G. (2003). On enfraudening the public sphere, the futility of empire and the future of knowledge after "America". *Policy Futures in Education, 1*(2), 488–503. http://www.wwwords.co.uk/pdf/validate.asp?j=pfie&vol=1&issue=3&year=2003&article=4_Smith_PFIE_1_3_web

Smith, S. (2013/14). Black feminism and intersectionality. *International Socialist Review* (91). http://isreview.org/issue/91/black-feminism-and-intersectionality

Smith, H. J., & Lander, V. (2012). Collusion or collision: Effects of teacher ethnicity in the teaching of critical whiteness. *Race, Ethnicity and Education, 15*(3). doi:10.1080/13613324.2011.585340.

Solórzano, D. G., & Yosso, T. J. (2002). Critical race methodology: Counter-storytelling as an analytical framework for education research. *Qualitative Inquiry, 8*(1), 23–44.

Solórzano, D., & Yosso, T. (2009). Counter-storytelling as an analytical frame-work for educational research. In E. Taylor, D. Gillborn, & G. Ladson-Billings (Eds.), *Foundations of critical race theory in education*. Abingdon: Routledge.

Solórzano, D., Allen, W. R., & Carroll, G. (2002). Keeping race in place. Racial microaggressions and campus racial climate at the University of California, Berkeley. *Chicano-Latino Law Review, 23*(15).

Southern Poverty Law Center (SPLC). (2015a, March 2). *Active Neo-Nazi Groups*. https://www.splcenter.org/fighting-hate/intelligence-report/2015/active-neo-nazi-groups

Southern Poverty Law Center (SPLC). (2015b). 892. https://www.splcenter.org/hate-map

Suarez-Villa, L. (2012). *Globalization and technocapitalism: The political economy of corporate power*. Farnham: Ashgate. https://books.google.co.uk/books?id=y-ChAgAAQBAJ&pg=PA146&lpg=PA146&dq=richard+d+wolff+on+capitalist++technologies+and+globalisation&source=bl&ots=hvLdjWoc1P&sig=bFLQ94BS8bUSkWeFw7lT9dQgo0k&hl=en&sa=X&ei=wmUeVbuvB8vWU9r3ggg&ved=0CD0Q6AEwBA#v=onepage&q=richard%20d%20wolff%20on%20capitalist%20%20technologies%20and%20globalisation&f=false

Suggett, J. (2015, December 27). Venezuela: Potential paths out of the economic crisis. *Venezuelanalysis*. http://venezuelanalysis.com/analysis/11790

Tatum, B. D. (1992). Talking about race, learning about racism: The applications of racial identity development theory. *Harvard Educational Review, 62*(1), 1–25.

Taylor, Keeanga-Yamahtta. (2011, January 4). Race, class and Marxism. *socialistworker.org*. https://socialistworker.org/2011/01/04/race-class-and-marxism

Telesur. (2014, September 17). Venezuela to present report on indigenous rights at UN. *venezuelanalysis.com*. https://venezuelanalysis.com/news/10916

Thatcher, M. (1986, October 10). Speech to Conservative Party Conference. *Margaret Thatcher Foundation*. http://www.margaretthatcher.org/document/106498

Thatcher, M. (1993). *The downing street years*. London: HarperCollinsPublishers.

The Real News. (2012, October 5). *Jimmy Carter says: Election process in Venezuela is the best in the world*. http://therealnews.com/t2/?option=com_content&task=view&id=31&Itemid=74&jumival=8935

Travis, A. (2015, December 30). Oliver Letwin blocked help for black youth after 1985 riots. *The Guardian*. http://www.theguardian.com/politics/2015/dec/30/oliver-letwin-blocked-help-for-black-youth-after-1985-riots?utm_source=esp&utm_medium=Email&utm_campaign=GU+Today+main+NEW+H&utm_term=146715&subid=14322859&CMP=EMCNEWEML6619I2

Trilling, D. (2013, April 10). Thatcher: The PM who brought racism in from the cold. *Verso blog*. http://www.versobooks.com/blogs/1282-thatcher-the-pm-who-brought-racism-in-from-the-cold

Tushnet, M. (1981). The dilemmas of liberal constitutionalism. *Ohio State Law Journal, 42*, 411–426.

Urrieta, L., & Villlena, S. A. (2013). The legacy of Derrick Bell and Latino/a education: A critical race testimonio. *Race, Ethnicity and Education, 16*(4), 514–535.

Urrieta, L., & Villlena, S. A. (2013). The legacy of Derrick Bell and Latino/a education: A critical race testimonio. *Race, Ethnicity and Education, 16*(4), 514–535.

Viola, M. J. (2016). W.E.B. Du Bois and Filipino/a American exposure programs to the Philippines: Race class analysis in an epoch of 'global apartheid'. *Race, Ethnicity and Education, 19*(3), 500–523.

Warmington, P. (2012). "A tradition in ceaseless motion": Critical race theory and black British intellectual spaces. *Race, Ethnicity and Education, 15*(1). doi:10.1080/13613324.2012.638861

Wolpe, H. (1988). *Race, class and the apartheid state*. London: James Currey, with OAU, UNESCO.

World Socialist Web Site (WSWS) Editorial Board. (2008, March 19). *Five years after the invasion of Iraq: A debacle for US Imperialism*. http://www.wsws.org/articles/2008/mar2008/iwar-m19.shtml#

Wright, C. (2012). Marxism and White Skin Privilege. http://libcom.org/library/marxism-white-skin-privilege-chriswright

Young, C., & Franco, J. (2013, April 12). No matter who wins in Venezuela, Chavez's legacy is secure. *Reuters*. http://blogs.reuters.com/great-debate/2013/04/12/no-matter-who-wins-in-venezuela-chavezs-legacy-is-secure/

Yuval-Davis, N. (2011). *Power, intersectionality and the politics of belonging*. Aalborg: Institut for Kultur og Global Studier, Aaloborg Universitet, Denmark. http://vbn.aau.dk/files/58024503/FREIA_wp_75.pdf

Index

Note: Page numbers followed by "n" denote notes.

© The Author(s) 2017
M. Cole, *New Developments in Critical Race Theory and Education*,
DOI 10.1057/978-1-137-53540-5

Roediger, D., 87
Rollock, N., 76, 78, 79
Romero, C., 174n8
Roof, D., 119
Rose, H., 114
Rose, S., 114
Rousseau, C. K., 33, 155
RSAs. *See* repressive state apparatuses (RSAs)
RT. *See* Race Traitor (RT)
'rule of law,' 21

S
Sabra, A., 66n8, 67n8
Said, E., 98
Salomon, A., 15
Sanders, B., 153, 169–72, 174n11
Sanguinetti, C., 158
Scatamburlo-D'Annibale, V., 19
schools' racist perceptions of parents of colour, 82–3
secondary multilingual learners, majoritarian stories in education of, 106–7
Second World War, 18
'self-condemnation,' 126
SEN. *See* special education needs (SEN)
Sivanandan, A., 90n4
Sleeter, C. E., 44, 45
Smith, H. J., 81
Smith, S., 78
social class, 76–8
social contract theory, 92n14
social-democratic party, 172
Socialist Equality Party, 64, 91n8
Sojourner Truth Organization (STO), 58
Solórzano, D. G., 72, 102–5, 113, 115, 118
Solty, I., 171

special education needs (SEN), 25
Stalinism, 14, 28, 34n1, 157
Stalin, J., 34n1
state neoliberalism, 116
Stefancic, J., 18, 49, 156
'stereotype threat,' 105
STO. *See* Sojourner Truth Organization (STO)
Stovall, D., 115, 116
structuralism, 35n2
student teachers of colour, recruiting and reclaiming, 119–21
Suggett, J., 165
superficial multiculturalism, 100
'symbolic violence,' 126

T
Tatum, B. D., 118
Taylor, K.-Y., 83
teacher education, 112–15
programs, 119, 120
teacher preparation programmes, 119
teacher 'racial' diversity, 113
Tea Party, 91n11
Thatcher, M., 1–3, 33, 138, 143, 150n1
The Condition of Postmodernity (Harvey), 138
"The Washington Consensus", 138
Thomas, C., 62–3
Torres, R., 5
transformative transition programs, 172
transmodernism, 13–14
transnational capitalism, 116
Trilling, D., 2
Troops to Teachers (TtT), 85
Trotsky, Leon, 60
TtT. *See* Troops to Teachers (TtT)
Tushnet, M., 14
twenty-first-century socialism in Venezuela, 26–9

white supremacy, 8n5, 11, 16, 17,
    36n8, 43, 45, 66n6, 67n9, 73,
    74, 76, 79, 80, 85–9, 91n7, 103,
    106–8, 118, 119, 126, 131, 180
white teacher educators, student
    teacher perceptions of, 81–2
'white-to-Hispanic' wealth ratio, 148
Williams, P., 110
working class, racialized fractions of
    in UK, 146–7
    in USA, 147–9
World Social Forum, 28
World Socialist Web Site (WSWS), 64,
    91n8
Wright, C., 51, 65n3
WSWS. *See* World Socialist Web Site
    (WSWS)

X
xeno-racialization, 17, 50
xeno-racism, 74, 87, 90n4

Y
Yosso, T., 72
young black men, knowledge worth
    knowing for/about, 115–16
Young, C., 27
Yukpa communities, 160
Yuval-Davis, N., 77

Z
Zionist Occupied Government
    (ZOG), 119

CPI Antony Rowe
Chippenham, UK
2017-02-24 09:45